POP TEAM EPIC

Bkub Okawa

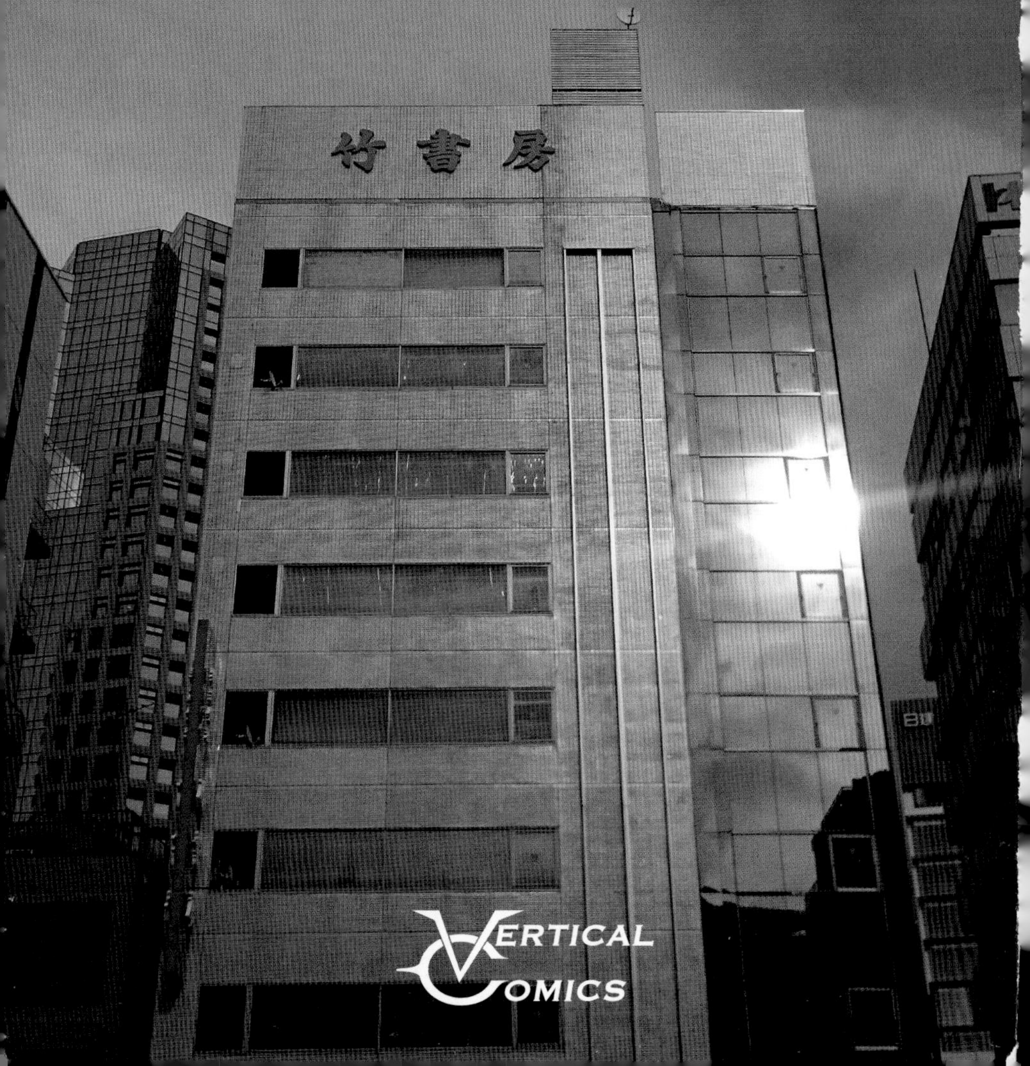
竹書房

VERTICAL COMICS

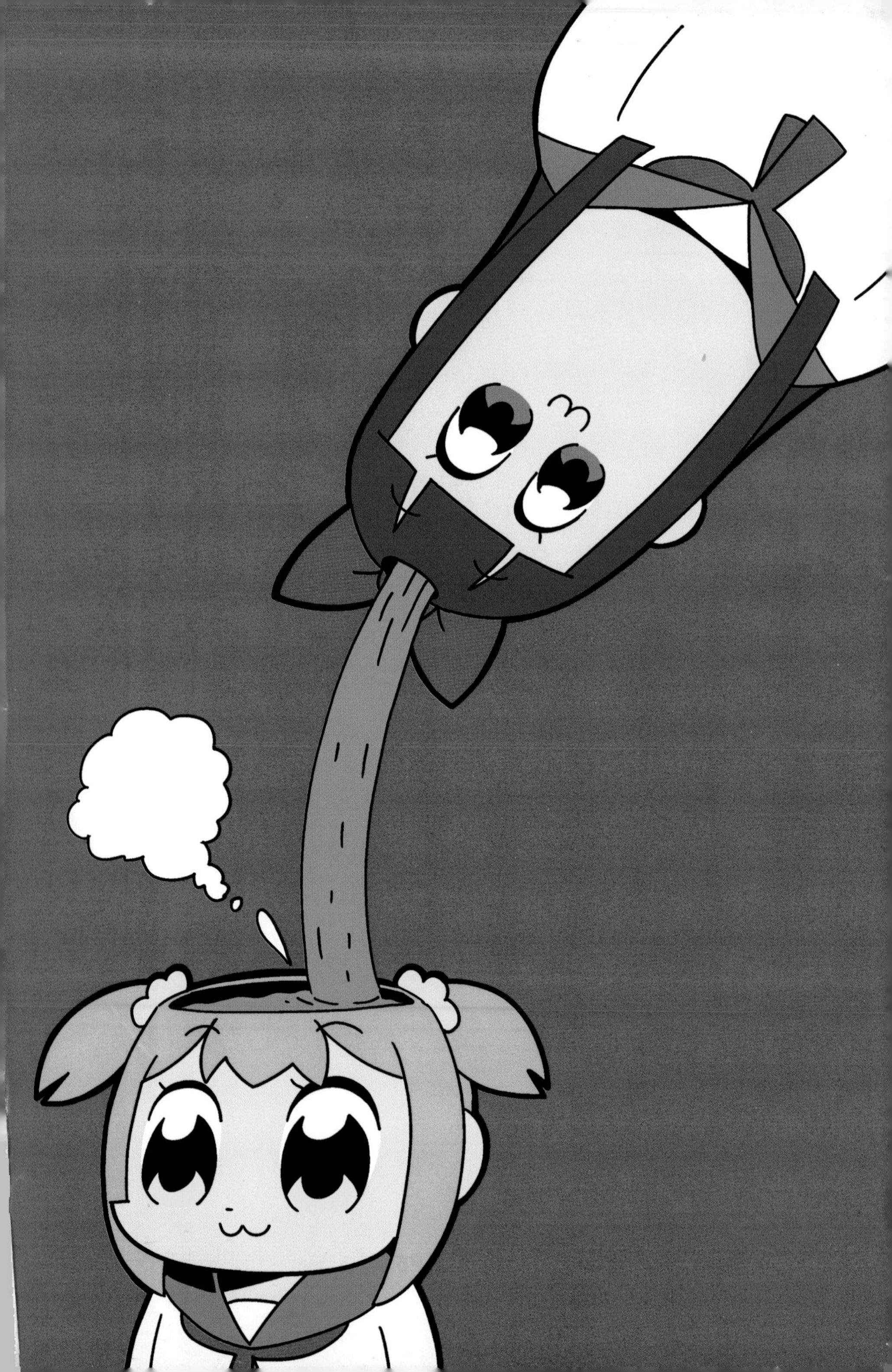

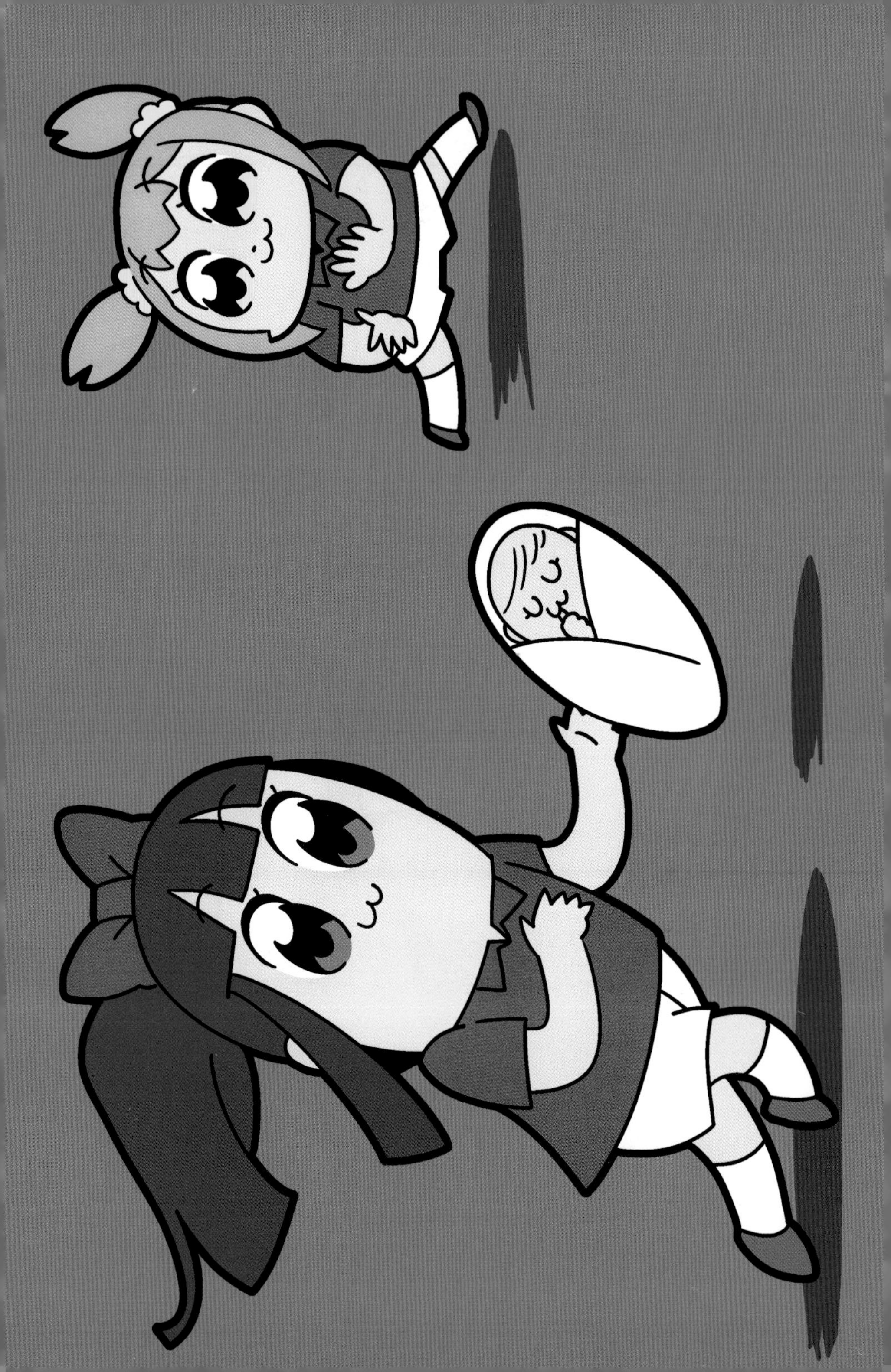

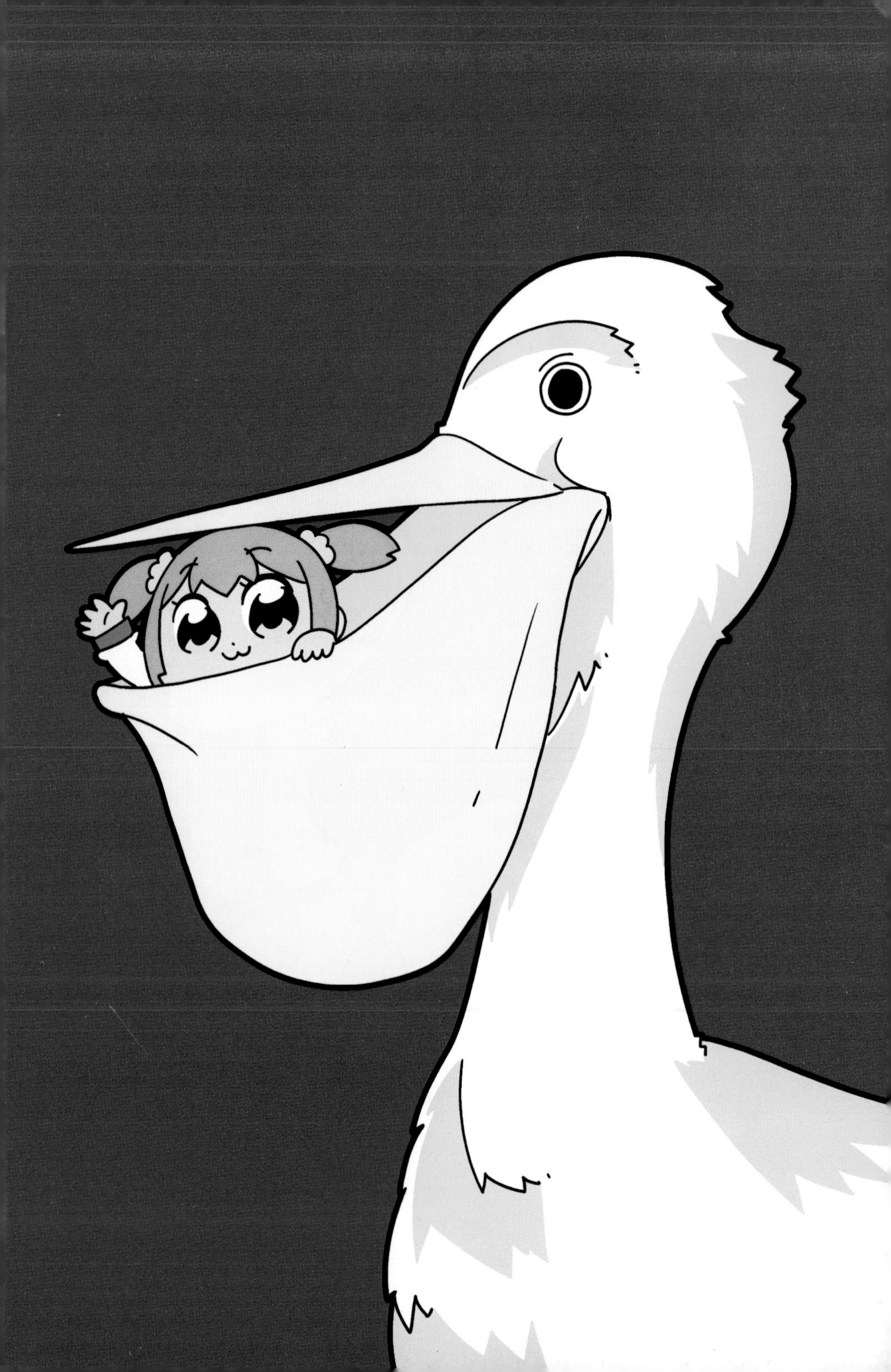

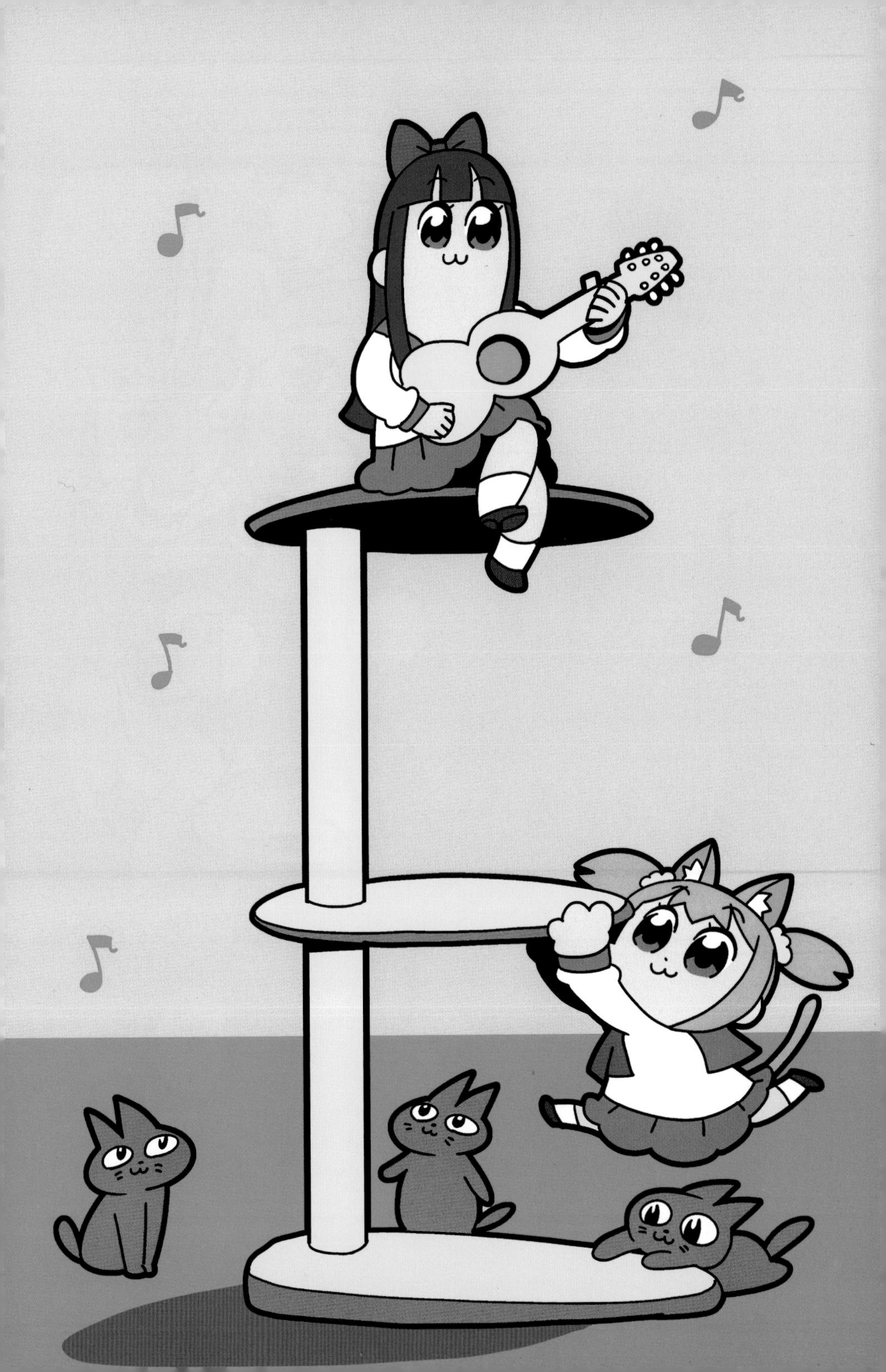

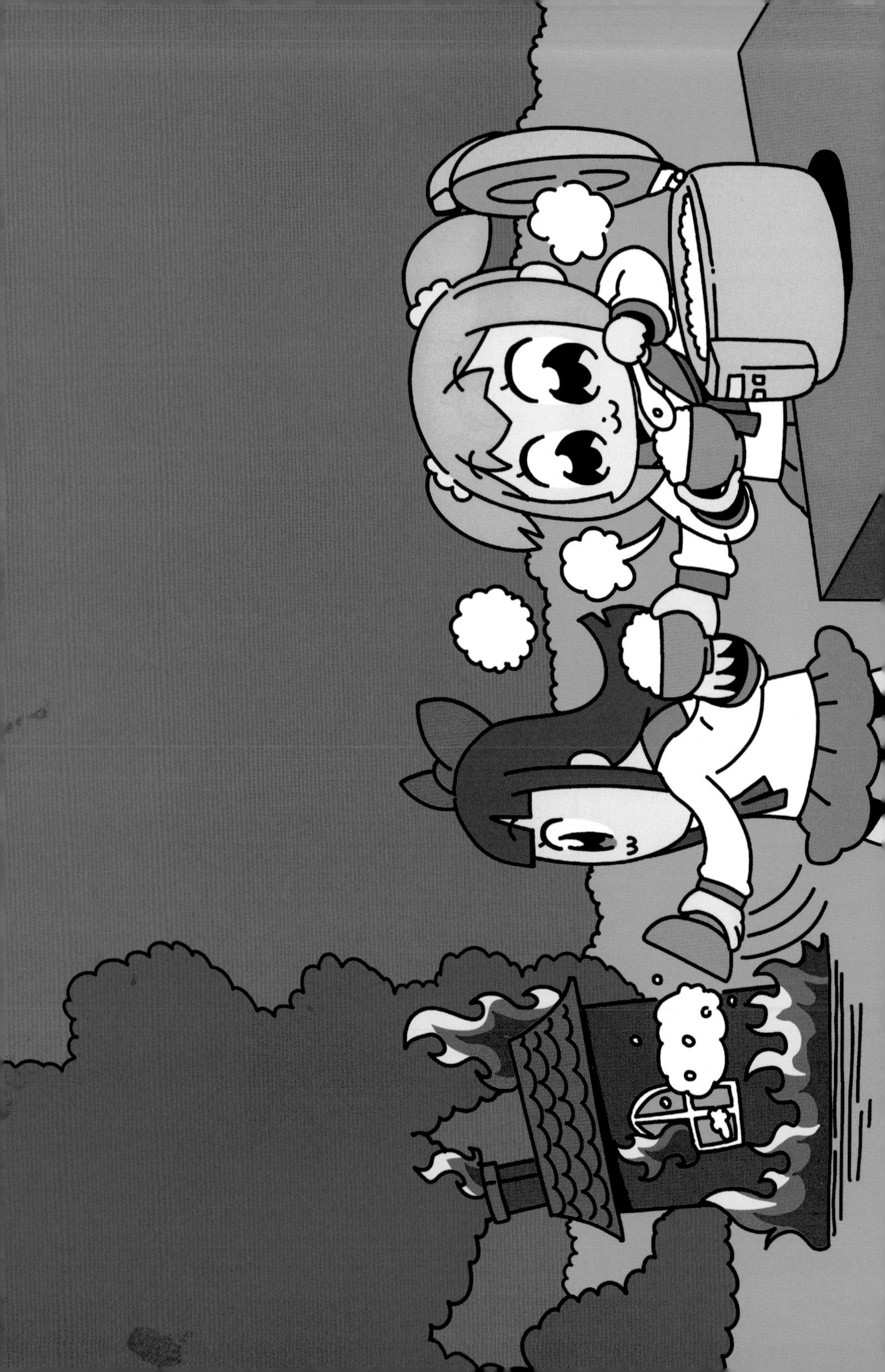

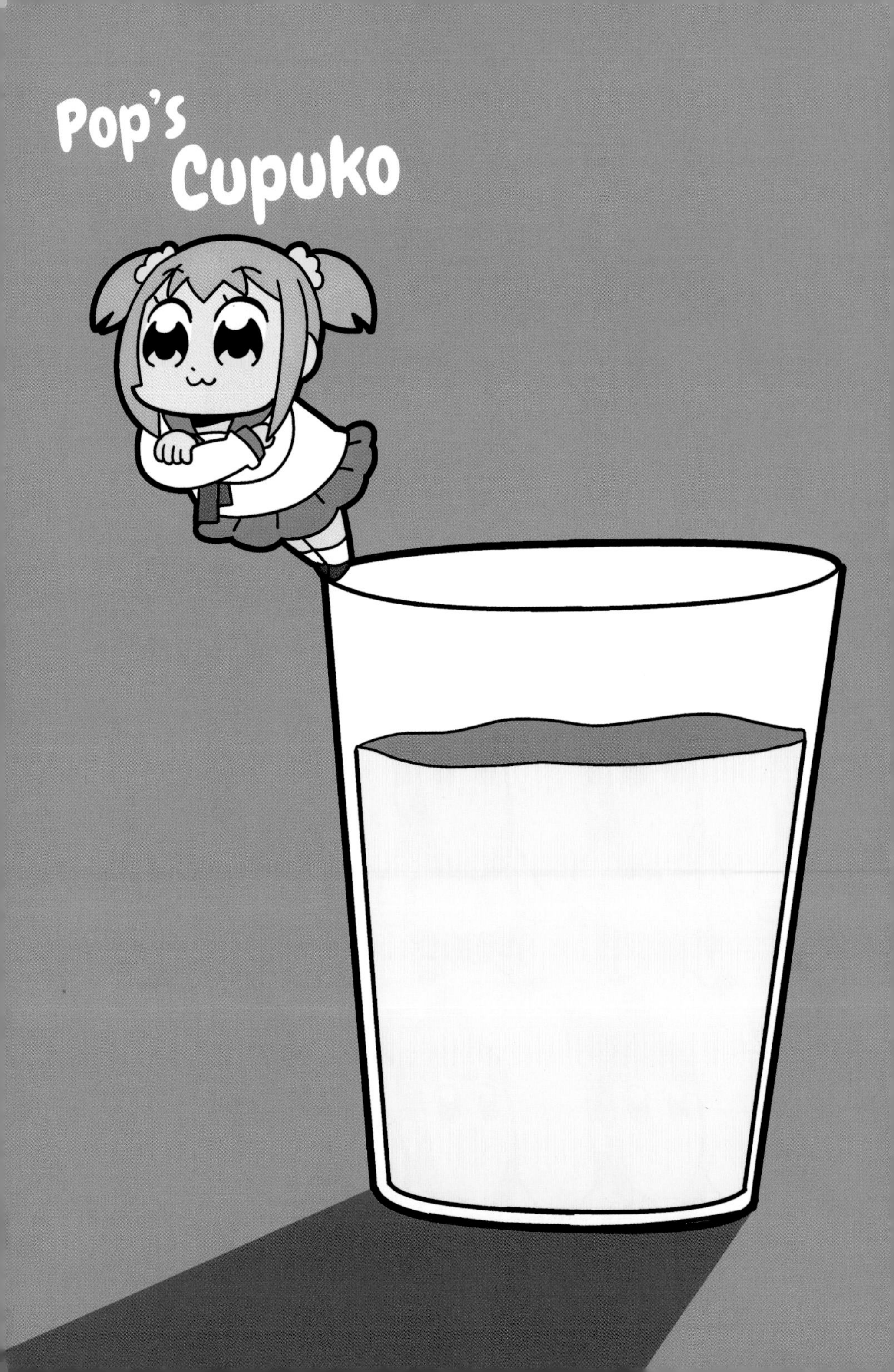
Pop's
Cupuko

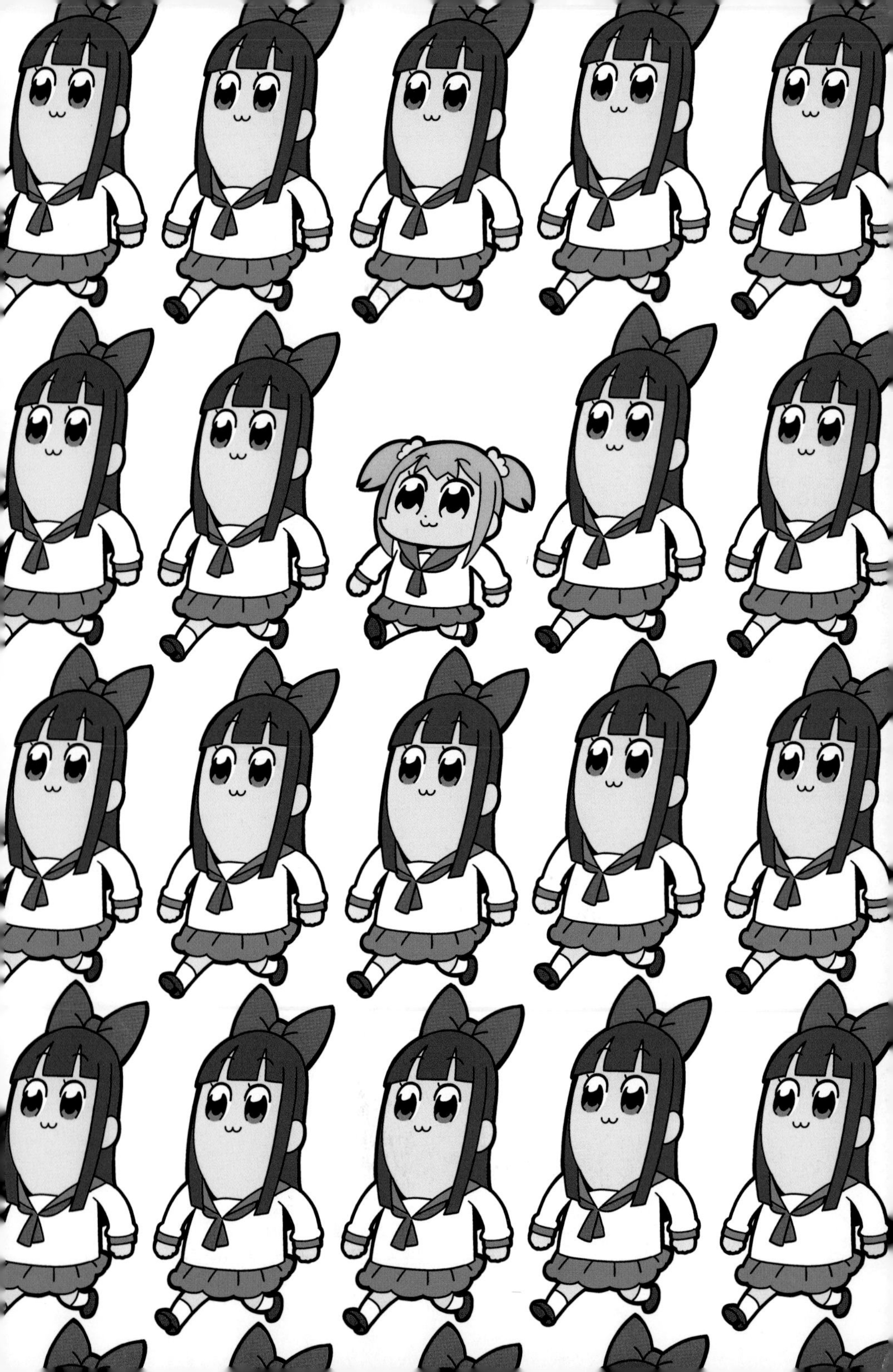

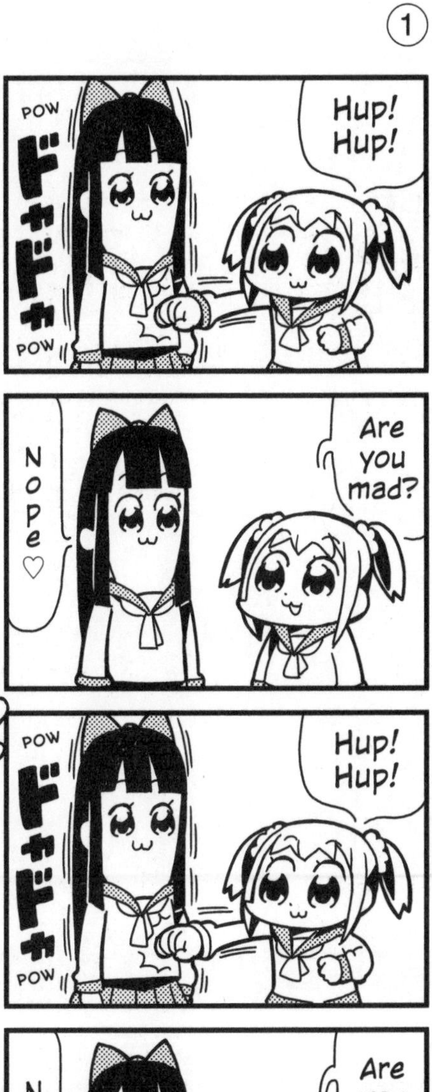
1
Hup! Hup!
POW
ドカドカ
POW
Are you mad?
Nope♡
Hup! Hup!
POW
ドカドカ
POW
Are you mad?
Nope♡

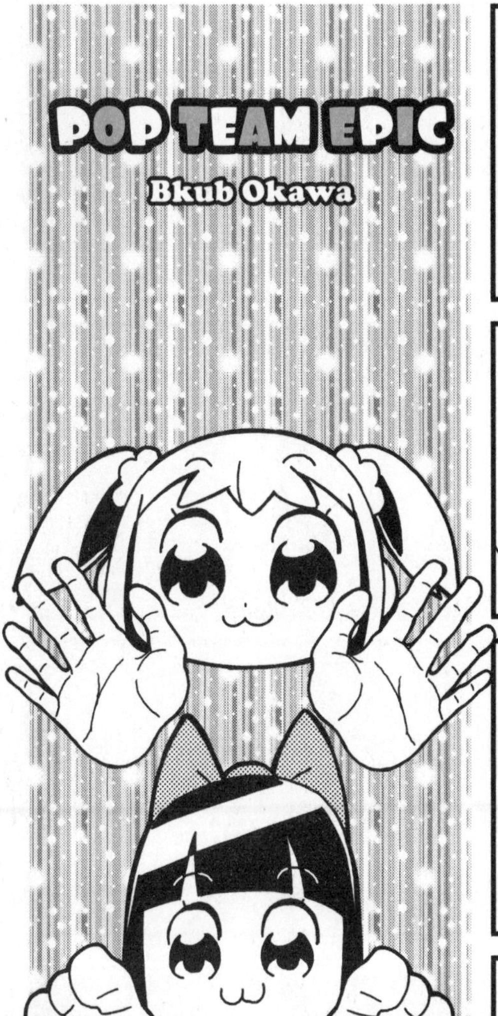
POP TEAM EPIC
Bkub Okawa

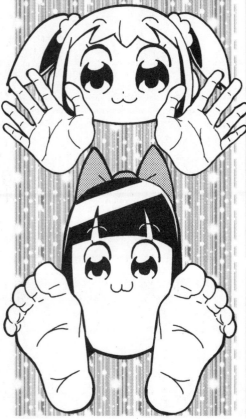

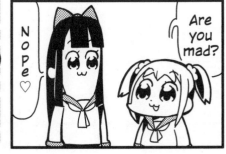

2

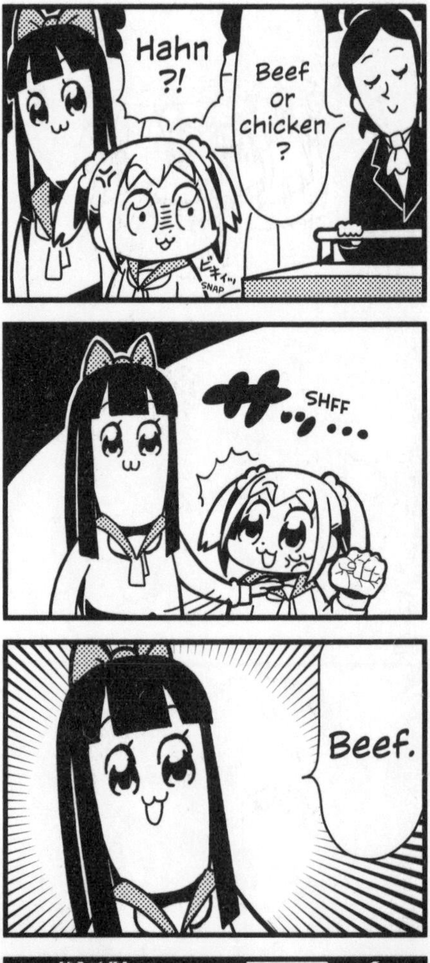
Beef or chicken ?
Hahn ?!
ビキィッ
SNAP
サッ…
SHFF...
Beef.
Yer lucky to be alive.
PEH

3

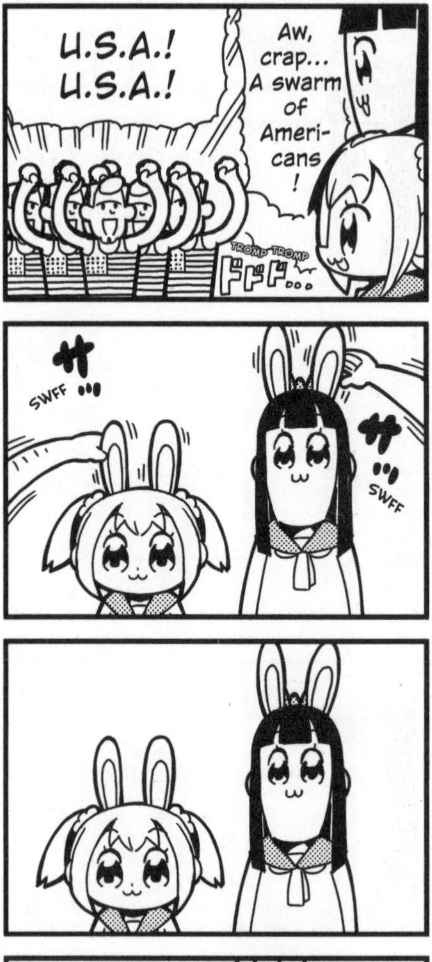
Aw, crap... A swarm of Americans !
U.S.A.! U.S.A.!
TROMP TROMP
ドドド...
サッ
SWFF
サッ
SWFF

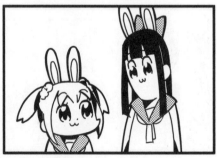

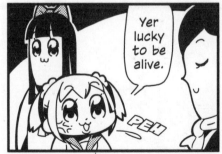

④

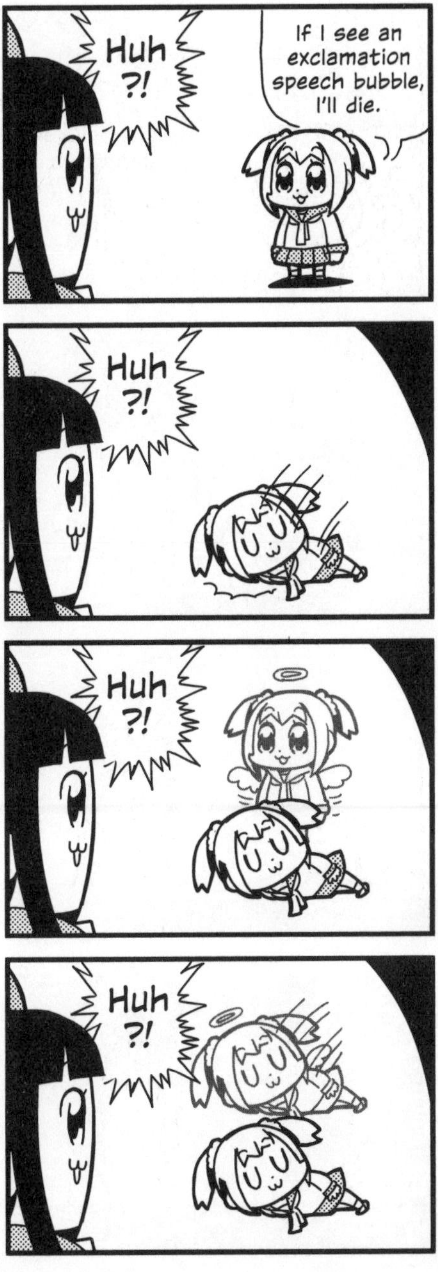
If I see an exclamation speech bubble, I'll die.
Huh ?!
Huh ?!
Huh ?!
Huh ?!

⑤

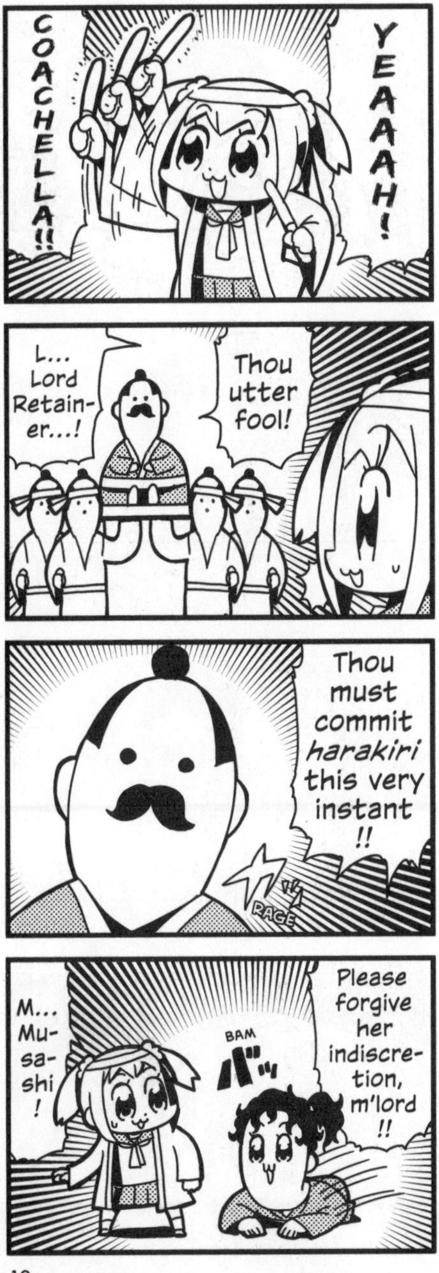
YEAAAAH!
COACHELLA!!
Thou utter fool!
L... Lord Retainer...!
Thou must commit *harakiri* this very instant !!
RAGE
Please forgive her indiscretion, m'lord !!
BAM
M... Musashi !

⑥

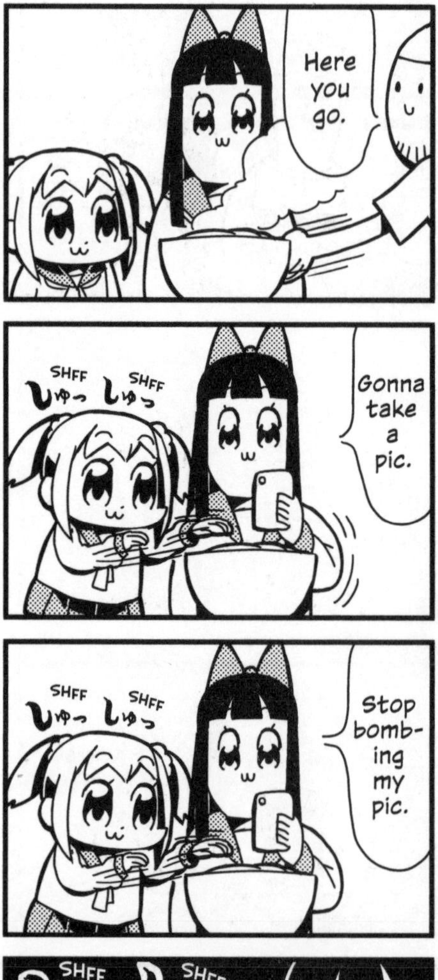
Here you go.
SHFF しゅっ SHFF しゅっ
Gonna take a pic.
SHFF しゅっ SHFF しゅっ
Stop bombing my pic.
SHFF しゅっ SHFF しゅっ

⑦

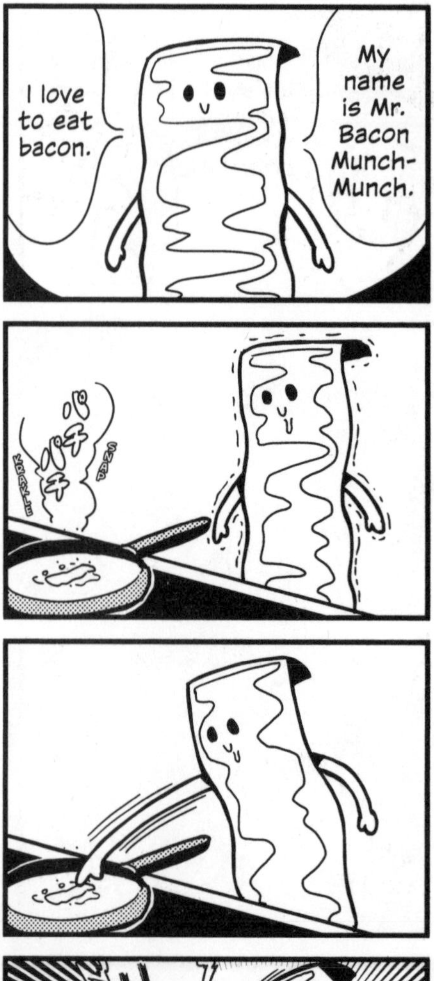
My name is Mr. Bacon Munch-Munch.
I love to eat bacon.
パチ パチ
SNAP
HOOTT!

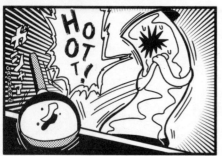

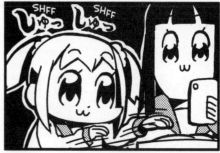

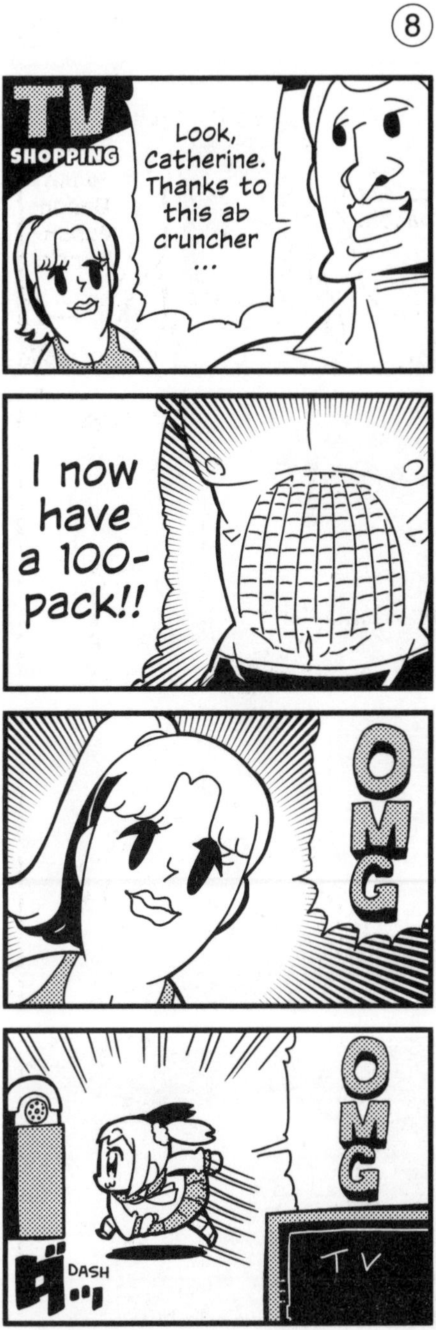
8
TV
SHOPPING
Look, Catherine. Thanks to this ab cruncher ...
I now have a 100-pack!!
OMG
OMG
TV
DASH

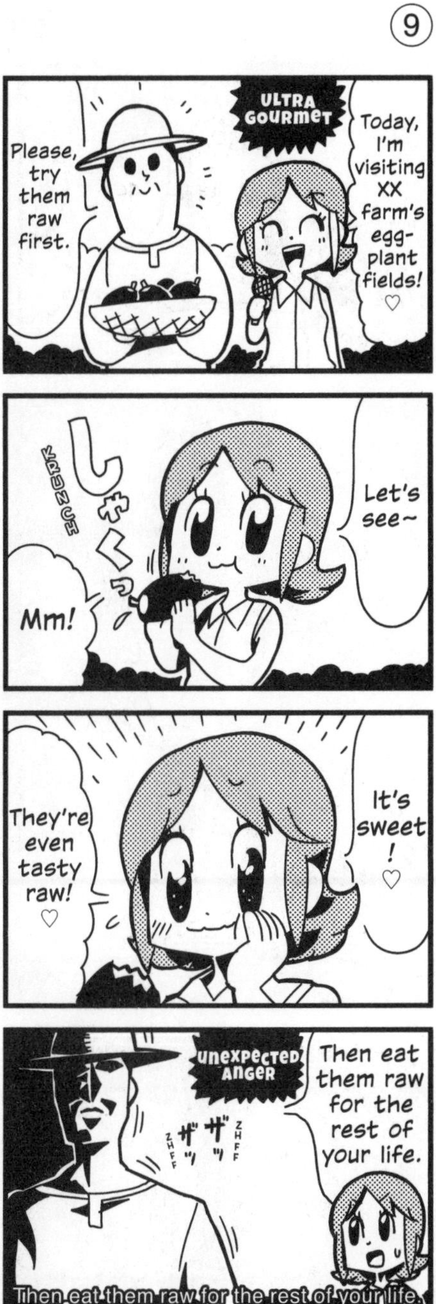
9
ULTRA GOURMET
Today, I'm visiting XX farm's egg-plant fields! ♡
Please, try them raw first.
Let's see~
しゃくっ
KRUNCH
Mm!
It's sweet! ♡
They're even tasty raw! ♡
UNEXPECTED ANGER
Then eat them raw for the rest of your life.
ザッ ZHFF
ザッ ZHFF
Then eat them raw for the rest of your life.

10

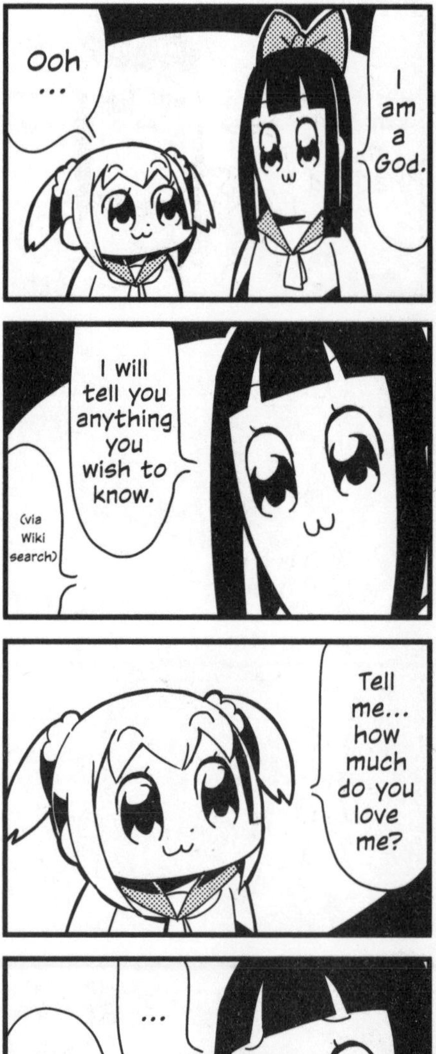
I am a God.
Ooh ...
I will tell you anything you wish to know.
(via Wiki search)
Tell me... how much do you love me?
...
I wuv you lots ♡

11

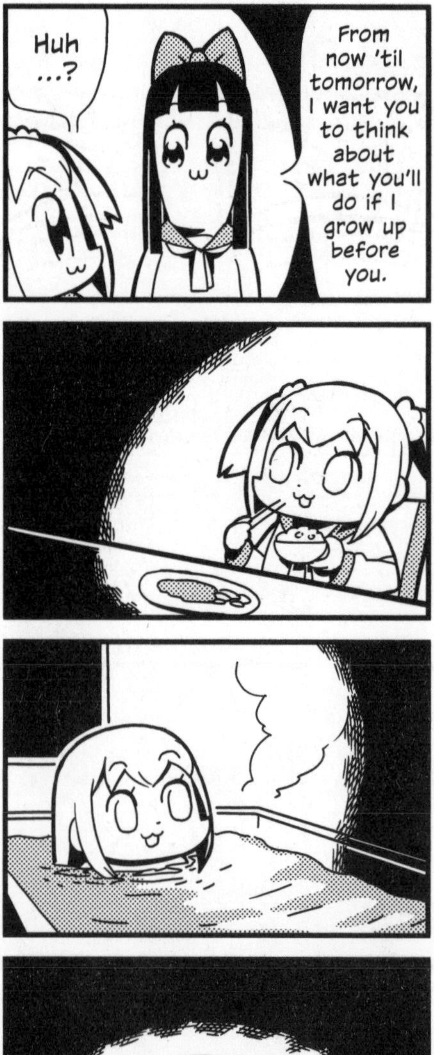
From now 'til tomorrow, I want you to think about what you'll do if I grow up before you.
Huh ...?

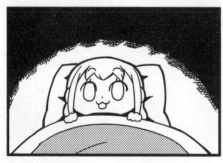

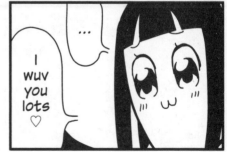

To be continued...

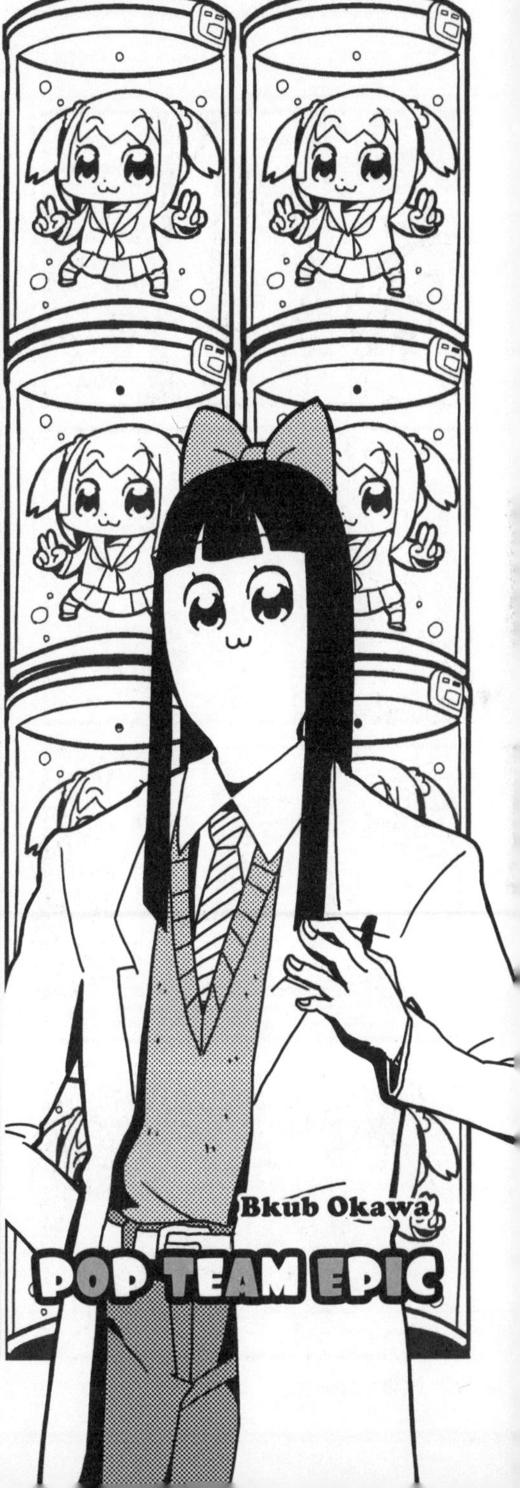
Bkub Okawa
POP TEAM EPIC

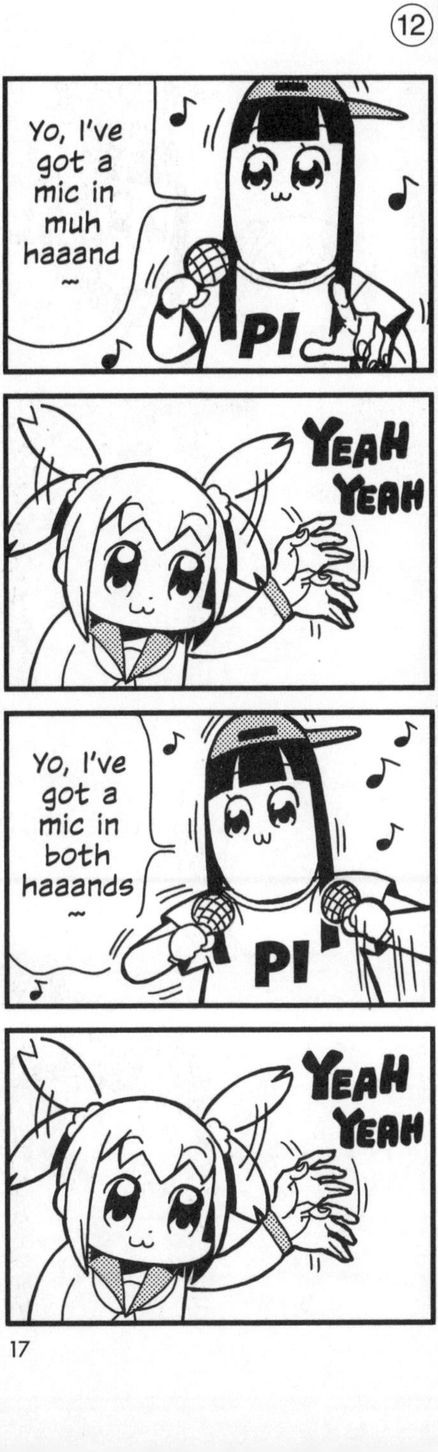
⑫
Yo, I've got a mic in muh haaand ~
PI
YEAH YEAH
Yo, I've got a mic in both haaands ~
PI
YEAH YEAH

13

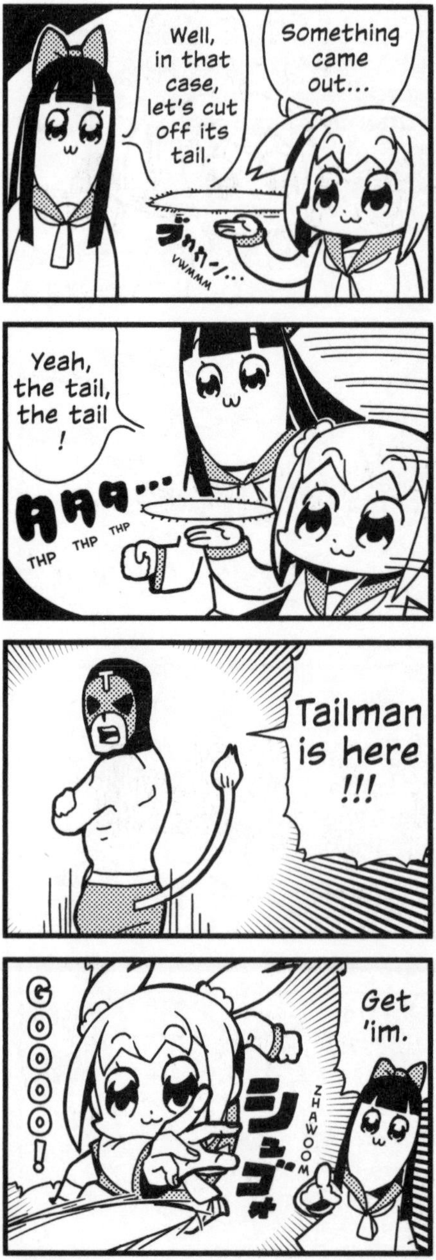
Something came out...
Well, in that case, let's cut off its tail.
VWMMM...
Yeah, the tail, the tail!
THP THP THP
Tailman is here!!!
Get 'im.
ZHAWOOM
GOOOOO!

14

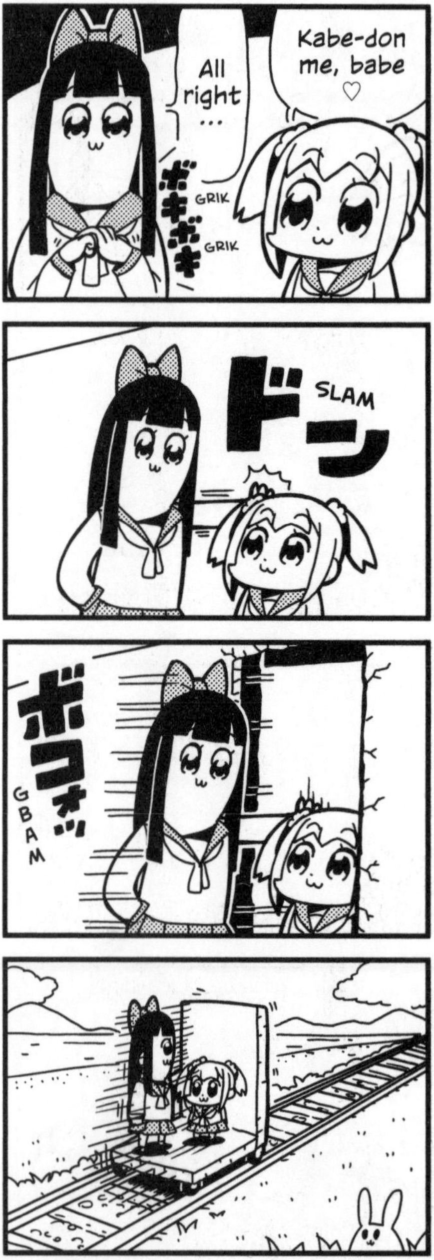
Kabe-don me, babe ♡
All right...
GRIK
GRIK
SLAM
GBAM

15

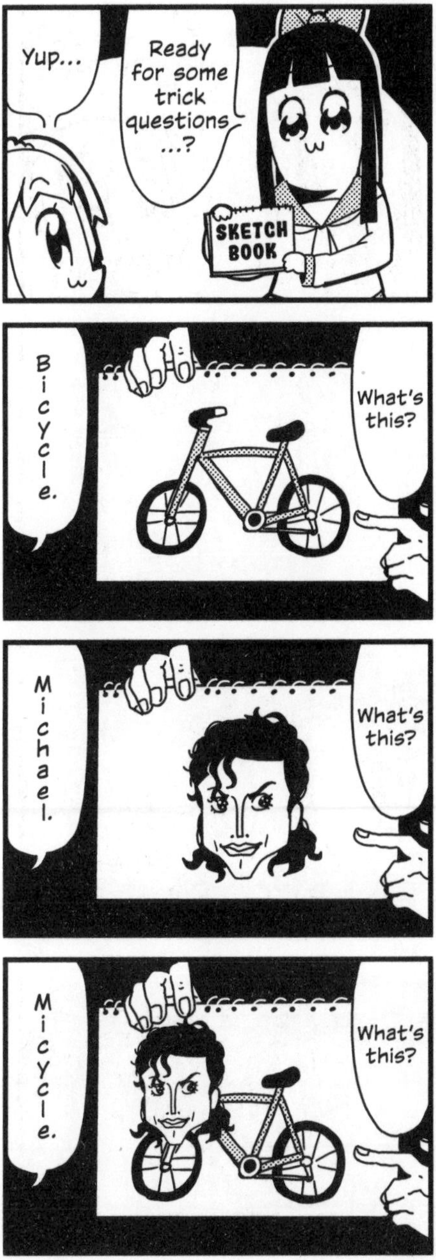
Ready for some trick questions ...?
Yup...
SKETCH BOOK
What's this?
Bicycle.
What's this?
Michael.
What's this?
Micycle.

16

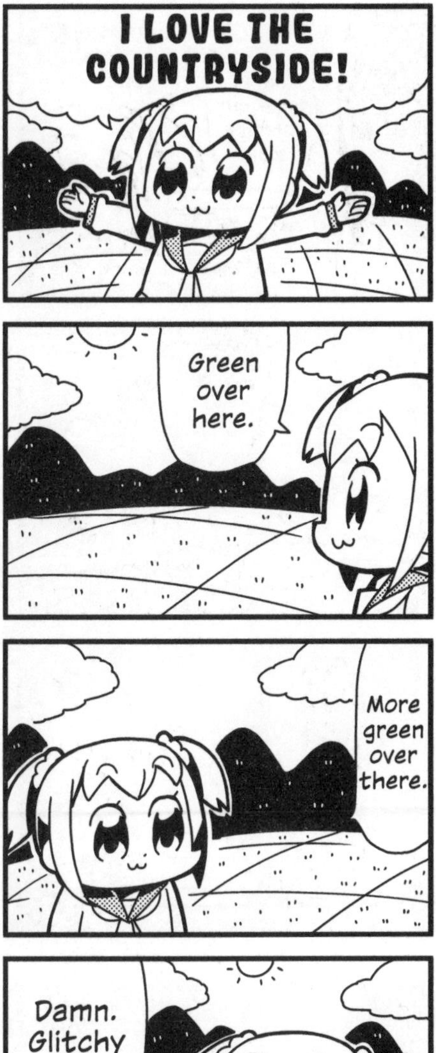
I LOVE THE COUNTRYSIDE!
Green over here.
More green over there.
Damn. Glitchy green all over.

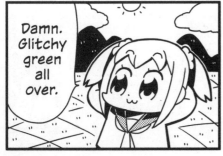

17

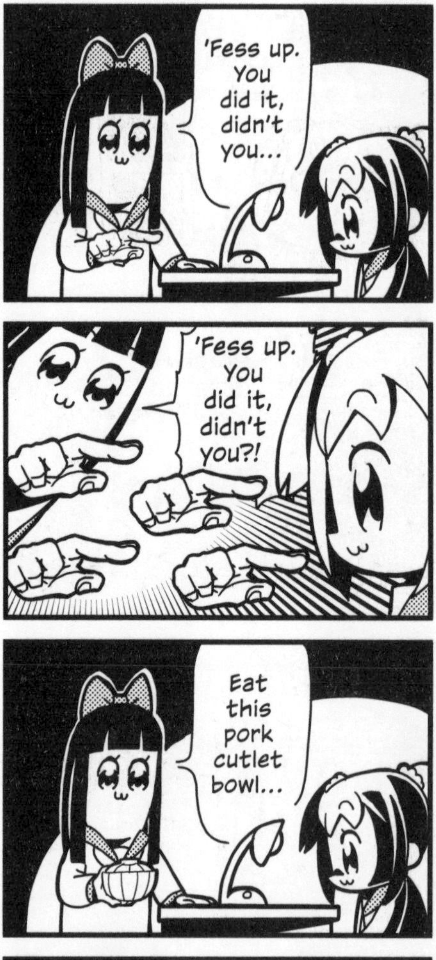
'Fess up. You did it, didn't you...
'Fess up. You did it, didn't you?!
Eat this pork cutlet bowl...
Eat this pork cutlet bowl !!

18

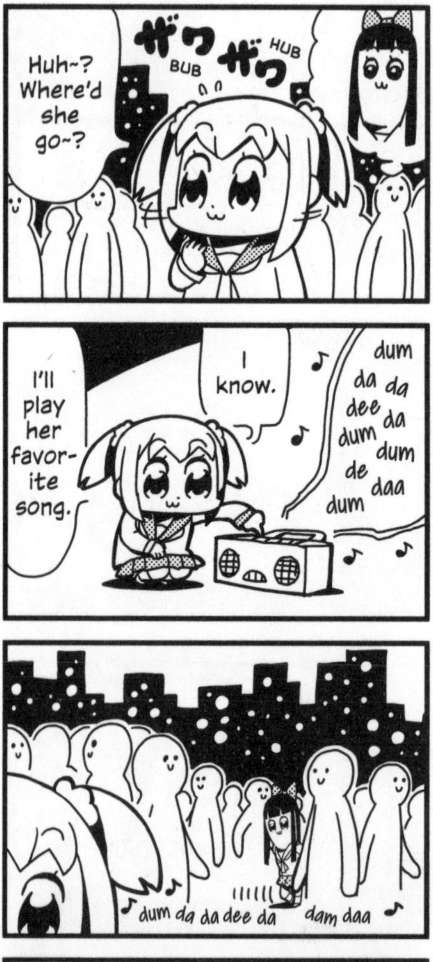
ザワ HUB
ザワ BUB
Huh~? Where'd she go~?
dum da da dee da dum dum de daa dum
I know.
I'll play her favorite song.
dum da da dee da dam daa
dum da da dee da daa

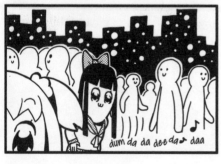

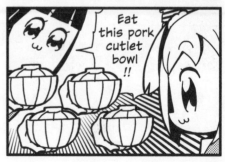

19

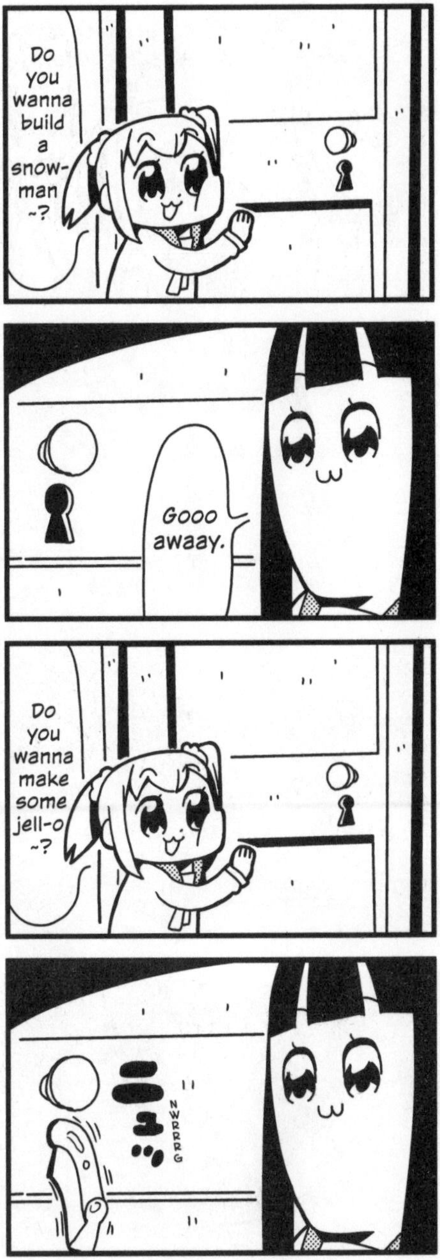
Do you wanna build a snowman ~?
Gooo awaay.
Do you wanna make some jell-o ~?
ニュッ
NWRRRG

20

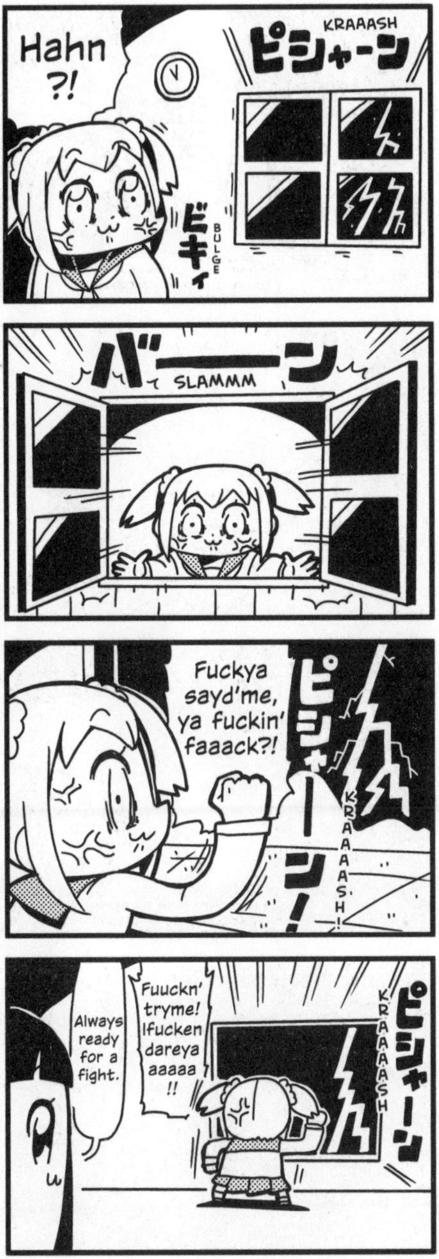
ピシャーン
KRAAASH
Hahn ?!
ビキィ
BULGE
バーーン
SLAMMM
ピシャーン!
KRAAAASH!
Fuckya sayd'me, ya fuckin' faaack?!
ピシャーン
KRAAAASH
Fuuckn' tryme! Ifucken dareya aaaaa !!
Always ready for a fight.

21

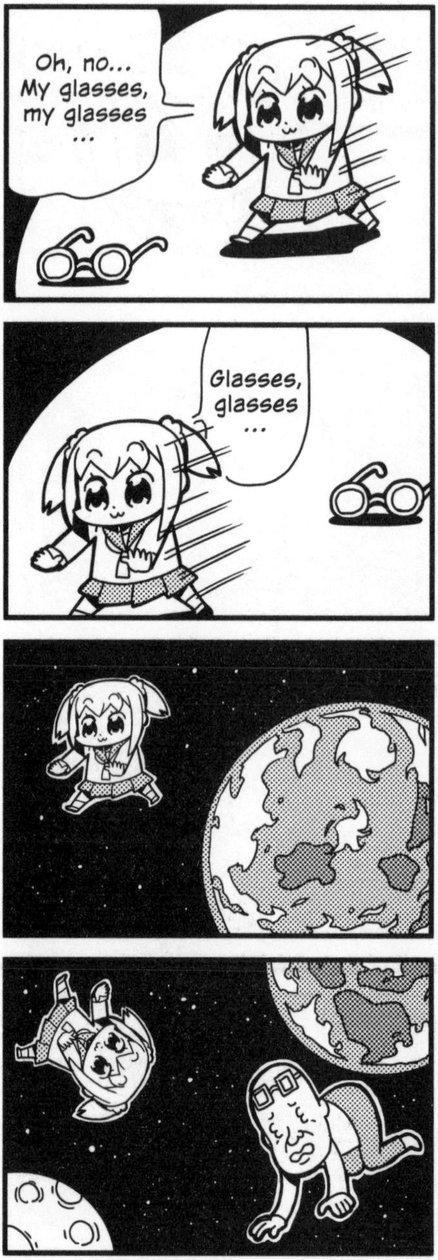
Oh, no... My glasses, my glasses ...
Glasses, glasses ...

22

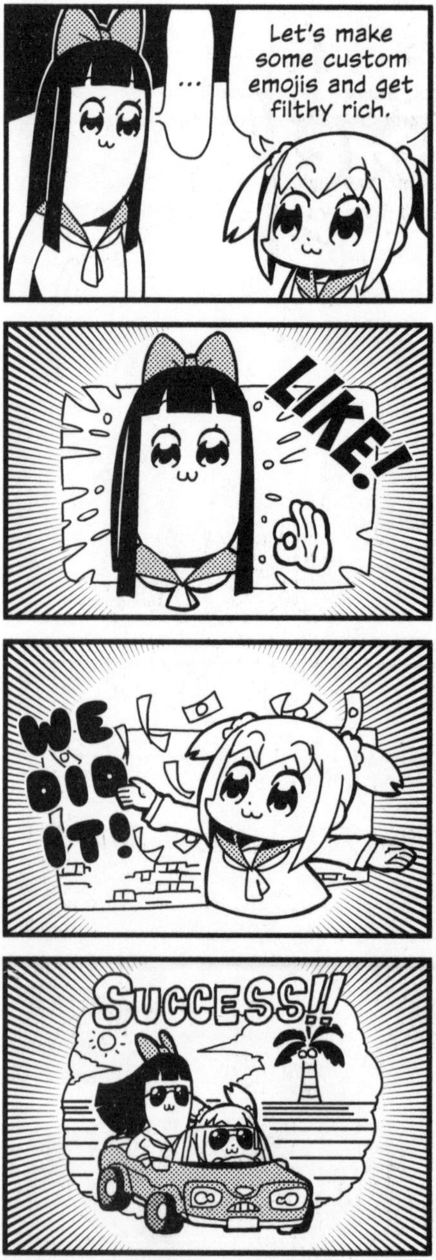
Let's make some custom emojis and get filthy rich.
...
LIKE!
WE DID IT!
SUCCESS!!

To be continued...

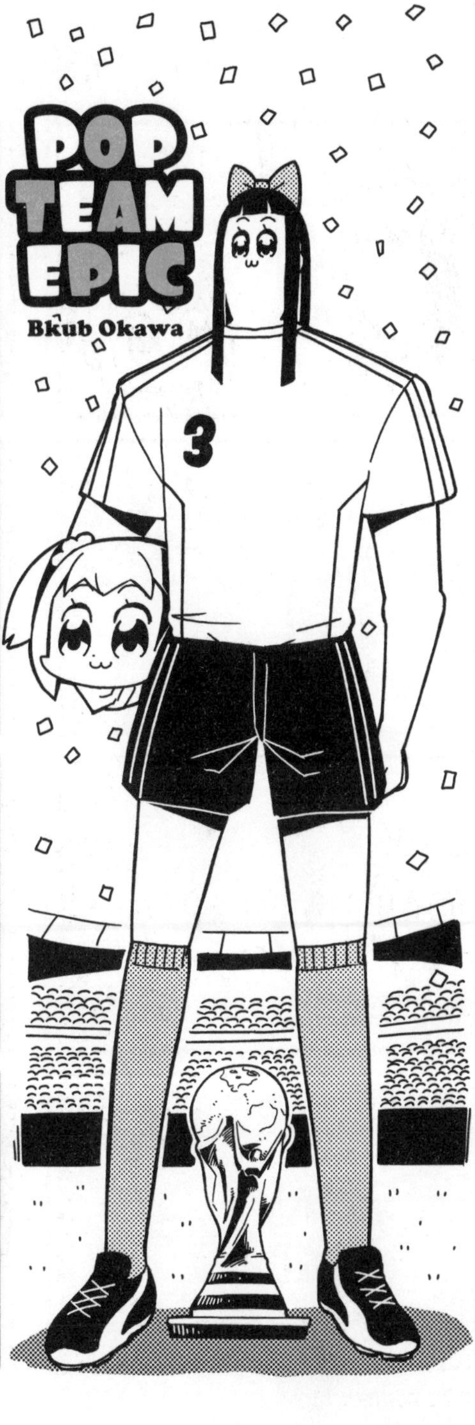
23
POP TEAM EPIC
Bkub Okawa
3

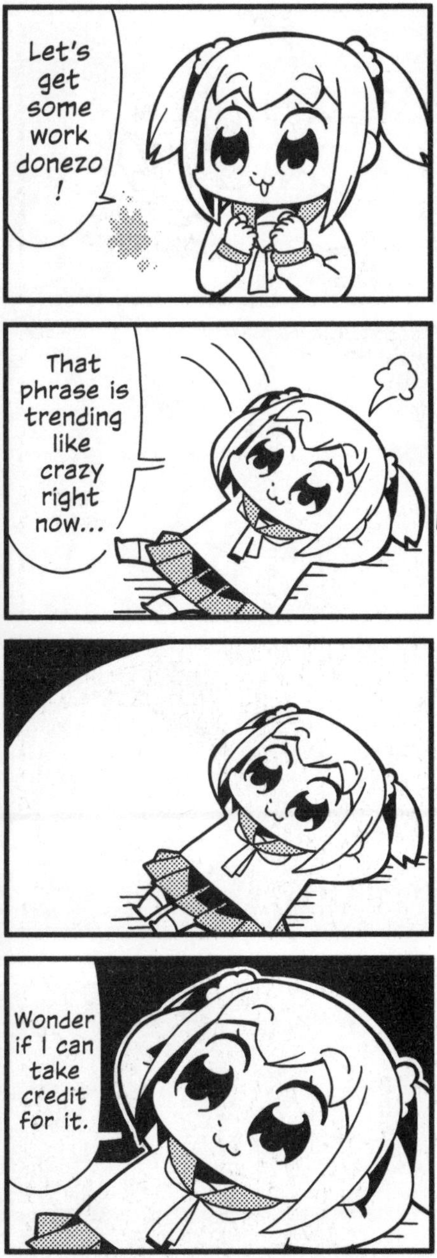
Let's get some work donezo!
That phrase is trending like crazy right now...
Wonder if I can take credit for it.

Ed note: We can hardly believe one of our own would write something so shameless.

(24)

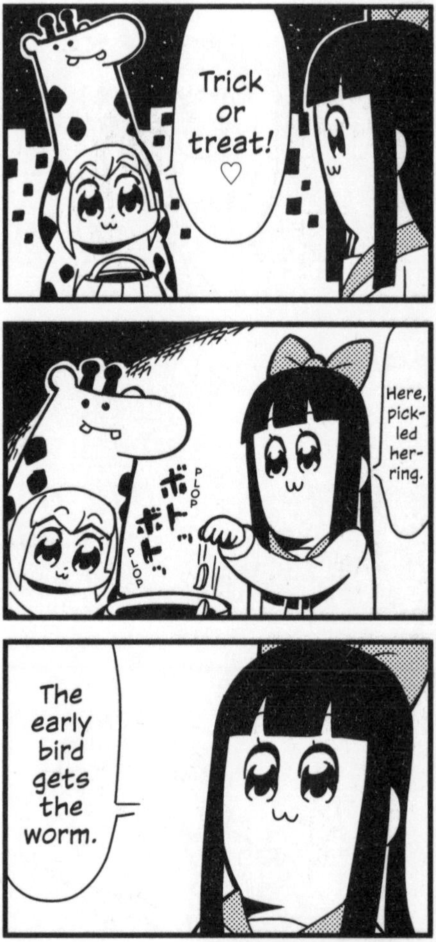
Trick or treat! ♡
Here, pick-led her-ring.
ボトッ PLOP
ボトッ PLOP
The early bird gets the worm.

(25)

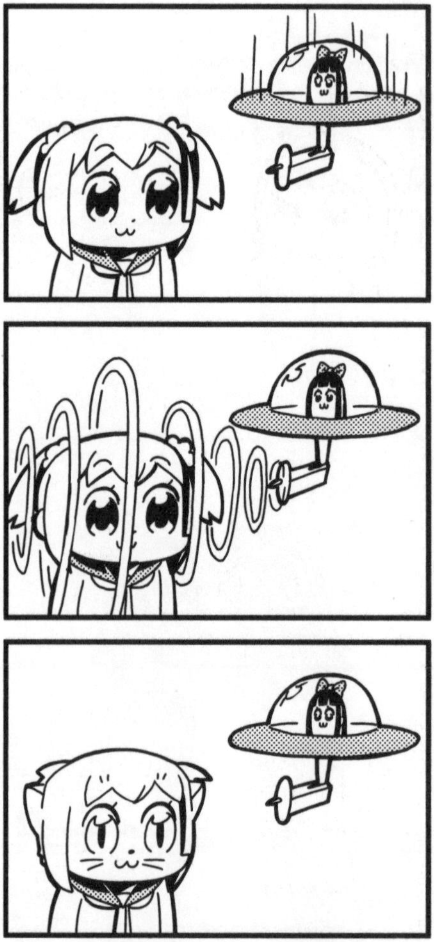

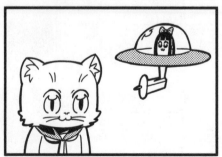

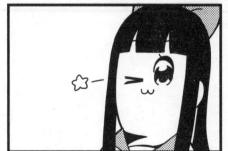

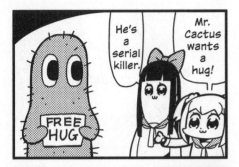

26

A rampaging bull!
MROOOO
Oh, shit.
I'm wearing red today!!
RED
It's okay!
Bulls don't care about the color, they charge at things that flutter.
MROooooo
Waaaah!
RED
WHAP
Didn't I just say ya don't fuckin' care about the color red?!

27

Mr. Cactus wants a hug!
He's a serial killer.
FREE HUG
FREE HUG
Mr. Needles, too!
They can kill each other.
Ready, set, hug!
What? Are ya scared, wuss?
You wanna hug, doncha, ya pussies?!
SFF
FREE HUG
SFF
Don't run away, ya fuckin' cowards!
FREE HUG

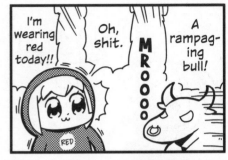

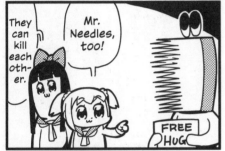

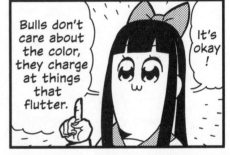

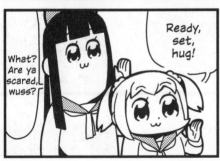

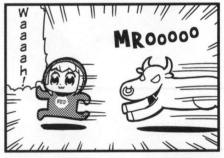

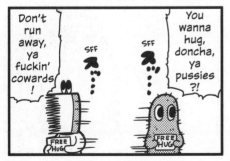

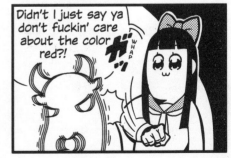

28

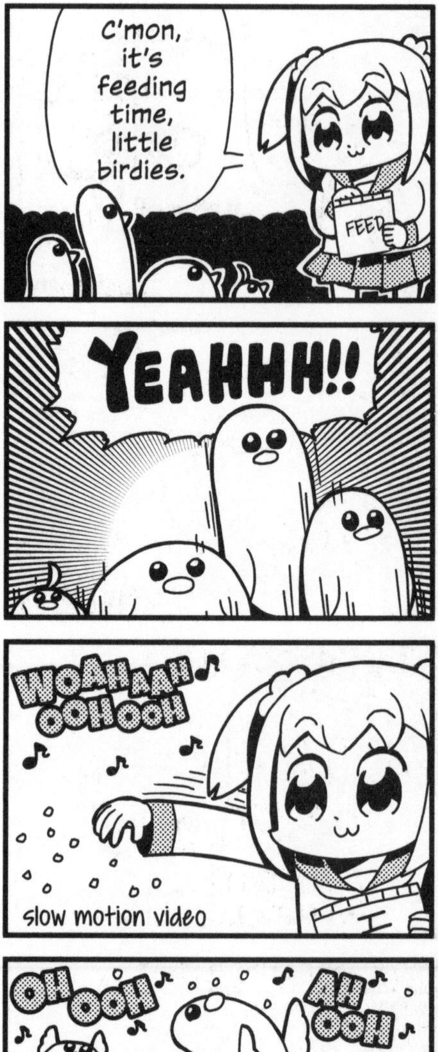
C'mon, it's feeding time, little birdies.
FEED
YEAHHH!!
WOAHAAH OOHOOH
slow motion video
OH OOH
AH OOH
slow motion video

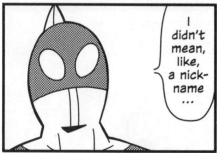

29

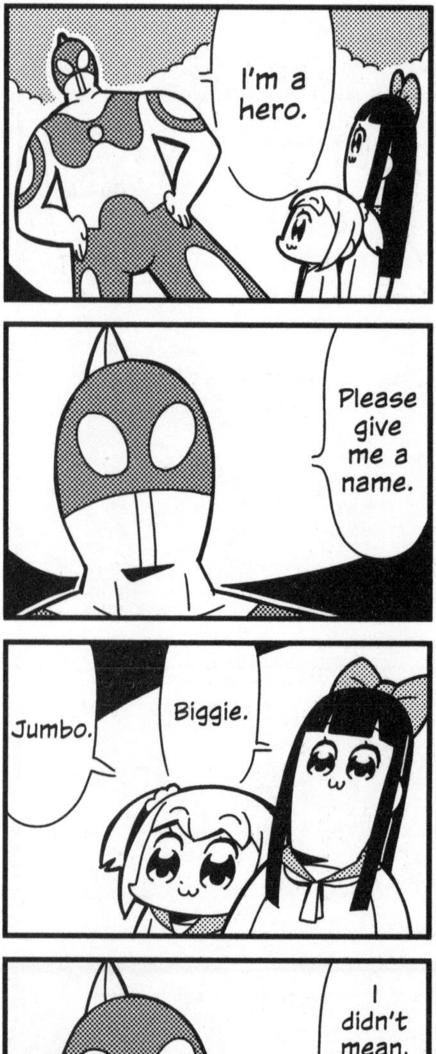
I'm a hero.
Please give me a name.
Biggie.
Jumbo.
I didn't mean, like, a nick-name ...

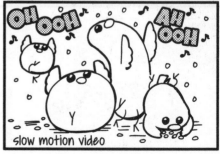

30

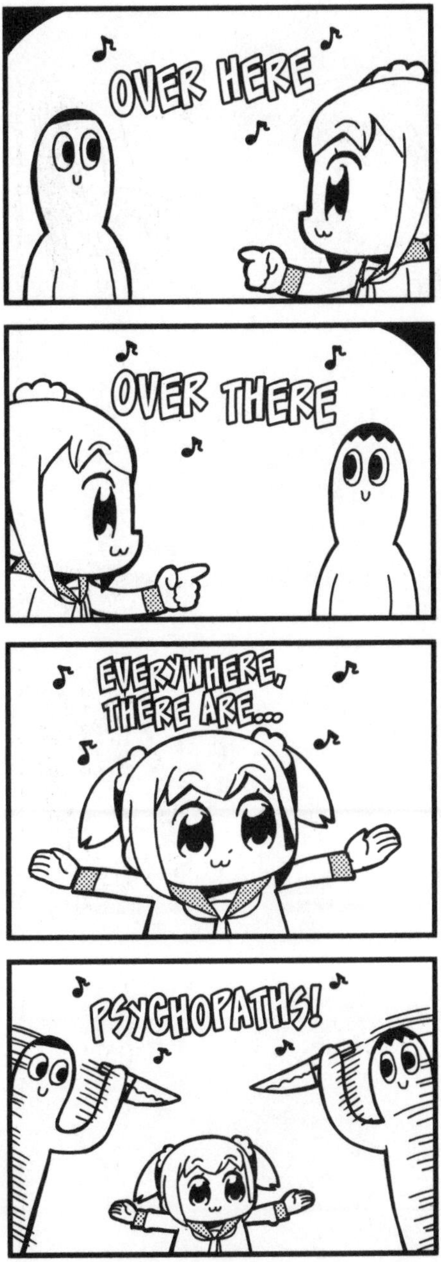
OVER HERE
OVER THERE
EVERYWHERE, THERE ARE...
PSYCHOPATHS!

31

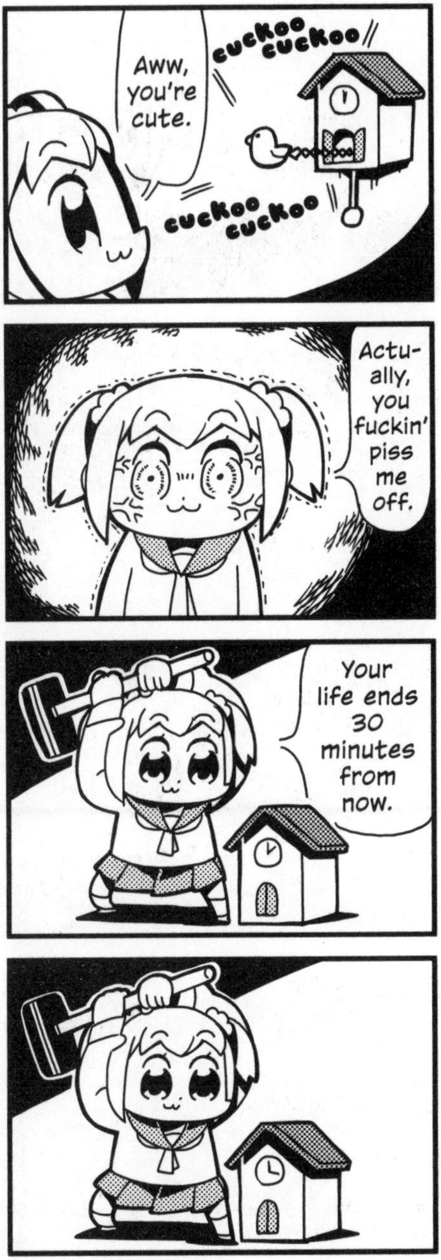
cuckoo cuckoo
Aww, you're cute.
cuckoo cuckoo
Actu-ally, you fuckin' piss me off.
Your life ends 30 minutes from now.

32

Fetch!
KLANK
Thank you ...
You gained karma.

33

DISMEMBERED Body-chan!
Episode 1: Hand
Hey there, Body-chan's Heart!
Hi there, Body-chan's Hand!
I went to look at a house the other day.
Did you buy it?
IT WAS OUT OF MY REACH.
BUT STILL IN YOUR HEART.
HAHAHAHA

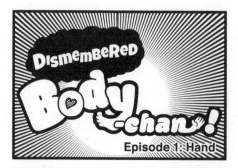

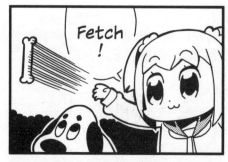

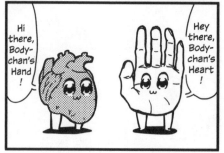

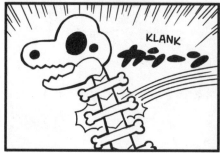

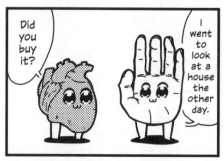

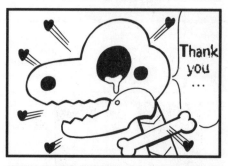

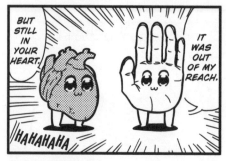

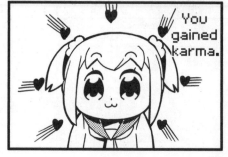

To be continued...

Hydro and wind energy are inefficient
Nuclear energy has many risks

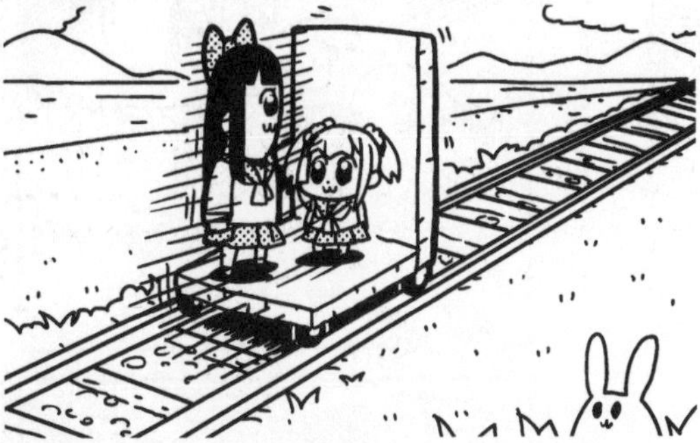

The green energy source of the future is...

Kabe-Don

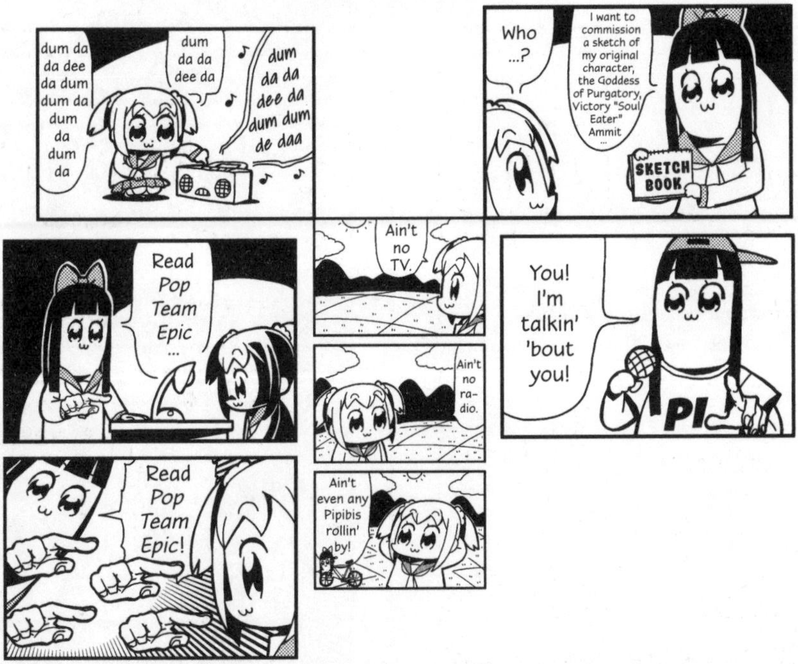
I want to commission a sketch of my original character, the Goddess of Purgatory, Victory "Soul Eater" Ammit ...
Who ...?
SKETCH BOOK
You! I'm talkin' 'bout you!
PI
Ain't no TV.
Ain't no radio.
Ain't even any Pipibis rollin' by!
dum da da dee da dum dum de daa
dum da da dee da
dum da da dee da dum dum da dum da dum da
Read Pop Team Epic ...
Read Pop Team Epic!

POP TEAM EPIC
HARD CORE

Row, row, row
Row, row, row your boat gently down the
Get the fuck outta my act!!
Aieeee?!
GRAB
Chill out! It's sung as a round!
Hurry up and run away!!

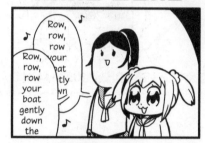

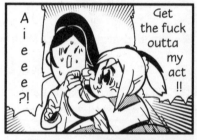

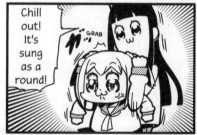

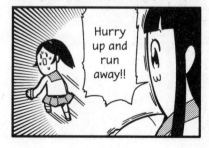

POP TEAM EPIC

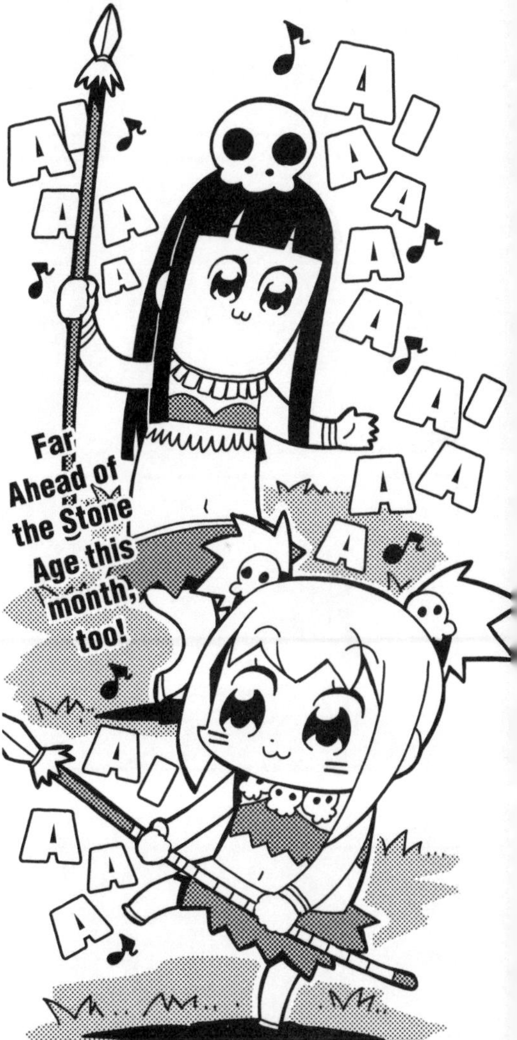
AIAAAAAAIAA
AIAAA
Far Ahead of the Stone Age this month, too!
AIAAAA

Bkub Okawa

(34)

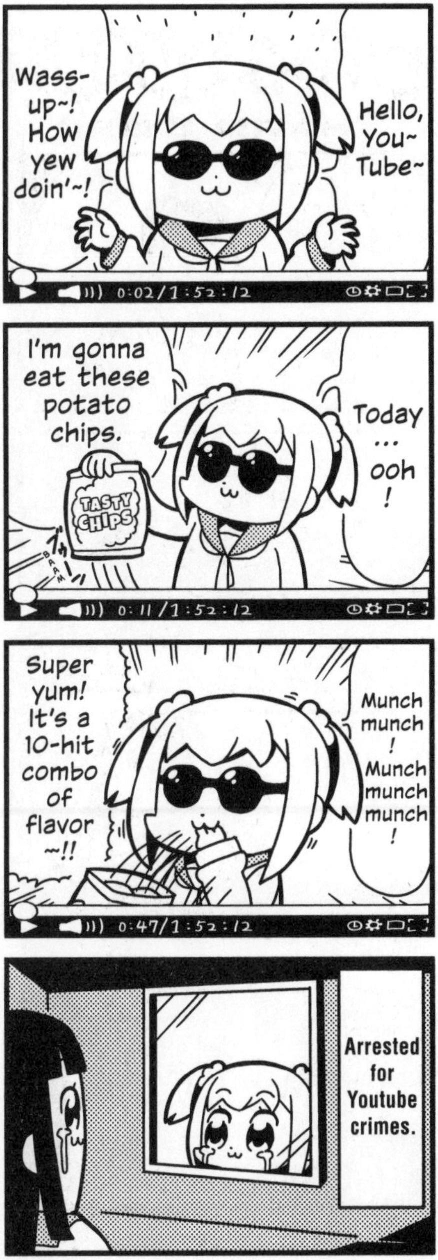
Hello, You~Tube~
Wass-up~! How yew doin'~!
0:02/1:52:12
Today... ooh!
I'm gonna eat these potato chips.
TASTY CHIPS
BAAAM
0:11/1:52:12
Munch munch! Munch munch munch!
Super yum! It's a 10-hit combo of flavor~!!
0:47/1:52:12
Arrested for Youtube crimes.

35

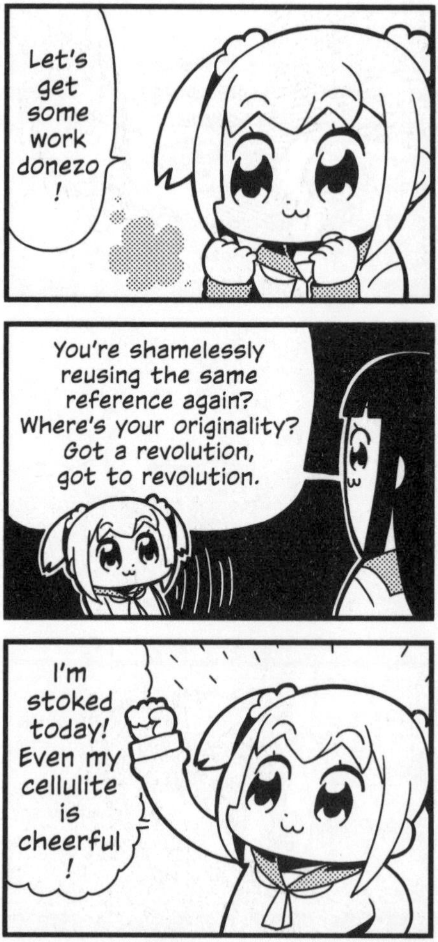
Let's get some work donezo!
You're shamelessly reusing the same reference again? Where's your originality? Got a revolution, got to revolution.
I'm stoked today! Even my cellulite is cheerful!
Cellulite is un-cheerful.
You don't need to phrase it like "diamond is unbreakable..."

36

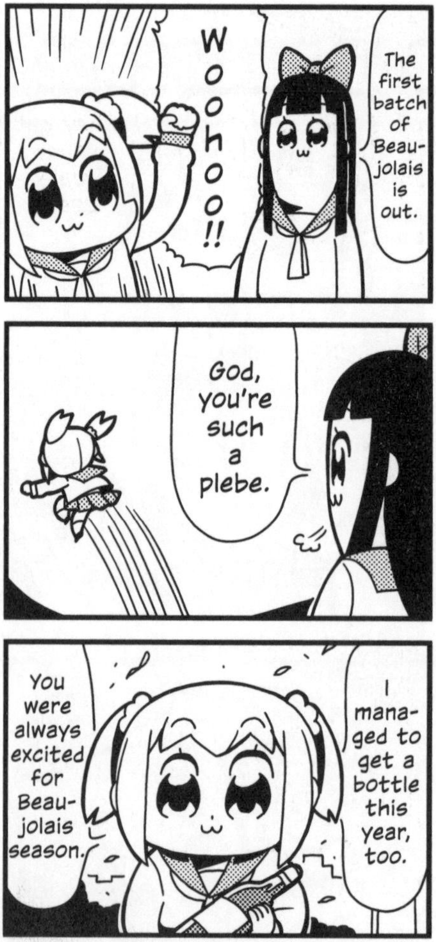
The first batch of Beaujolais is out.
Woohooo!!
God, you're such a plebe.
I managed to get a bottle this year, too.
You were always excited for Beaujolais season.
How is it?
They say this year's batch is top notch.

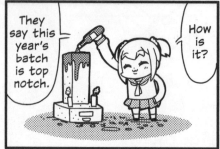

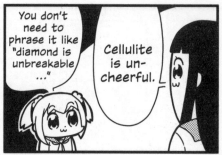

37

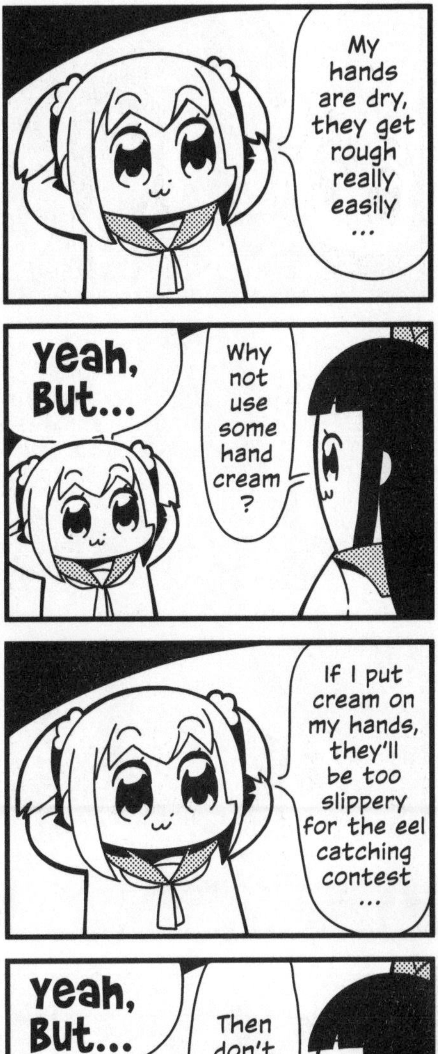

My hands are dry, they get rough really easily ...
Why not use some hand cream?
Yeah, But...
If I put cream on my hands, they'll be too slippery for the eel catching contest ...
Then don't use hand cream.
Yeah, But...

38

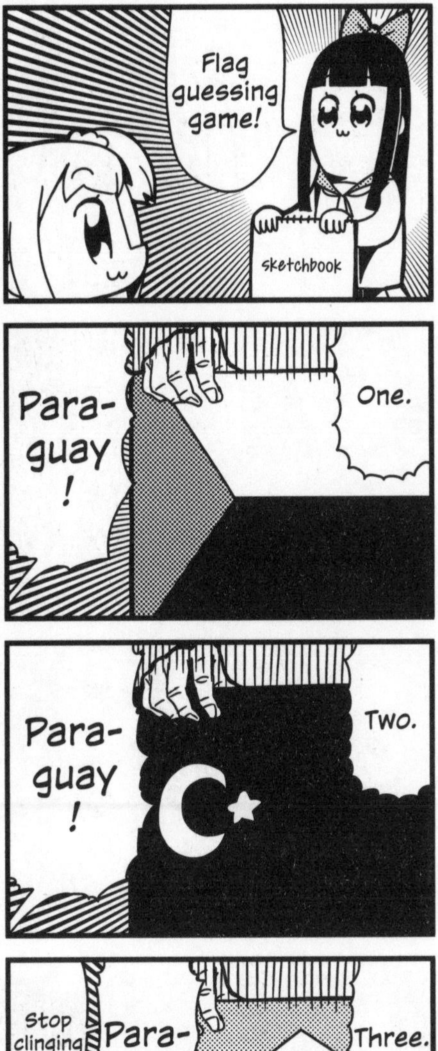

Flag guessing game!
sketchbook
One.
Paraguay!
Two.
Paraguay!
Three.
Paraguay!
Stop clinging to Paraguay.
ORDEN E PROGRESSO

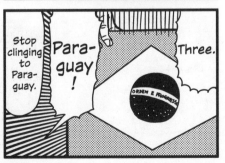

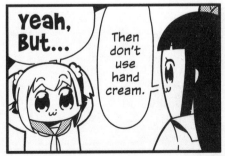

39

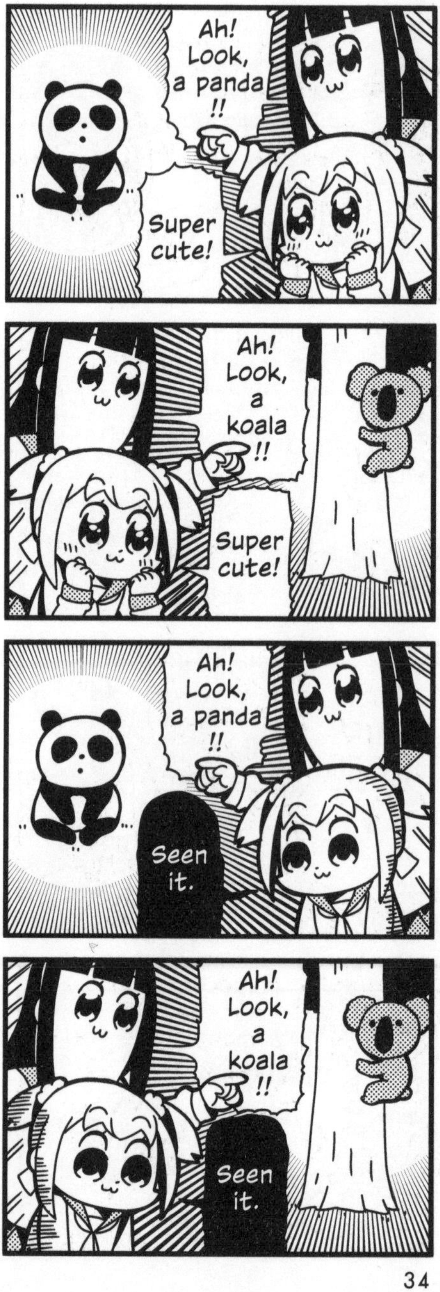
Ah! Look, a panda!!
Super cute!
Ah! Look, a koala!!
Super cute!
Ah! Look, a panda!!
Seen it.
Ah! Look, a koala!!
Seen it.

40

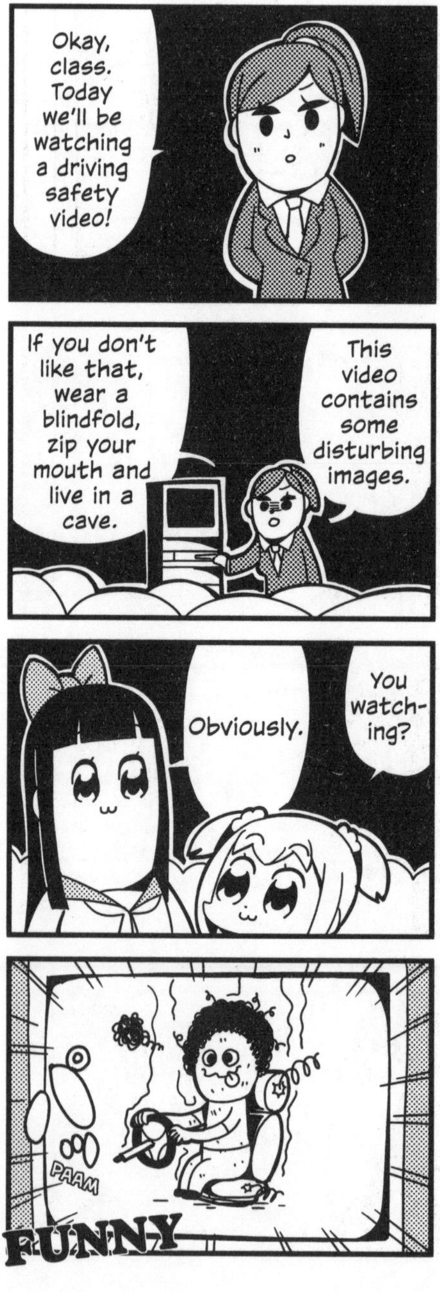
Okay, class. Today we'll be watching a driving safety video!
This video contains some disturbing images.
If you don't like that, wear a blindfold, zip your mouth and live in a cave.
You watch-ing?
Obviously.
PAAM
FUNNY

41

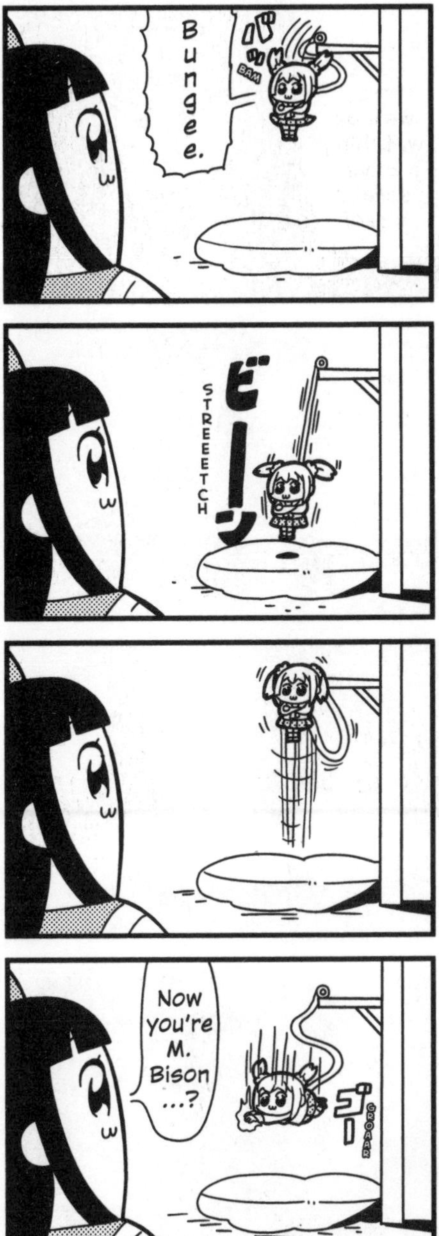
Bungee.
BAM
STREEETCH
Now you're M. Bison ...?
GROAAR

42

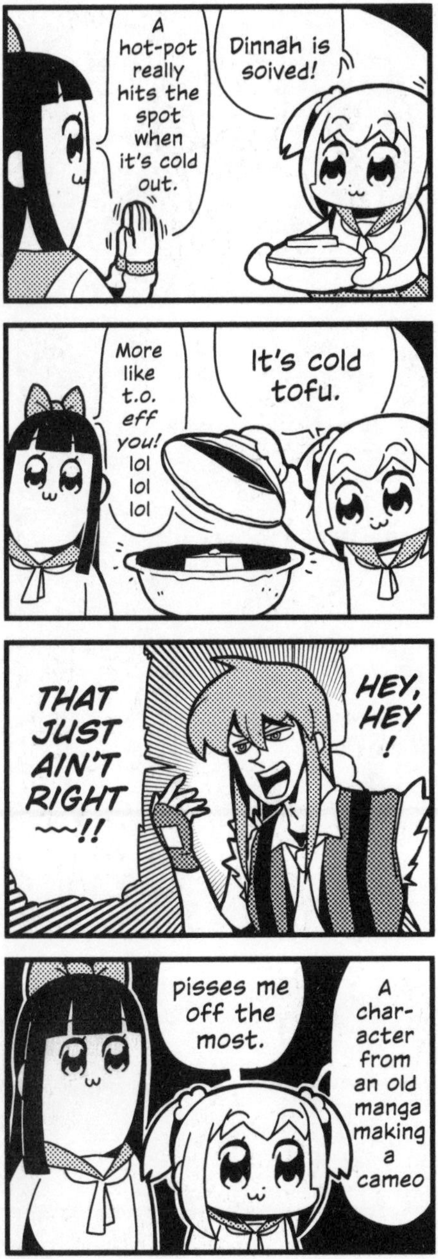
Dinnah is soived!
A hot-pot really hits the spot when it's cold out.
It's cold tofu.
More like t.o. eff you! lol lol lol
HEY, HEY!
THAT JUST AIN'T RIGHT ~~!!
A character from an old manga making a cameo
pisses me off the most.

43

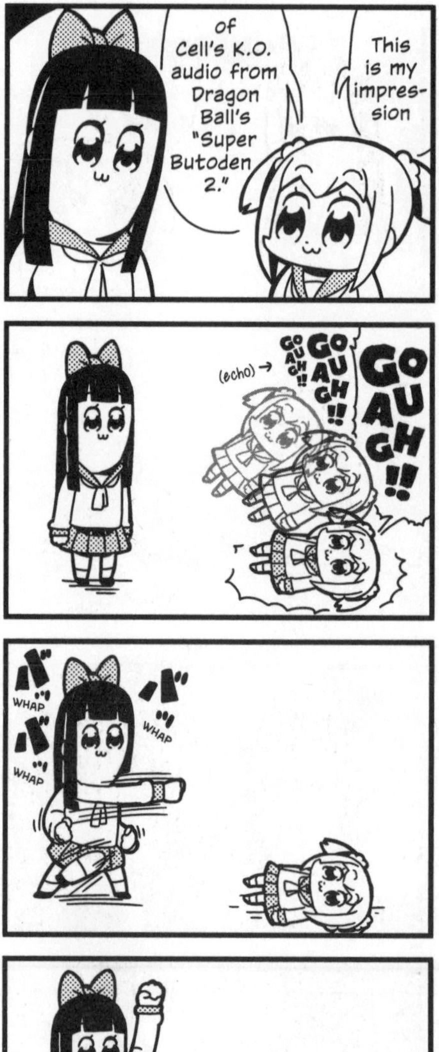
This is my impression
of Cell's K.O. audio from Dragon Ball's "Super Butoden 2."
(echo) →
GO AUGH!!
GO AUGH!!
GO AUGH!!
WHAP
WHAP
WHAP

44

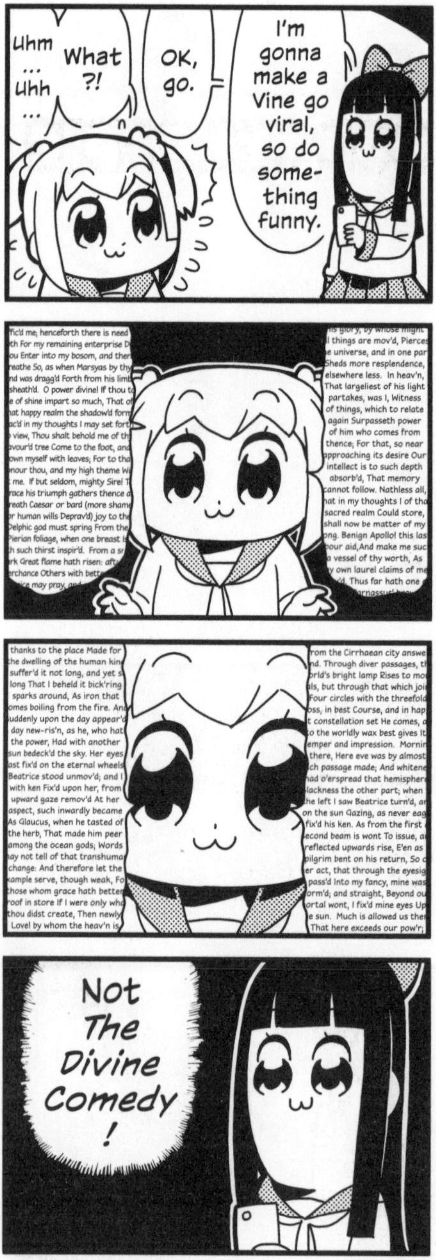
I'm gonna make a Vine go viral, so do some-thing funny.
OK, go.
What?!
Uhm ... Uhh ...
Not The Divine Comedy!

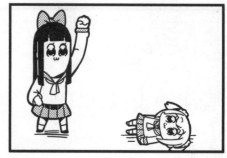

To be continued...

POP TEAM EPIC

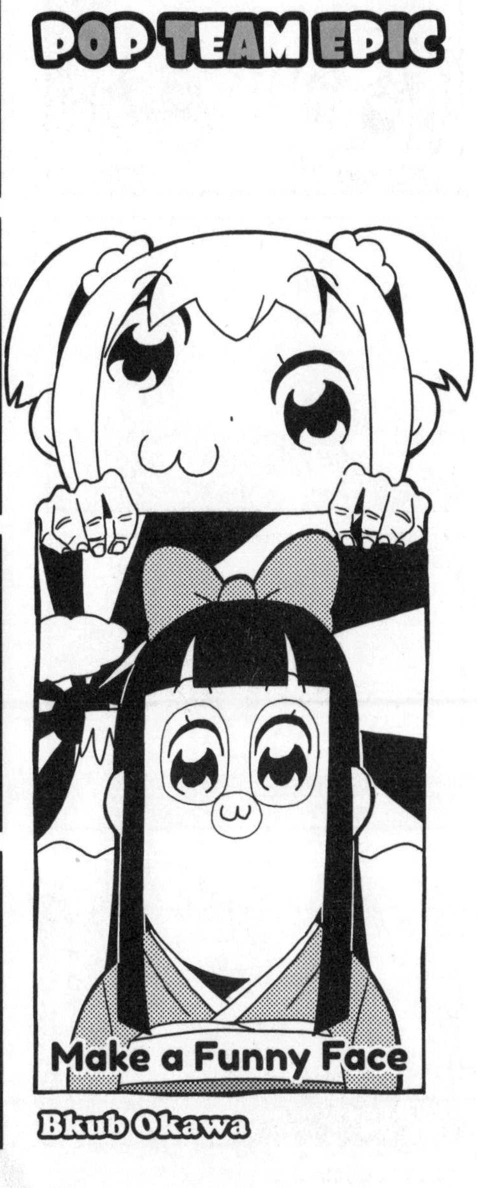

Make a Funny Face

Bkub Okawa

45

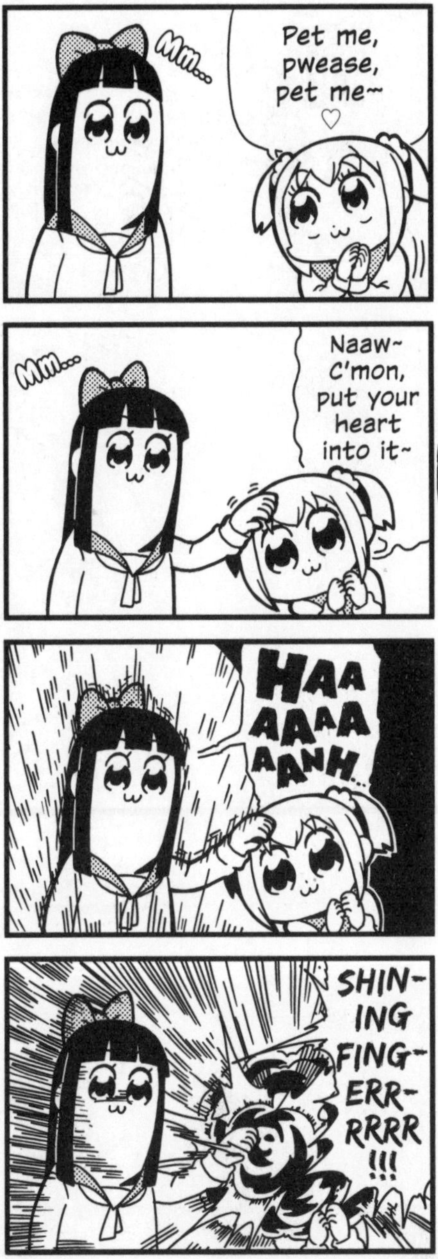

Pet me, pwease, pet me~ ♡
Mm...
Naaw~ C'mon, put your heart into it~
Mm...
HAAAAAAAANH...
SHIN-ING FING-ERR-RRRR !!!

46

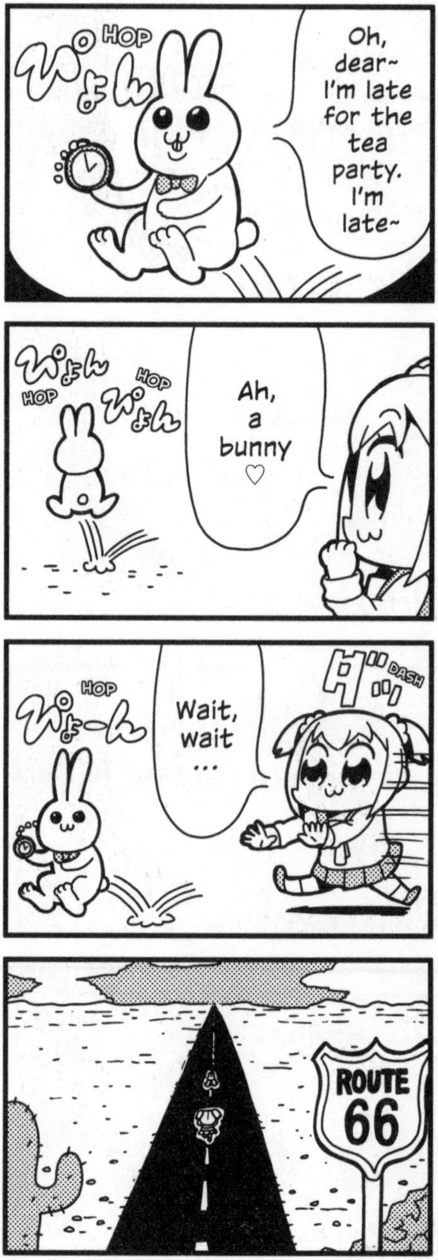
ぴょん
HOP
Oh, dear~ I'm late for the tea party. I'm late~
ぴょん
HOP
ぴょん
HOP
Ah, a bunny ♡
ぴょーん
HOP
DASH
Wait, wait ...
ROUTE 66

47

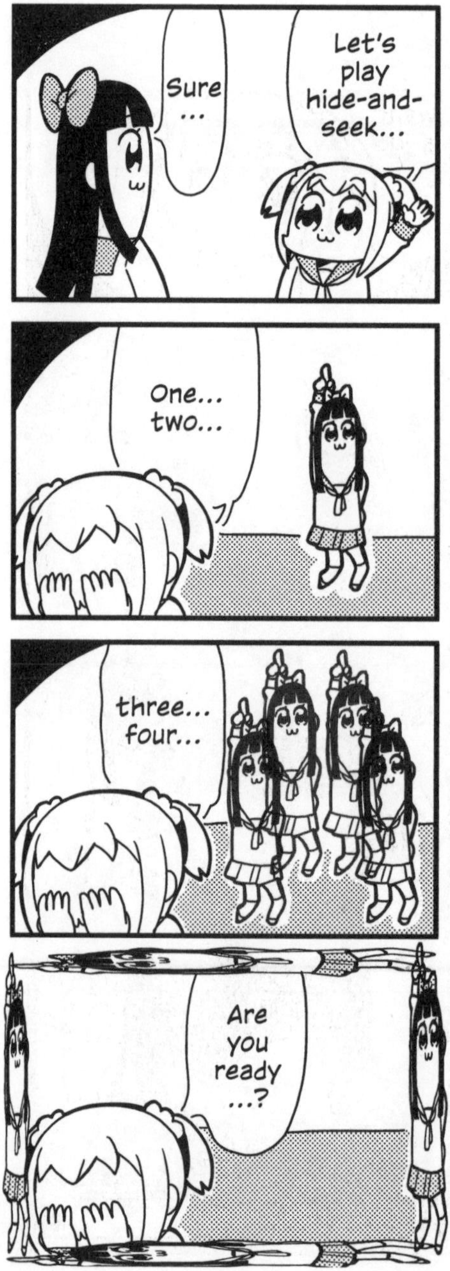
Let's play hide-and-seek...
Sure ...
One... two...
three... four...
Are you ready ...?

48

Aah ...
I want a job ...
I could put you to work.
Yay! I'm game.
All right, here's your advance.
Yeesss.

49

*Lucky items in Japan
1: Mount Fuji
2: Hawk
3: Egg-Plant
4: Elf

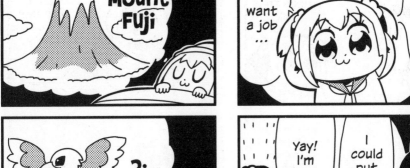

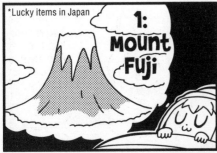

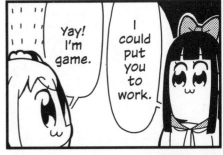

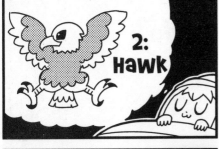

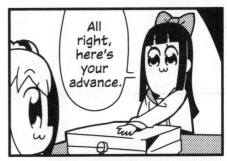

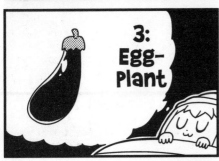

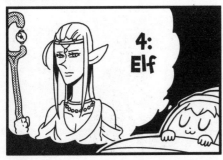

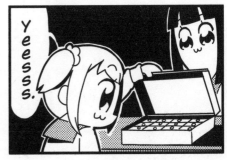

50

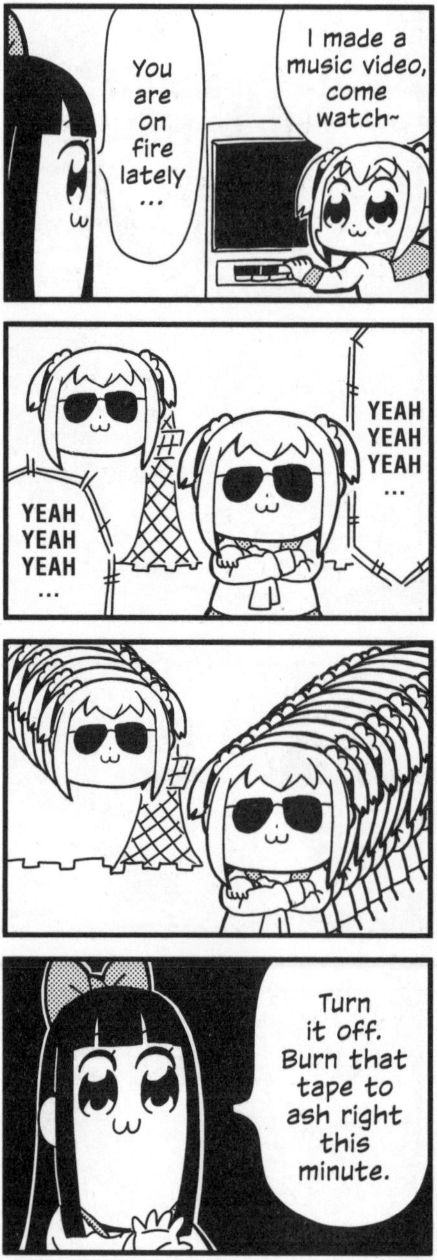

I made a music video, come watch~
You are on fire lately ...
YEAH YEAH YEAH ...
YEAH YEAH YEAH ...
Turn it off. Burn that tape to ash right this minute.

51

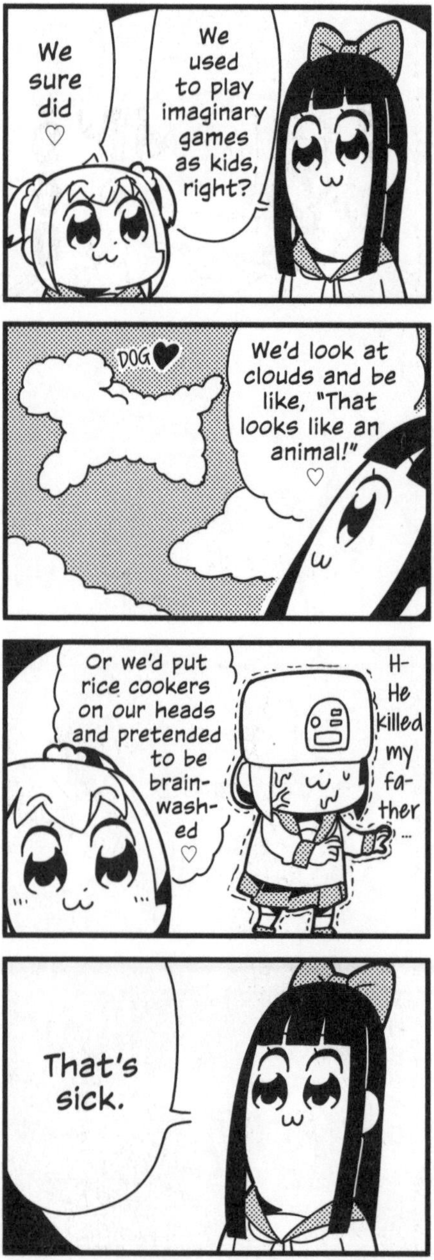

We used to play imaginary games as kids, right?
We sure did ♡
DOG ♥
We'd look at clouds and be like, "That looks like an animal!" ♡
H-He killed my fa-ther ...
Or we'd put rice cookers on our heads and pretended to be brain-wash-ed ♡
That's sick.

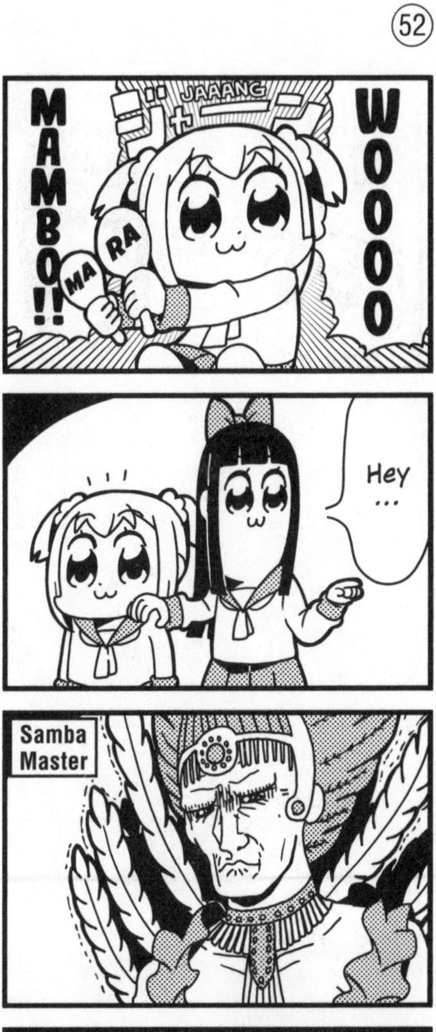
52
WOOOO
JAAANG
MAMBO!!
RA
MA
Hey ...
Samba Master
My casual mambo hurt the Samba Master.

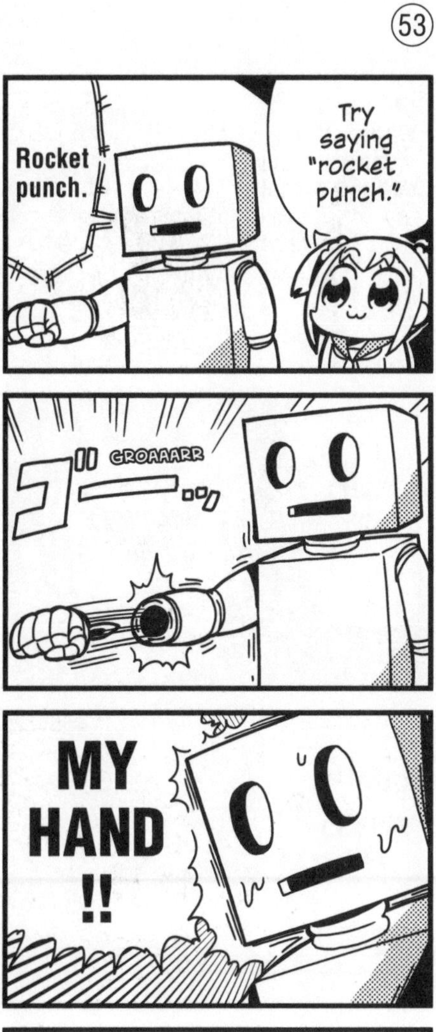
53
Try saying "rocket punch."
Rocket punch.
GROAAARR
MY HAND !!
That's fuckin' funny.
MY HAND!!!
GROAAR

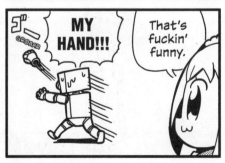

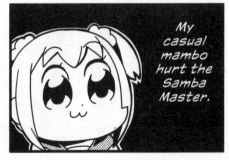

54

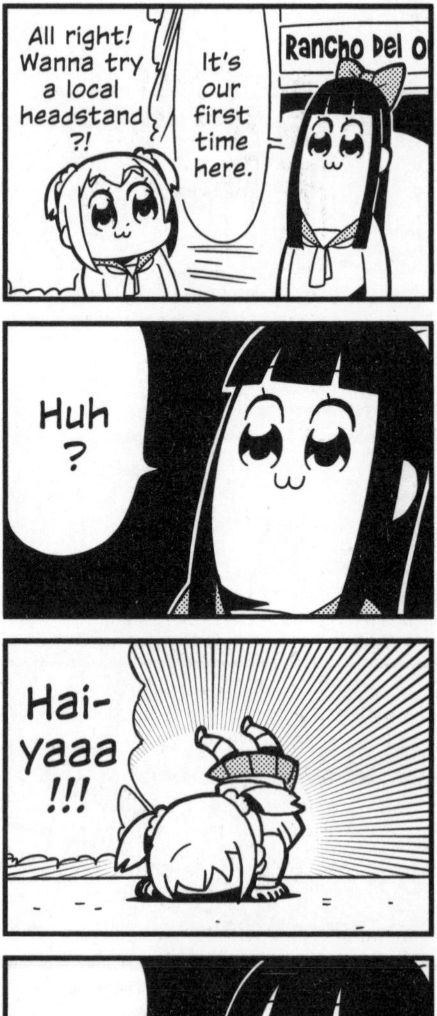
Rancho Del O
It's our first time here.
All right! Wanna try a local headstand?!
Huh?
Hai-yaaa!!!
Huh?

55

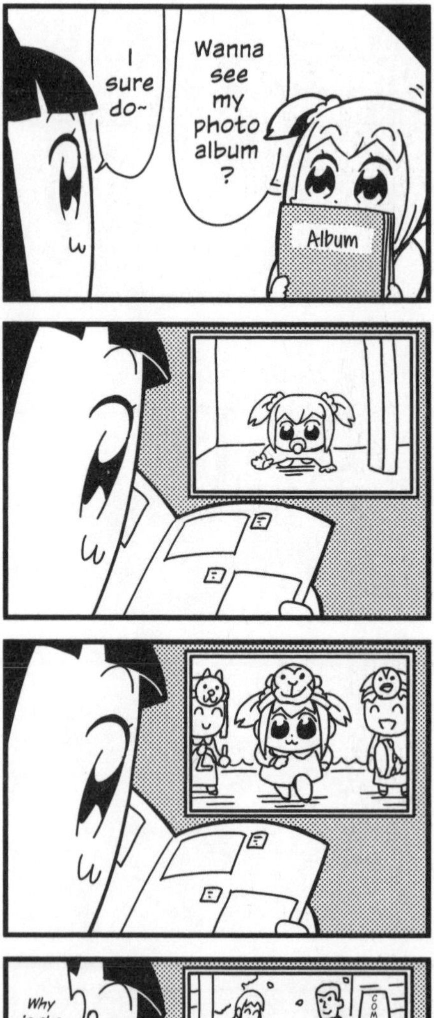
Wanna see my photo album?
I sure do~
Album
COMMENCEMENT
Why is she running towards the camera in every shot.

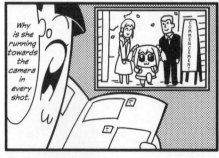

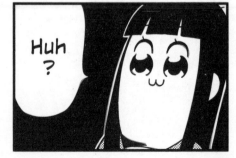

To be continued...

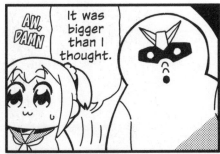

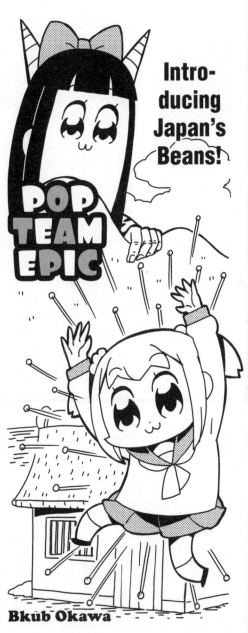

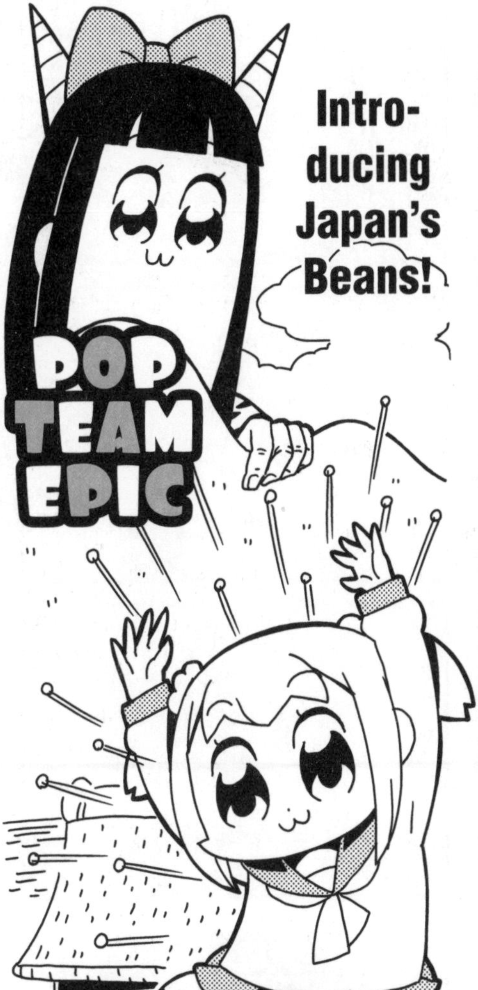
Introducing Japan's Beans!
POP TEAM EPIC
Bkub Okawa

56

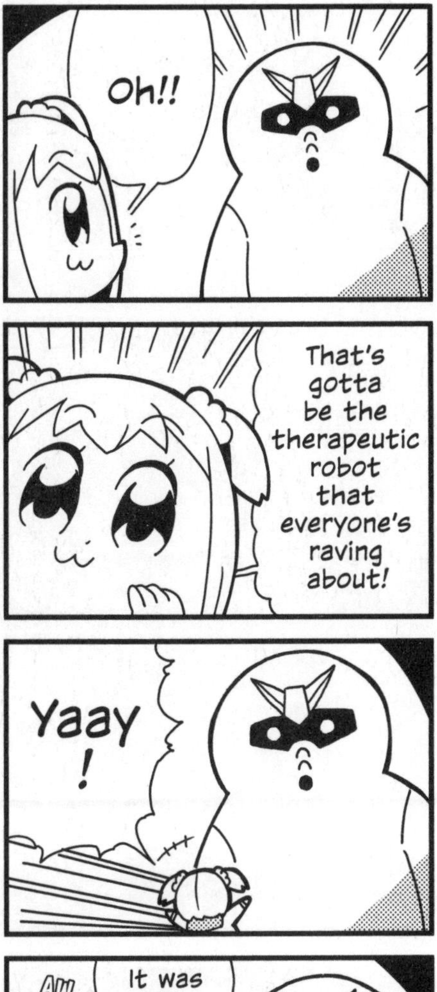
Oh!!
That's gotta be the therapeutic robot that everyone's raving about!
Yaay!
It was bigger than I thought.
AW, DAMN

57

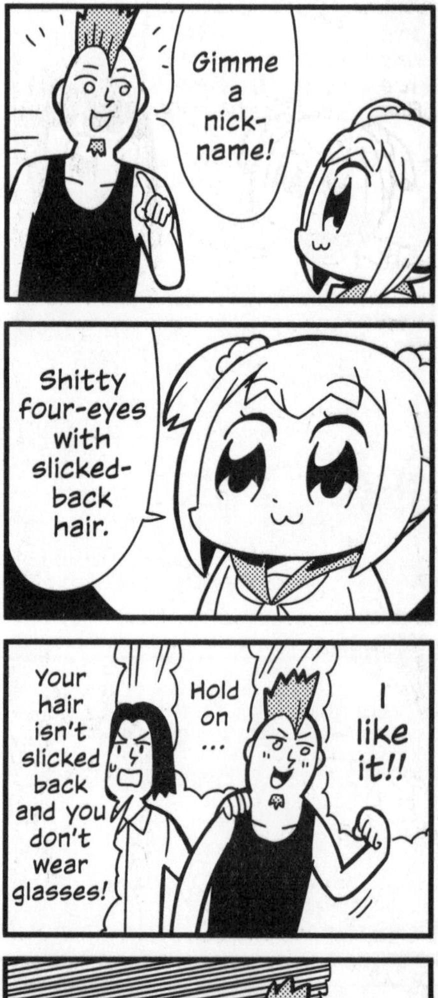
Gimme a nick-name!
Shitty four-eyes with slicked-back hair.
I like it!!
Hold on ...
Your hair isn't slicked back and you don't wear glasses!
Shut up! It's fine!

58

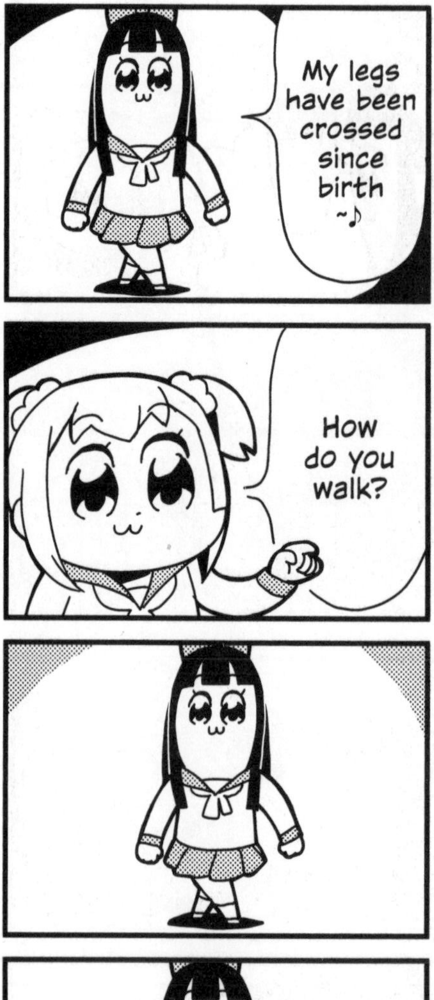
My legs have been crossed since birth ~♪
How do you walk?
BAM

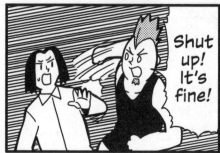

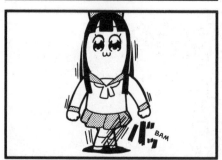

59

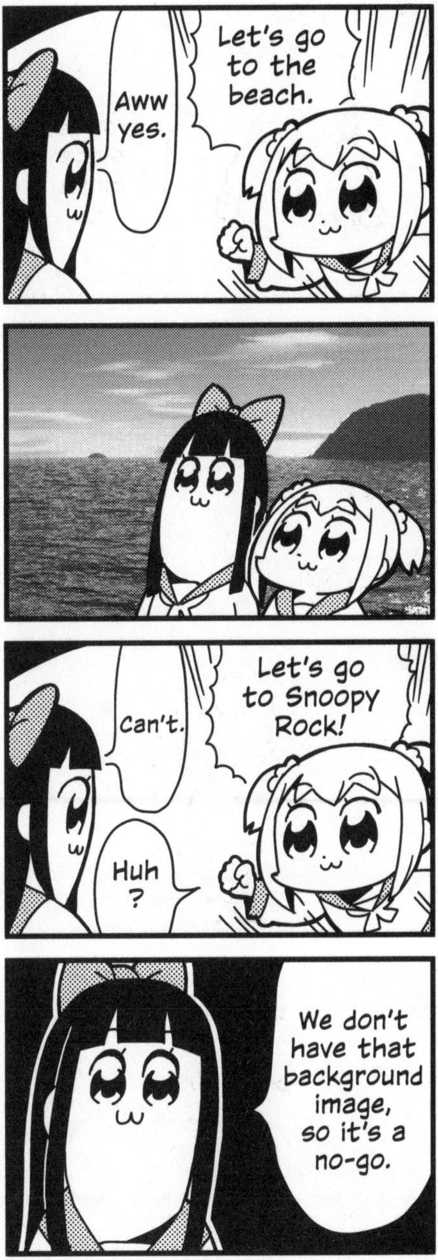
Let's go to the beach.
Aww yes.
Let's go to Snoopy Rock!
Can't.
Huh?
We don't have that background image, so it's a no-go.

60

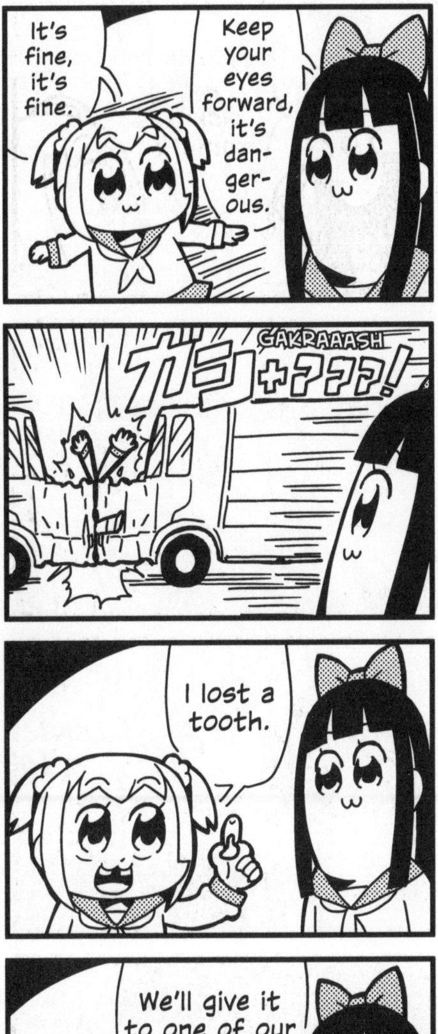
Keep your eyes forward, it's dangerous.
It's fine, it's fine.
GAKRAAASH
ガシャァァァ!
I lost a tooth.
We'll give it to one of our readers.

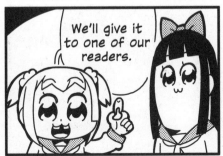

61

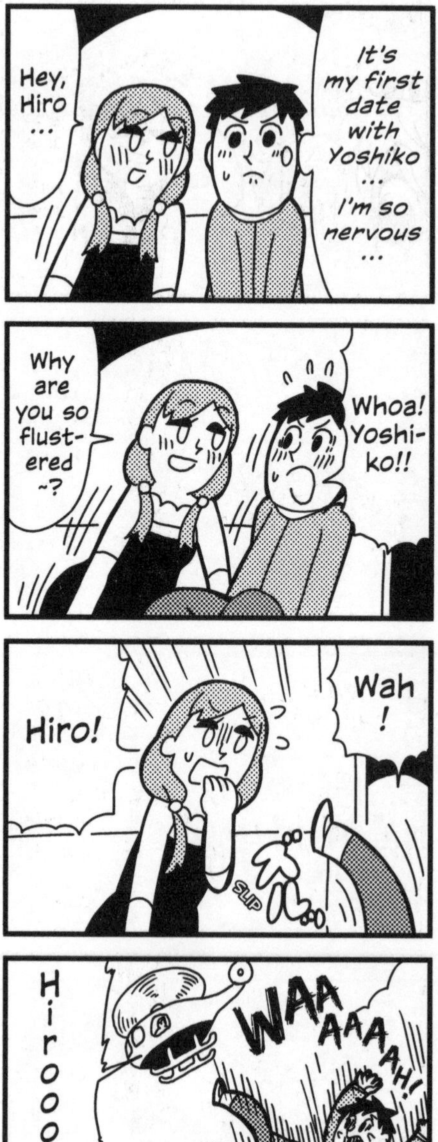
It's my first date with Yoshiko ... I'm so nervous ...
Hey, Hiro ...
Whoa! Yoshiko!!
Why are you so flustered ~?
Wah!
Hiro!
SLIP
WAAAAAAH!!
Hirooooo!!!

62

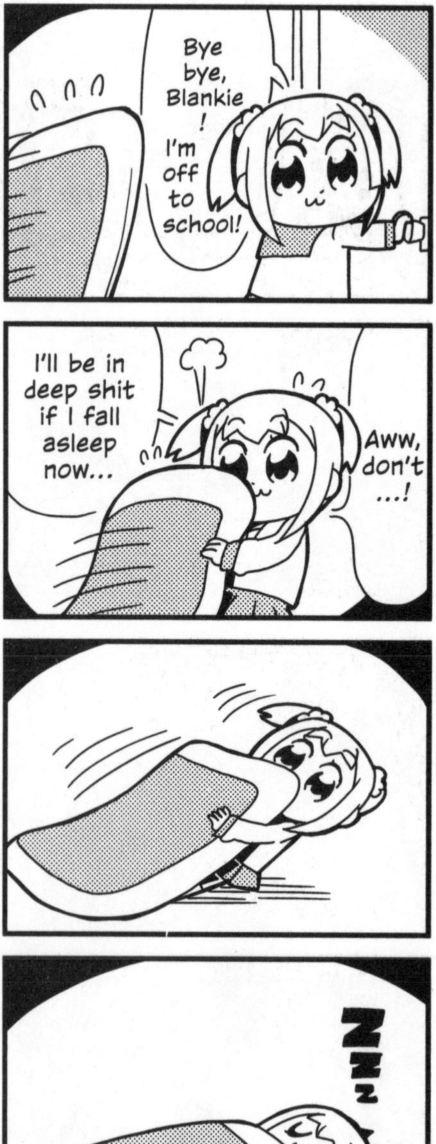
Bye bye, Blankie! I'm off to school!
Aww, don't ...!
I'll be in deep shit if I fall asleep now...
Zzz

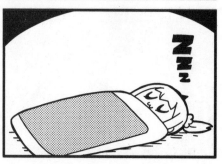

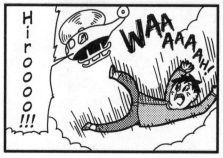

63

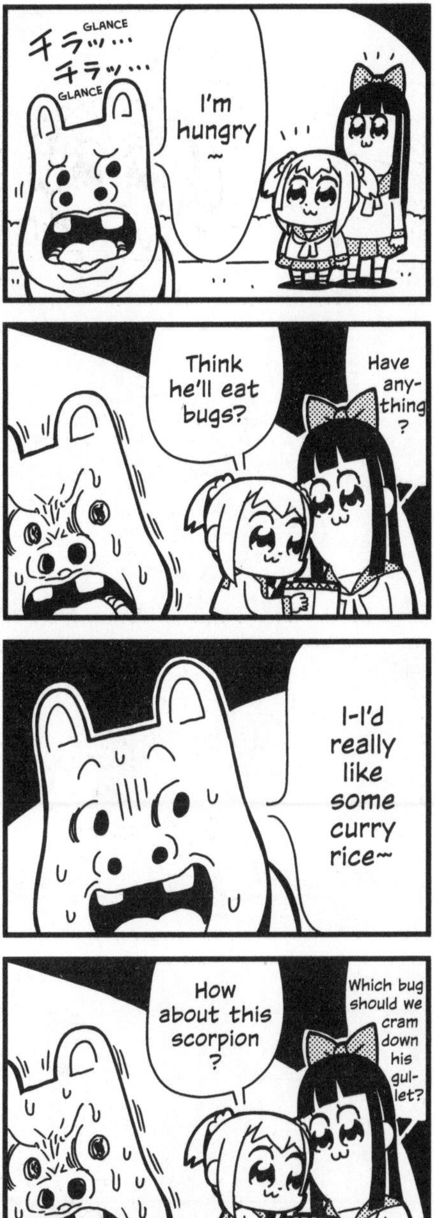
チラッ…
GLANCE
チラッ…
GLANCE
I'm hungry ~
Have anything?
Think he'll eat bugs?
I-I'd really like some curry rice~
Which bug should we cram down his gullet?
How about this scorpion?

64

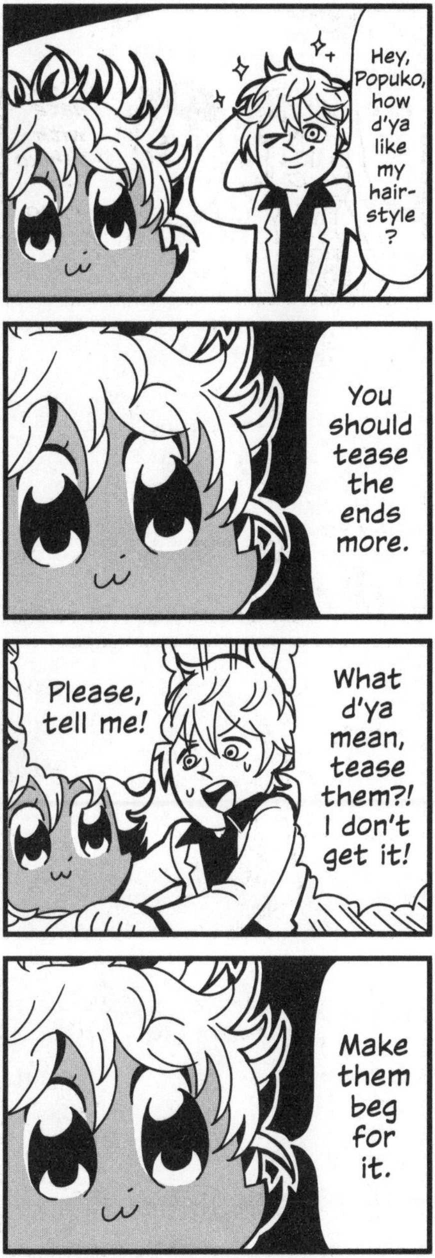
Hey, Popuko, how d'ya like my hair-style?
You should tease the ends more.
What d'ya mean, tease them?! I don't get it!
Please, tell me!
Make them beg for it.

65

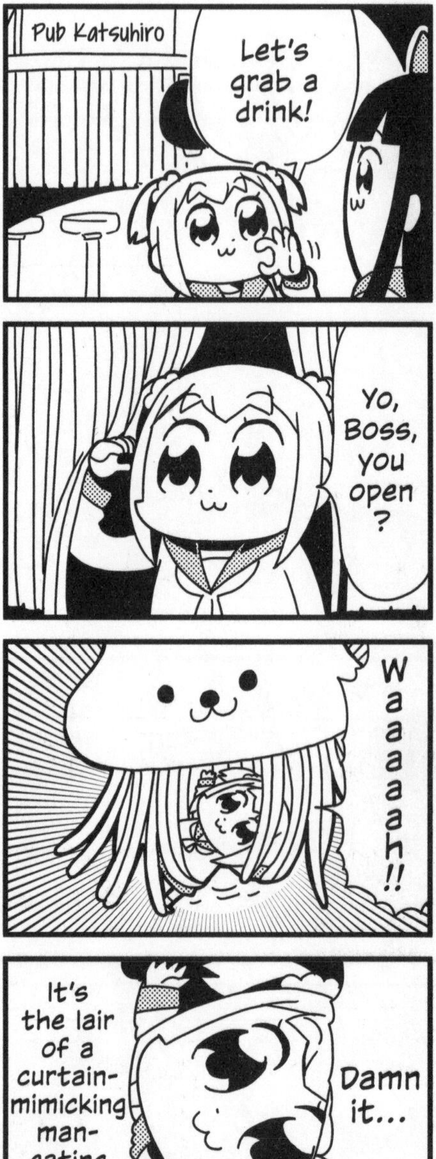
Pub Katsuhiro
Let's grab a drink!
Yo, Boss, you open?
Waaaaaah!!
It's the lair of a curtain-mimicking man-eating jellyfish!!
Damn it...

66

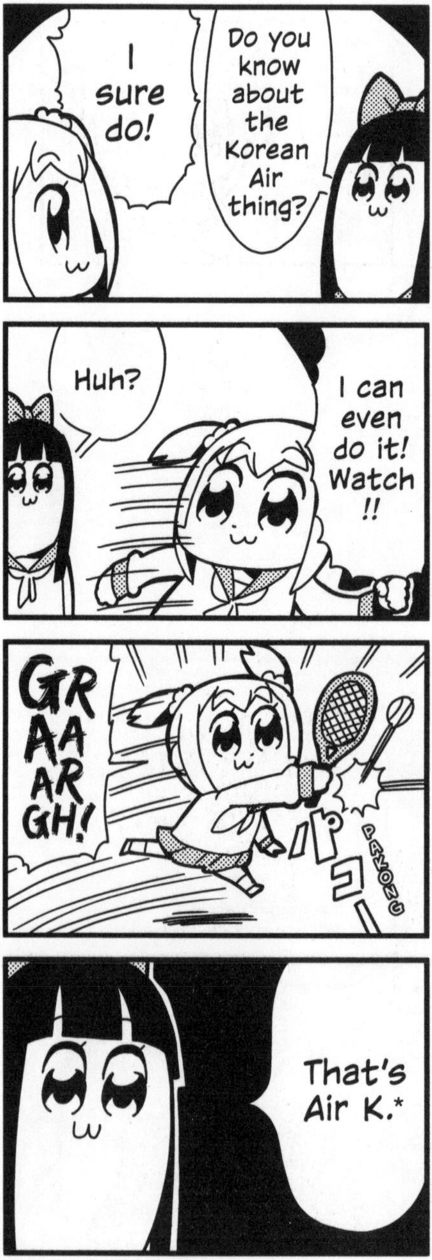
Do you know about the Korean Air thing?
I sure do!
I can even do it! Watch!!
Huh?
GRAAARGH!
PAKONG
That's Air K.*

To be continued...

*Tennis player Kei Nishikori's signature move

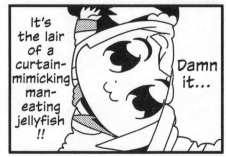

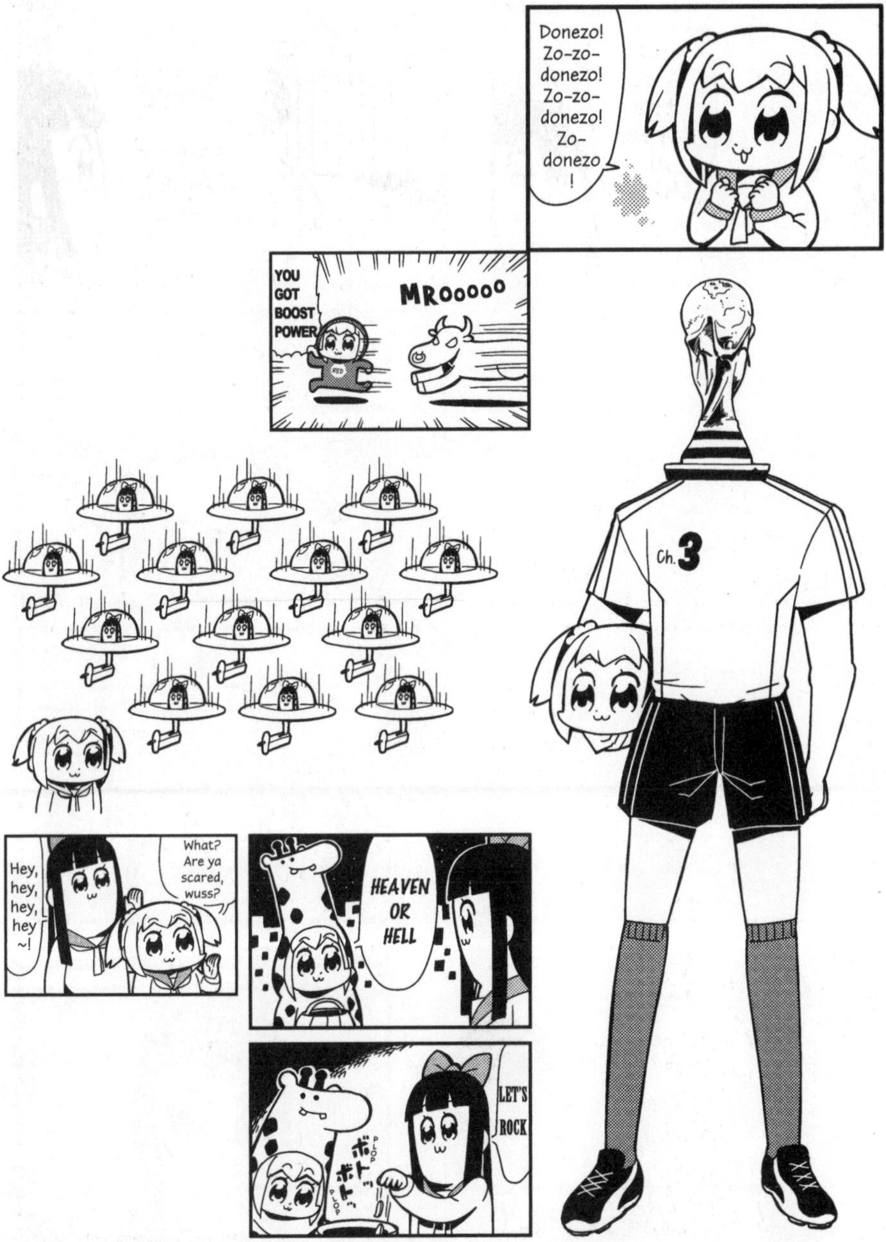
Donezo! Zo-zo-donezo! Zo-zo-donezo! Zo-donezo!
Ch. 3
YOU GOT BOOST POWER
MROOOOO
HEAVEN OR HELL
LET'S ROCK
ボトッ PLOP
ボトッ PLOP
What? Are ya scared, wuss?
Hey, hey, hey, hey~!

POP TEAM EPIC
HARD CORE

No one can beat my smile!
Oh ho... But can you beat mine?

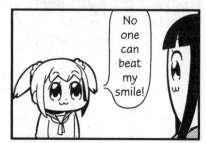

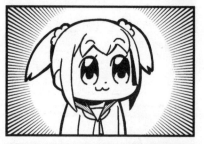

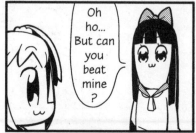

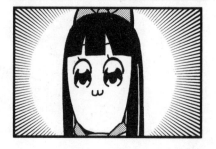

POP TEAM EPIC

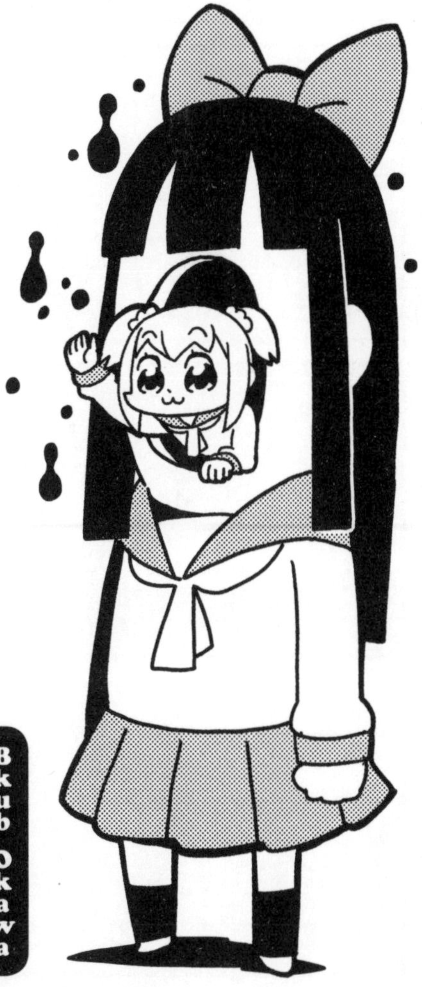

Bkub Okawa

(67)

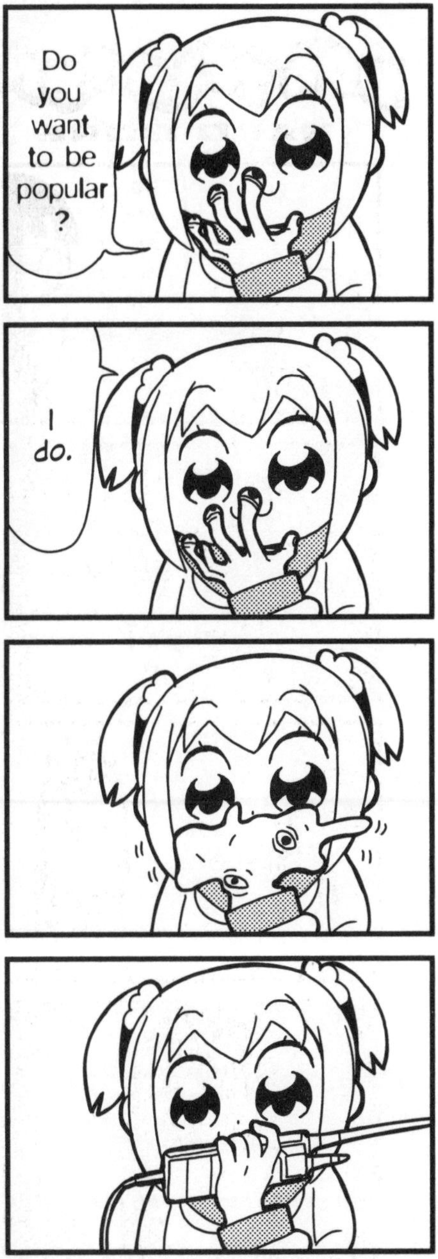
Do you want to be popular?
I do.

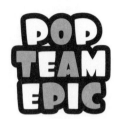

68

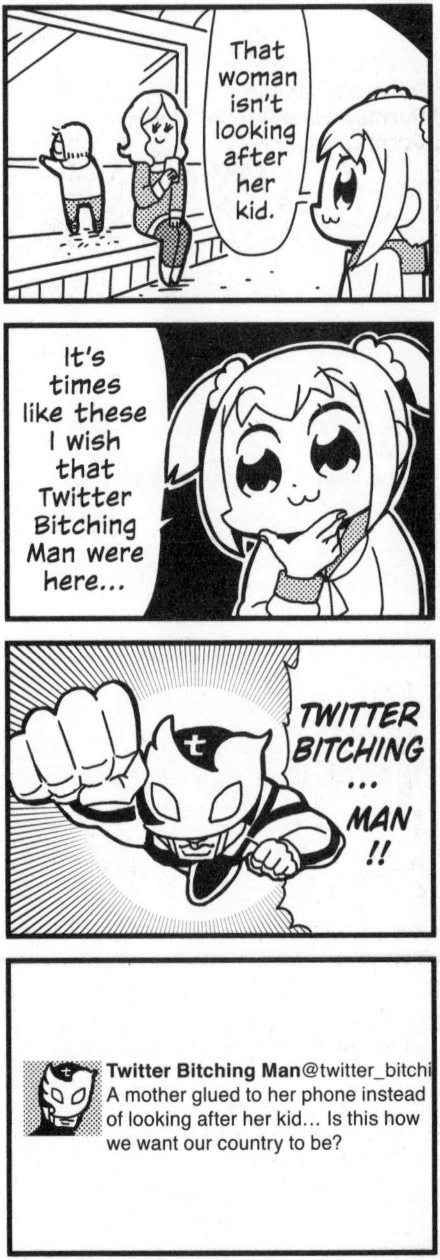
That woman isn't looking after her kid.
It's times like these I wish that Twitter Bitching Man were here...
TWITTER BITCHING ... MAN !!
Twitter Bitching Man@twitter_bitchi
A mother glued to her phone instead of looking after her kid... Is this how we want our country to be?

69

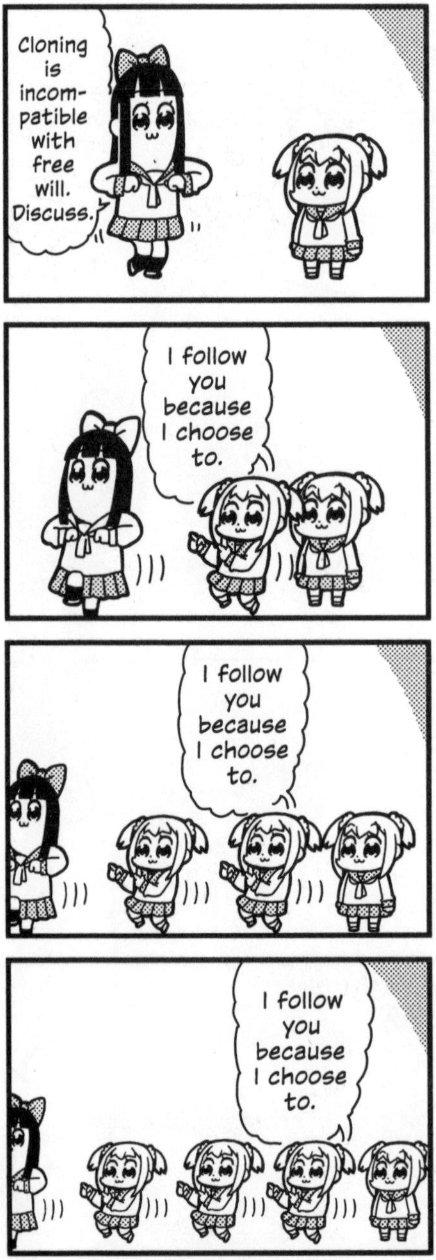
Cloning is incompatible with free will. Discuss.
I follow you because I choose to.
I follow you because I choose to.
I follow you because I choose to.

70

PAKO PAKO PAKO PAKO
PAKO PAKO PAKO PAKO PAKO
PAKO PAKO
PAKO PAKO
PAKO PAKO PAKO
SWEEEE

71

Frère Jacques, Frère Jacques, Dormez-vous? Dormez-vous? ~♪
Who was this Frère Jacques anyway?
Dunno. It's a mystery to us ignorant millennials.
But I know I can count on John Frieda.

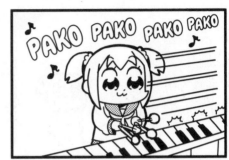

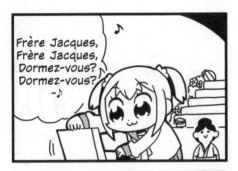

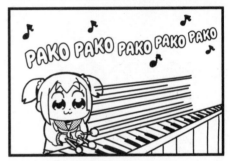

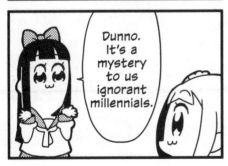

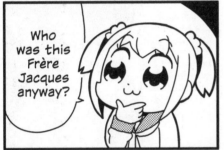

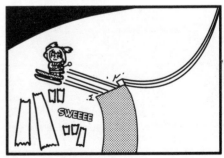

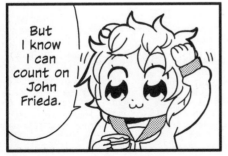

72

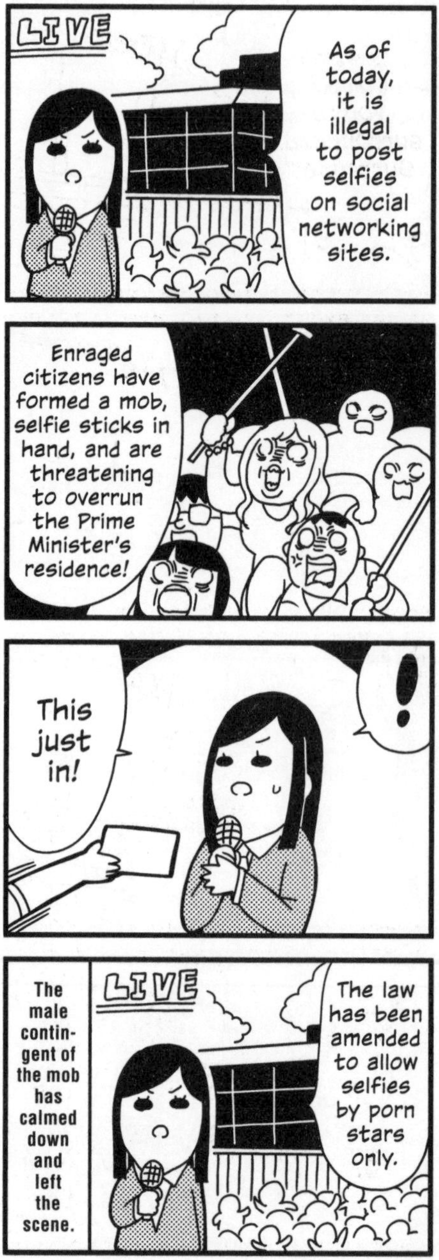
LIVE
As of today, it is illegal to post selfies on social networking sites.
Enraged citizens have formed a mob, selfie sticks in hand, and are threatening to overrun the Prime Minister's residence!
!
This just in!
LIVE
The law has been amended to allow selfies by porn stars only.
The male contingent of the mob has calmed down and left the scene.

73

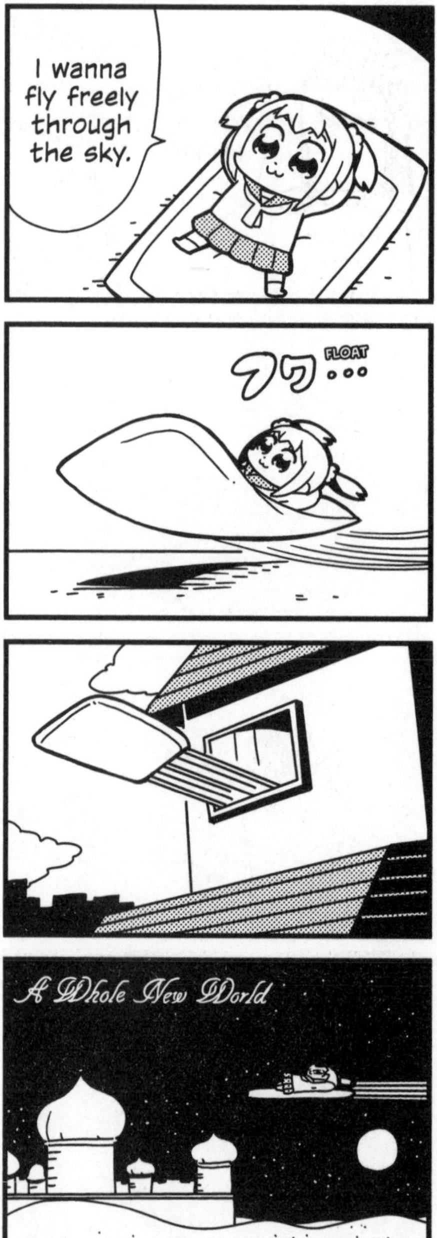
I wanna fly freely through the sky.
フワ...
FLOAT
A Whole New World

74

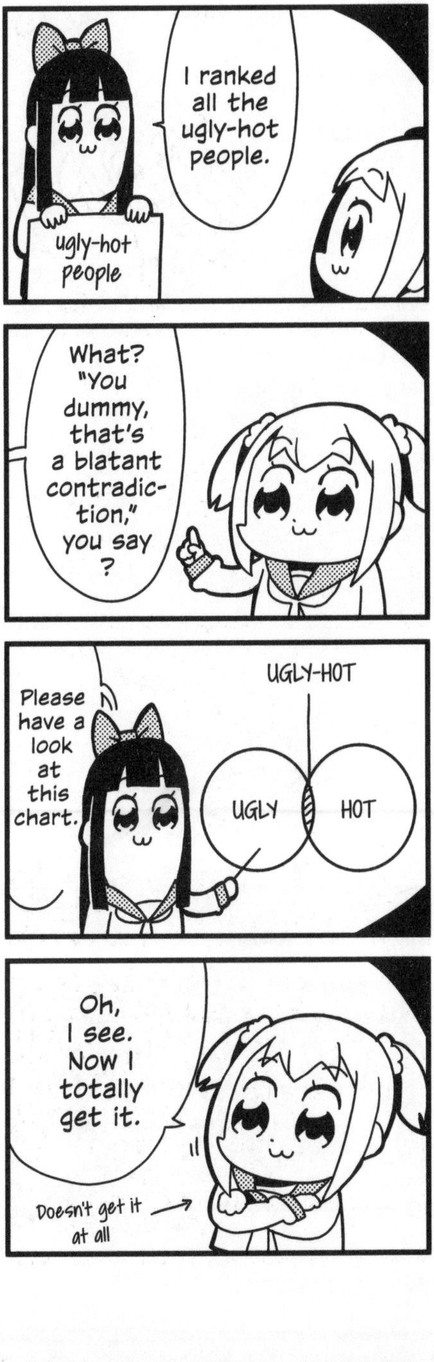
I ranked all the ugly-hot people.
ugly-hot people
What? "You dummy, that's a blatant contradic-tion," you say?
Please have a look at this chart.
UGLY-HOT
UGLY
HOT
Oh, I see. Now I totally get it.
Doesn't get it at all

75

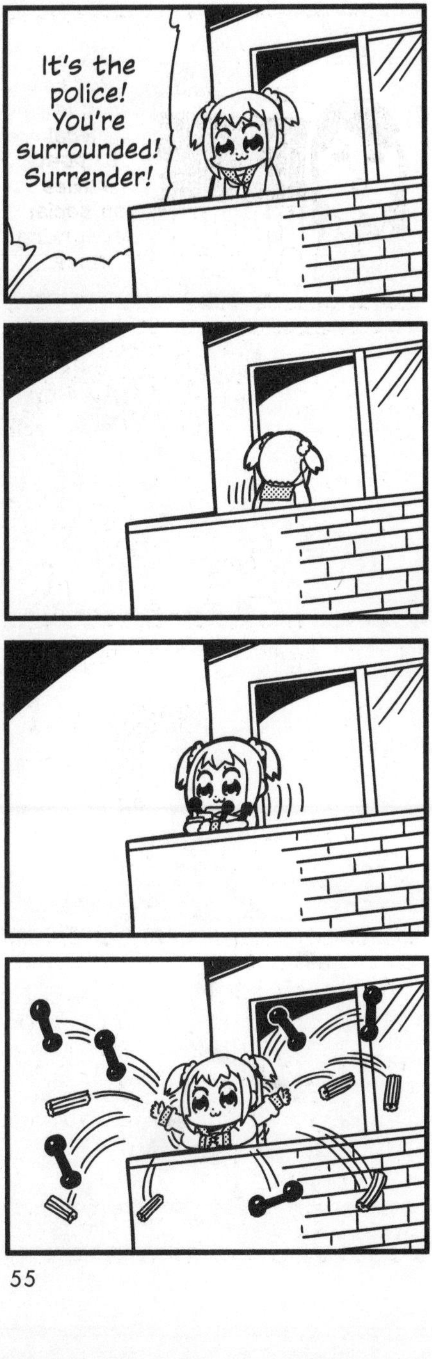
It's the police! You're surrounded! Surrender!

76

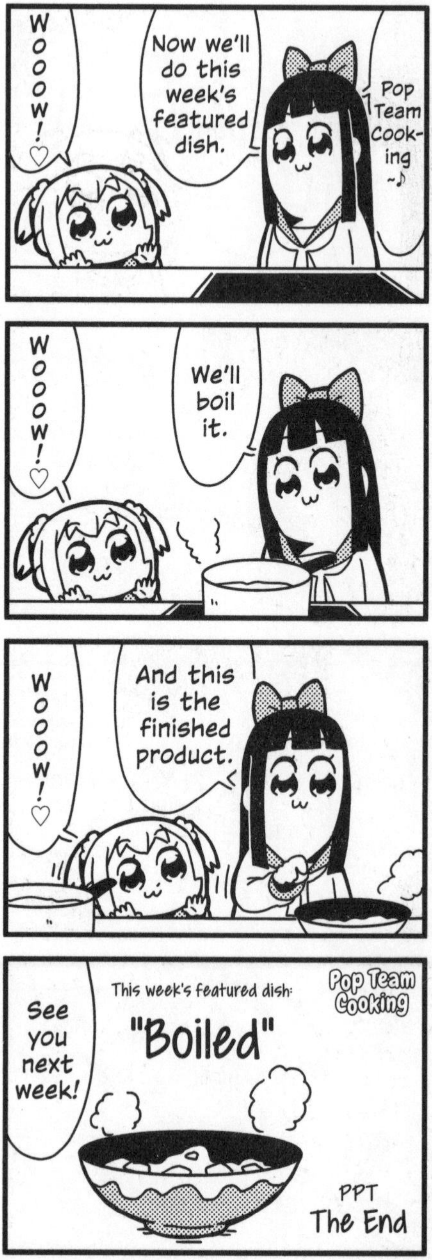
Pop Team Cooking ~♪
Now we'll do this week's featured dish.
WOOOOW!♡
We'll boil it.
WOOOOW!♡
And this is the finished product.
WOOOOW!♡
Pop Team Cooking
This week's featured dish:
"Boiled"
See you next week!
PPT The End

77

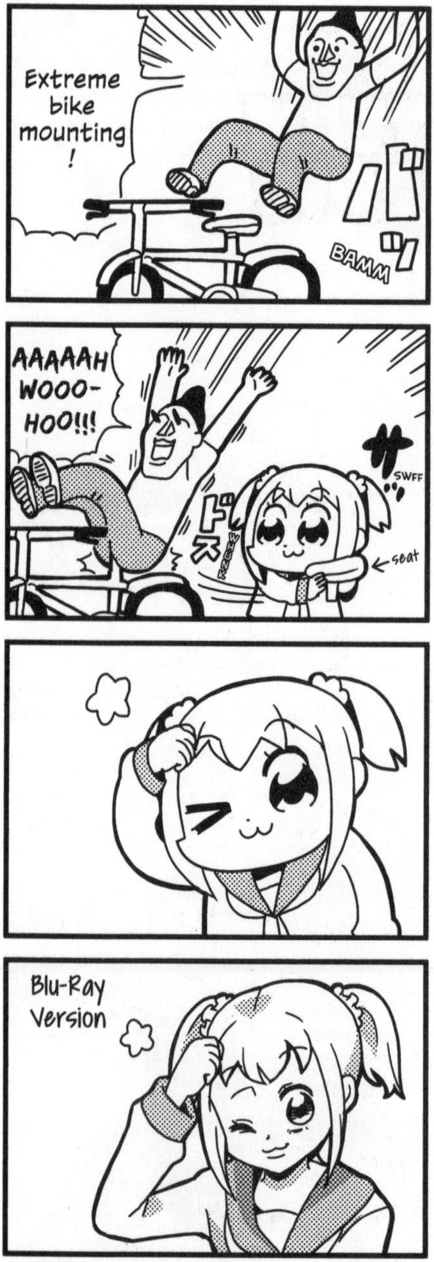
Extreme bike mounting!
BAMM
AAAAAH WOOO-HOO!!!
SWFF
seat
Blu-Ray Version

To be continued...

We've got fan mail.

"*Pop Team Epic* uses too much copypaste. It's stupid. Learn something from better manga artists."

... All right!

That really struck home ...

We won't rely on copypaste anymore!

POP TEAM EPIC

Bkub Okawa

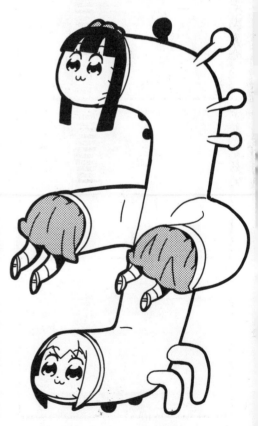

79

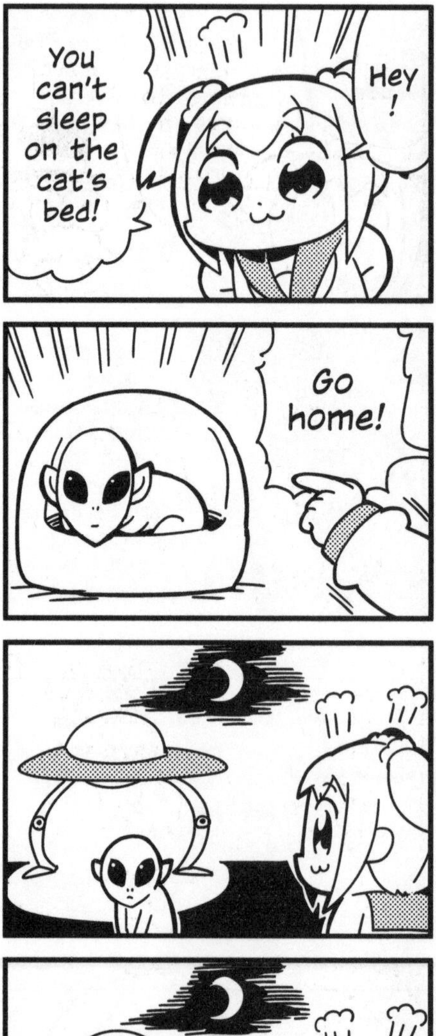
Hey!
You can't sleep on the cat's bed!
Go home!

80

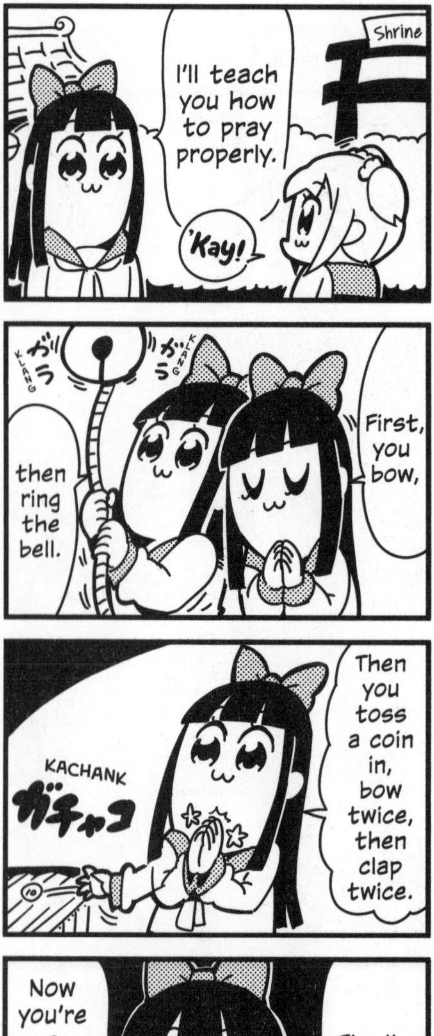
Shrine
I'll teach you how to pray properly.
'Kay!
KLANG ガラ
First, you bow,
then ring the bell.
KLANG ガラ
Then you toss a coin in, bow twice, then clap twice.
KACHANK ガチャコ
Finally, bow again, and voilà!
Now you're a bona-fide prayer master, too.

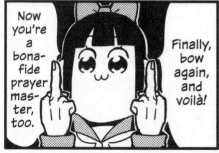

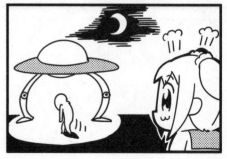

81

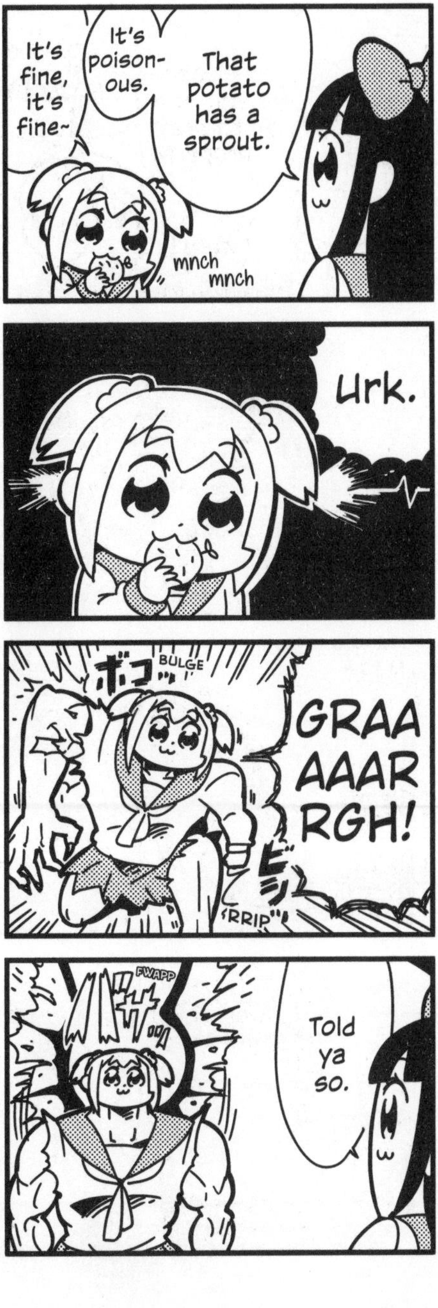
That potato has a sprout.
It's poison-ous.
It's fine, it's fine~
mnch mnch
Urk.
GRAAAAARRGH!
BULGE
RRIP
FWAPP
Told ya so.

82

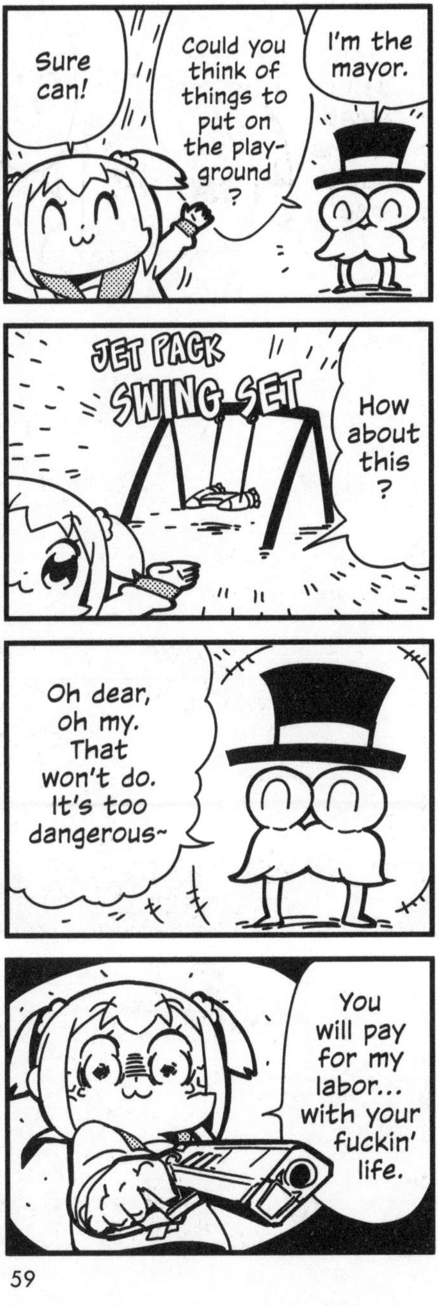
I'm the mayor.
Could you think of things to put on the play-ground?
Sure can!
How about this?
JET PACK SWING SET
Oh dear, oh my. That won't do. It's too dangerous~
You will pay for my labor... with your fuckin' life.

83

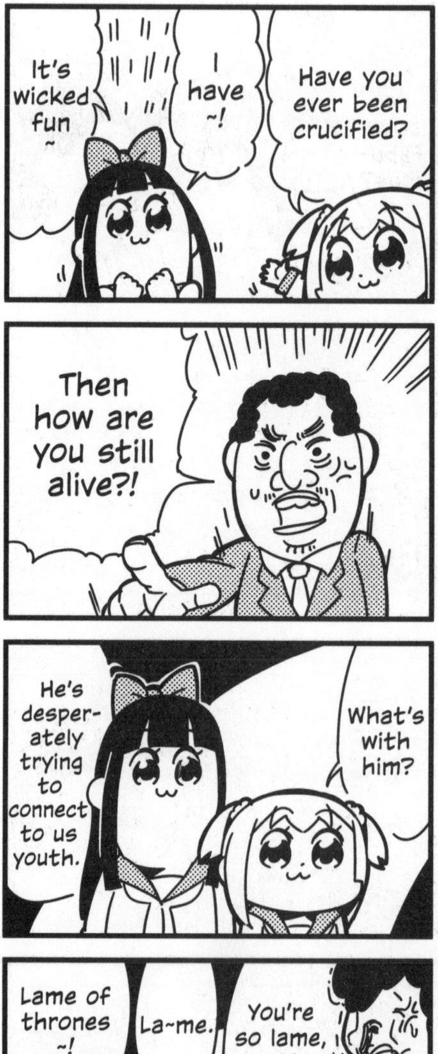
Have you ever been crucified?
I have~!
It's wicked fun~
Then how are you still alive?!
What's with him?
He's desperately trying to connect to us youth.
You're so lame, old man~!
La~me.
Lame of thrones~!

84

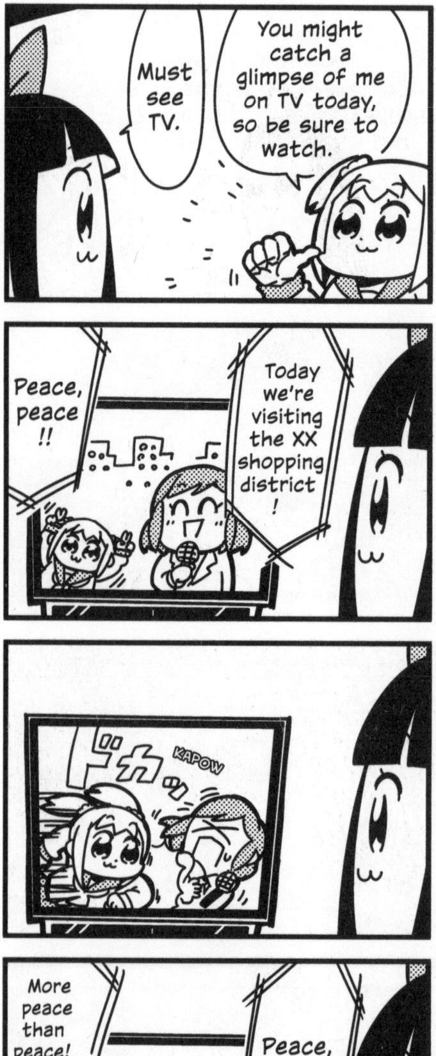
You might catch a glimpse of me on TV today, so be sure to watch.
Must see TV.
Today we're visiting the XX shopping district!
Peace, peace!!
ドカッ
KAPOW
Peace, peace!!
More peace than peace! 3 Peace!!

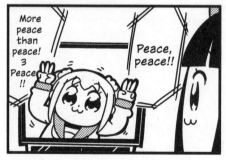

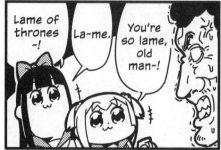

85

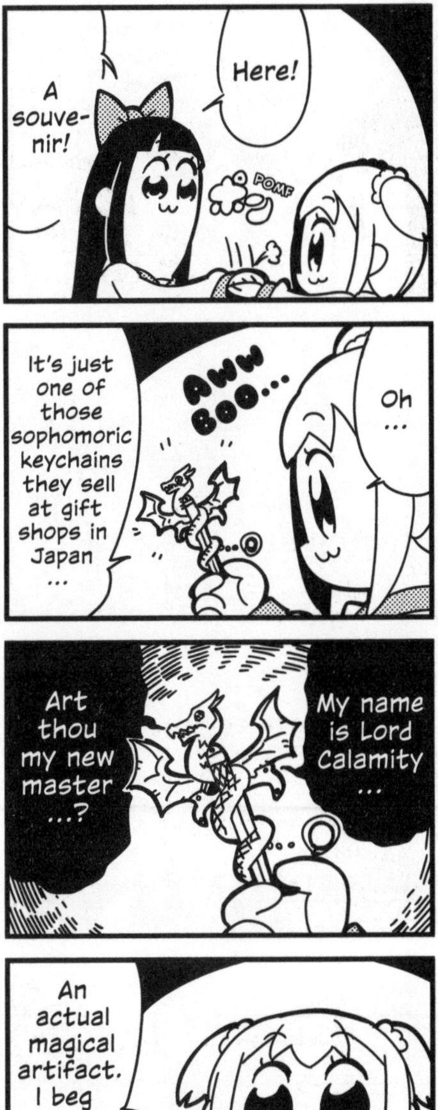
Here!
A souvenir!
POMF
Oh ...
AWW BOO...
It's just one of those sophomoric keychains they sell at gift shops in Japan ...
My name is Lord Calamity ...
Art thou my new master ...?
An actual magical artifact. I beg your pardon.

86

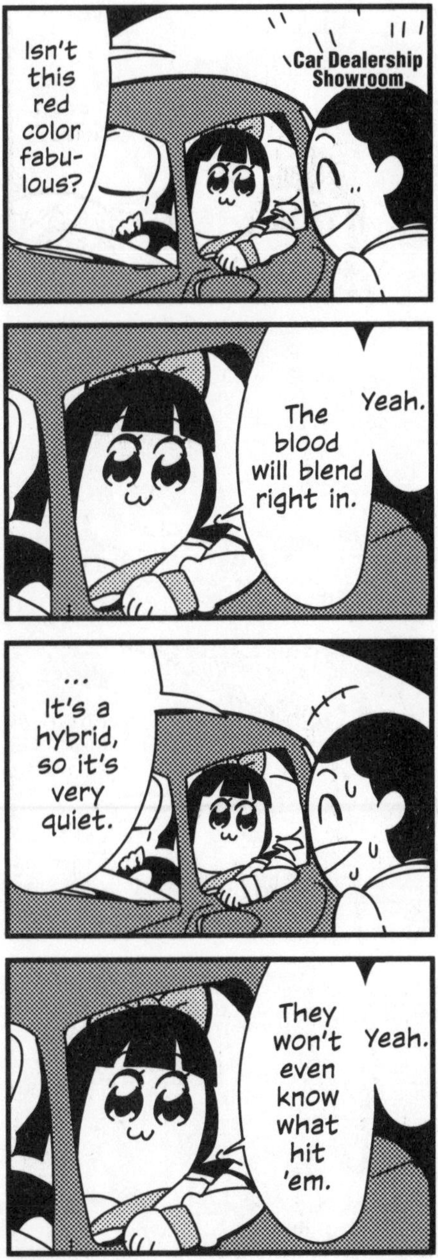
Car Dealership Showroom
Isn't this red color fabulous?
Yeah.
The blood will blend right in.
... It's a hybrid, so it's very quiet.
Yeah.
They won't even know what hit 'em.

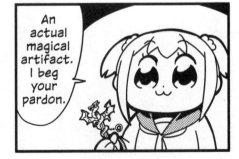

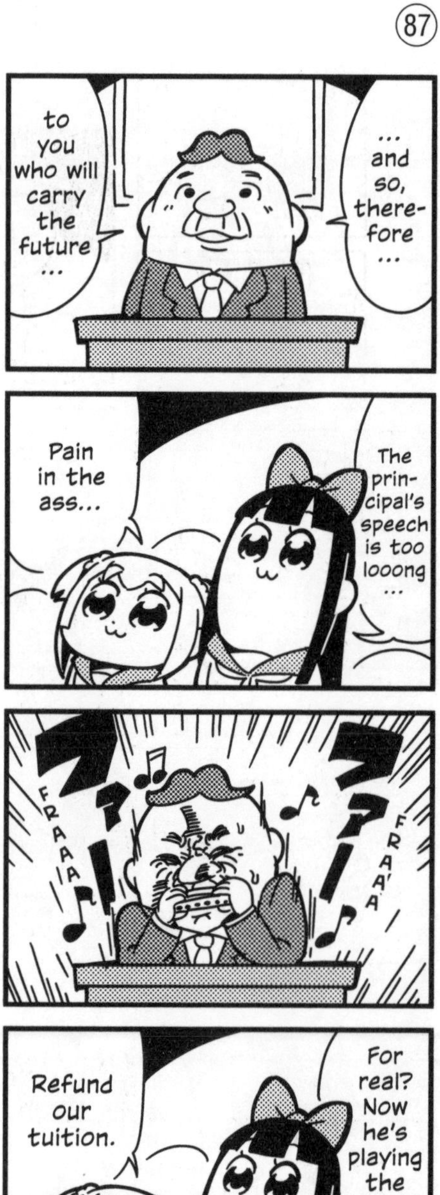
87
... and so, therefore ...
to you who will carry the future ...
The principal's speech is too looong ...
Pain in the ass...
FRAAAA
FRAAA
For real? Now he's playing the harmonica.
Refund our tuition.

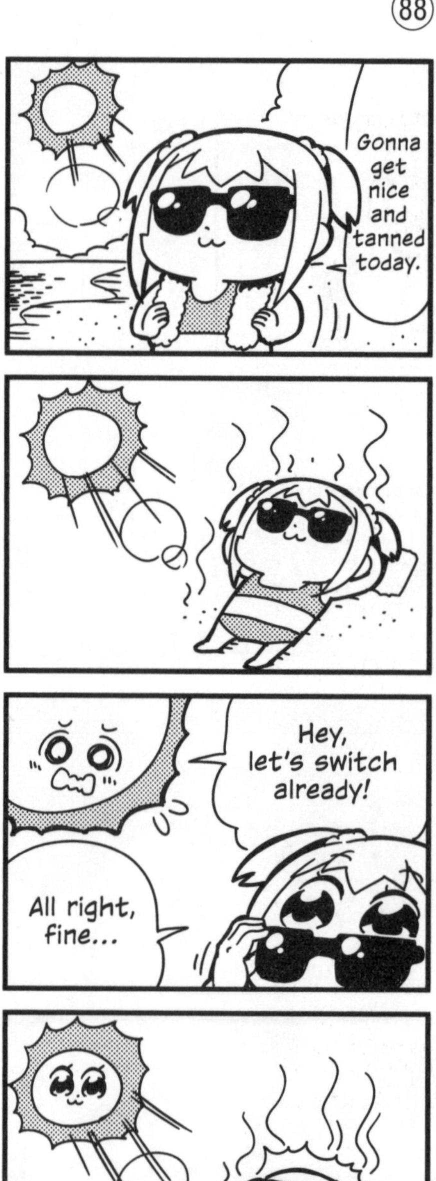
88
Gonna get nice and tanned today.
Hey, let's switch already!
All right, fine...

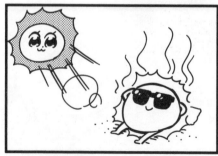

To be continued...

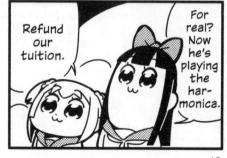

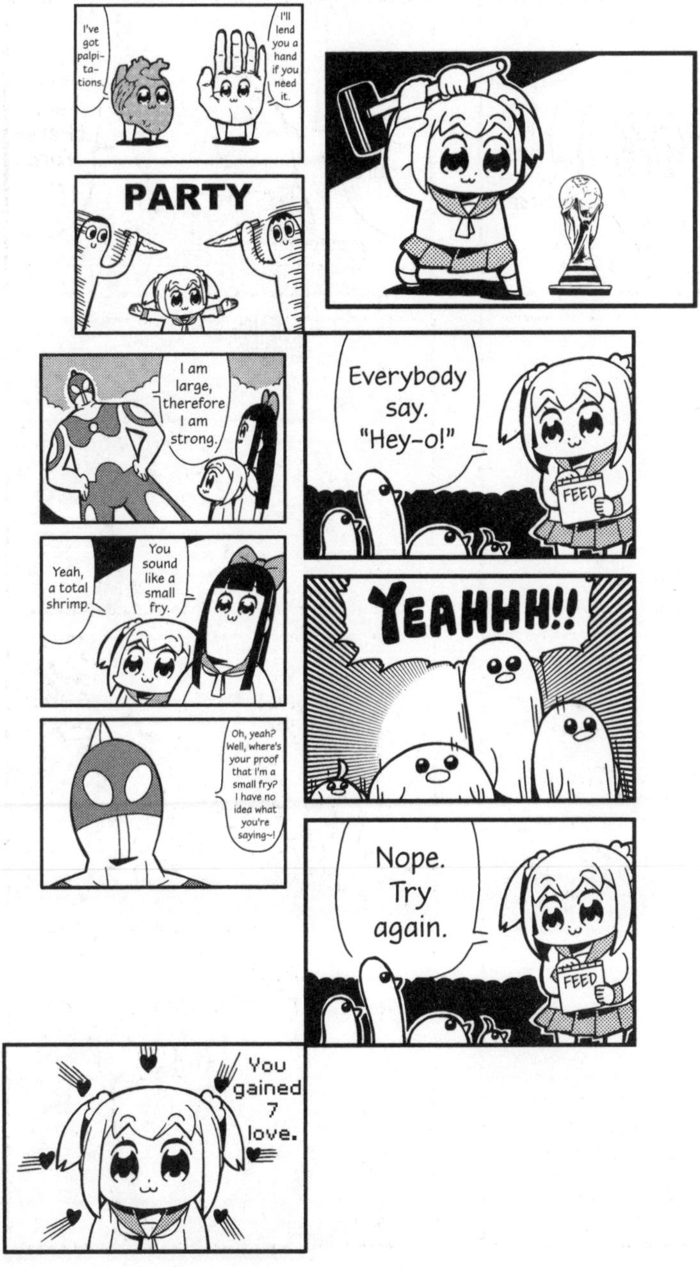
Everybody say. "Hey-o!"
FEED
YEAHHH!!
Nope. Try again.
FEED
I'll lend you a hand if you need it.
I've got palpi-ta-tions.
PARTY
I am large, therefore I am strong.
You sound like a small fry.
Yeah, a total shrimp.
Oh, yeah? Well, where's your proof that I'm a small fry? I have no idea what you're saying~!
You gained 7 love.

This list.
What about it?
Do it.
Do what?
WHUNK
DO IT.

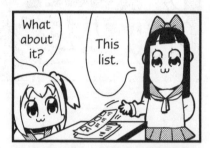

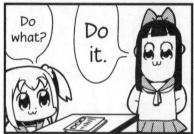

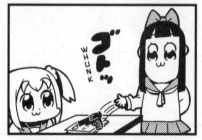

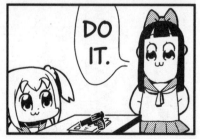

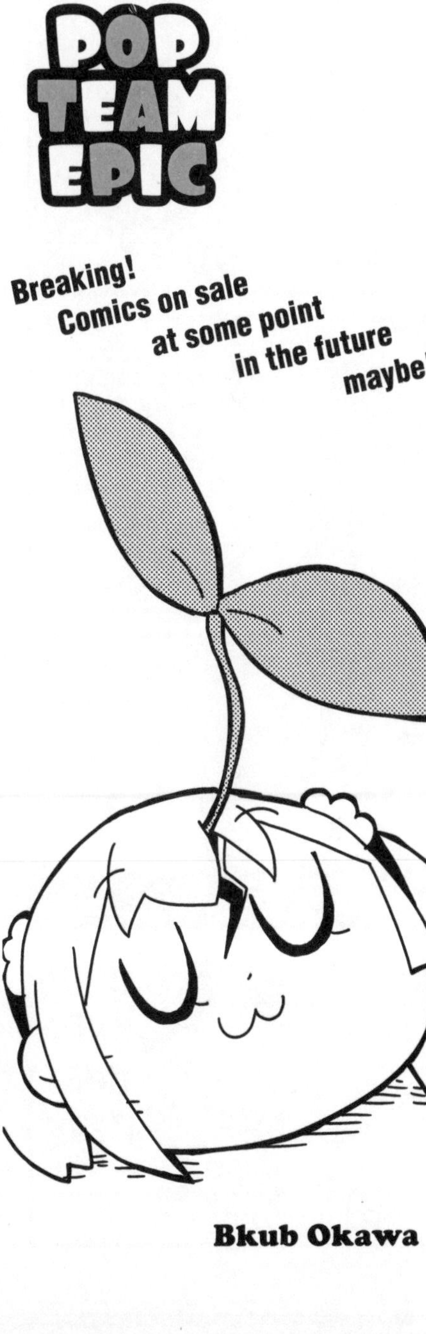
POP TEAM EPIC
Breaking! Comics on sale at some point in the future maybe!
Bkub Okawa

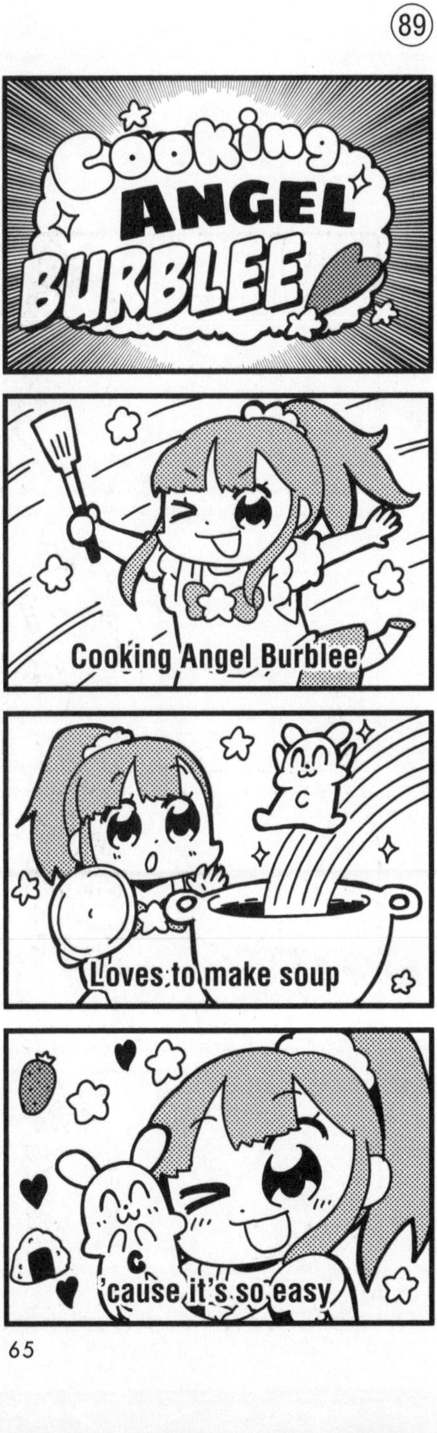
89
Cooking ANGEL BURBLEE
Cooking Angel Burblee
Loves to make soup
'cause it's so easy

90

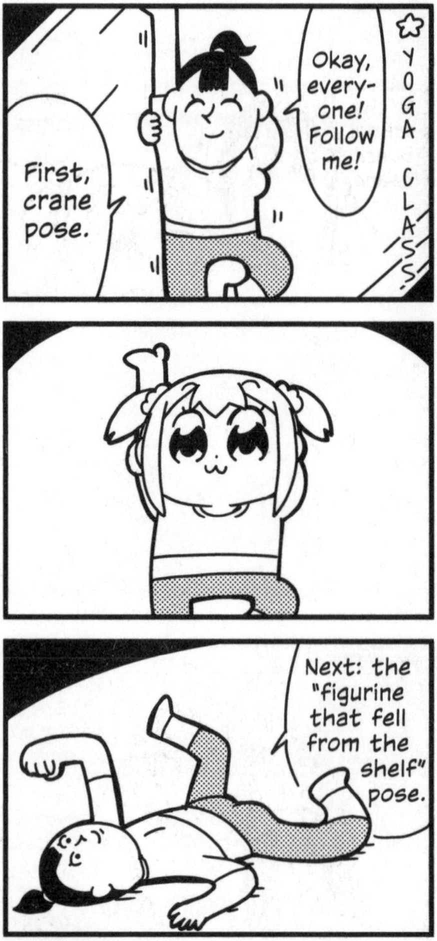
YOGA CLASS
Okay, everyone! Follow me!
First, crane pose.
Next: the "figurine that fell from the shelf" pose.

91

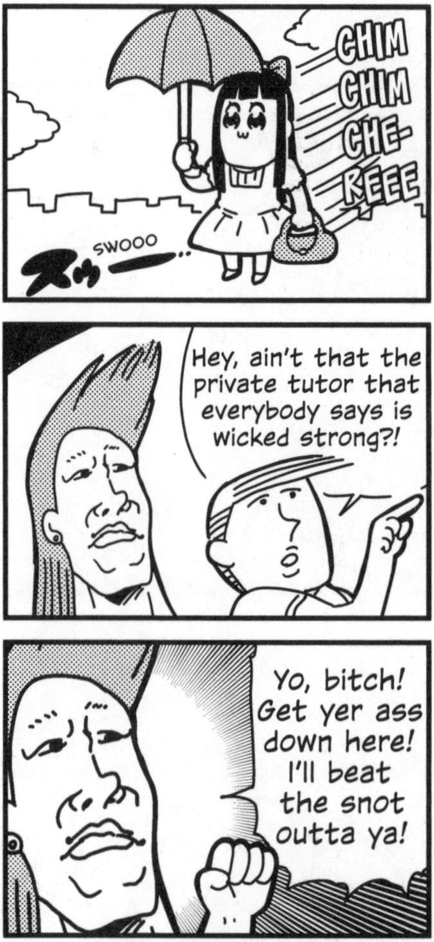
CHIM CHIM CHE-REEE
SWOOO
Hey, ain't that the private tutor that everybody says is wicked strong?!
Yo, bitch! Get yer ass down here! I'll beat the snot outta ya!
CHIM CHIM CHE-REEE
⇩+B

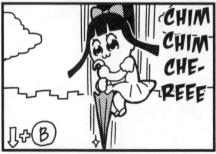

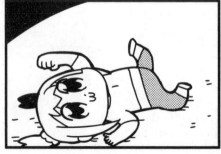

92

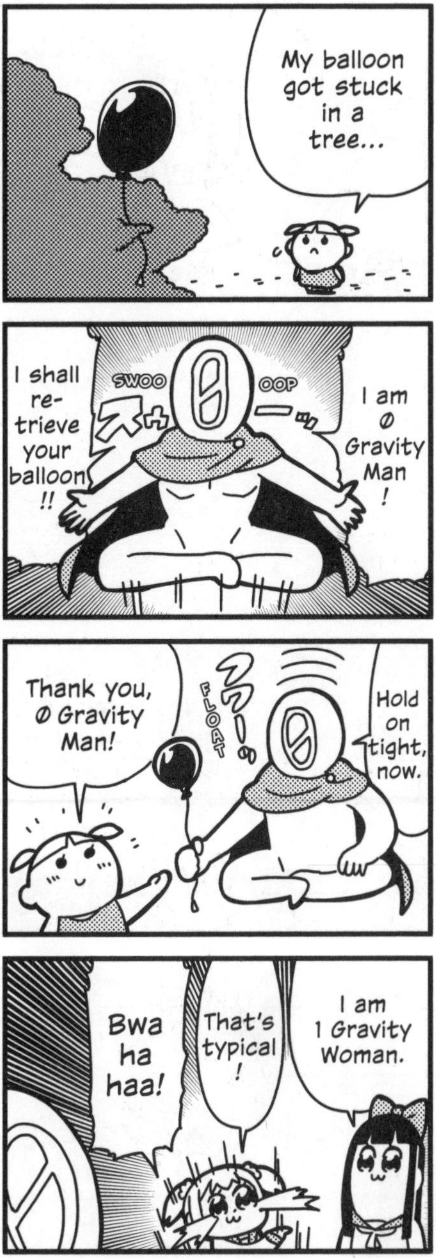
My balloon got stuck in a tree...
I am Ø Gravity Man!
SWOOOOP
I shall re-trieve your balloon!!
Hold on tight, now.
FLOAT
Thank you, Ø Gravity Man!
I am 1 Gravity Woman.
That's typical!
Bwa ha haa!

93

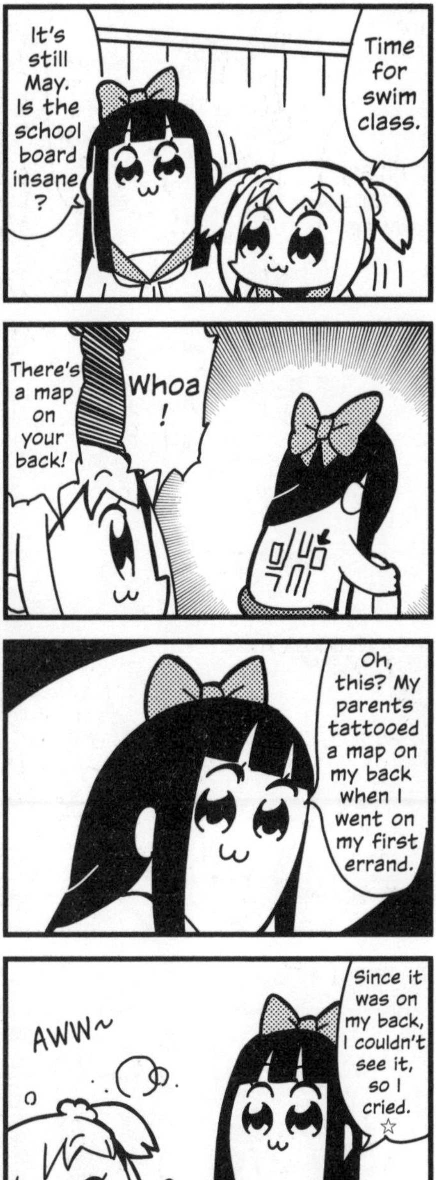
Time for swim class.
It's still May. Is the school board insane?
Whoa!
There's a map on your back!
Oh, this? My parents tattooed a map on my back when I went on my first errand.
Since it was on my back, I couldn't see it, so I cried. ☆
AWW~

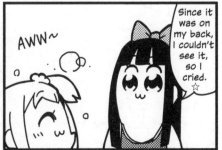

94

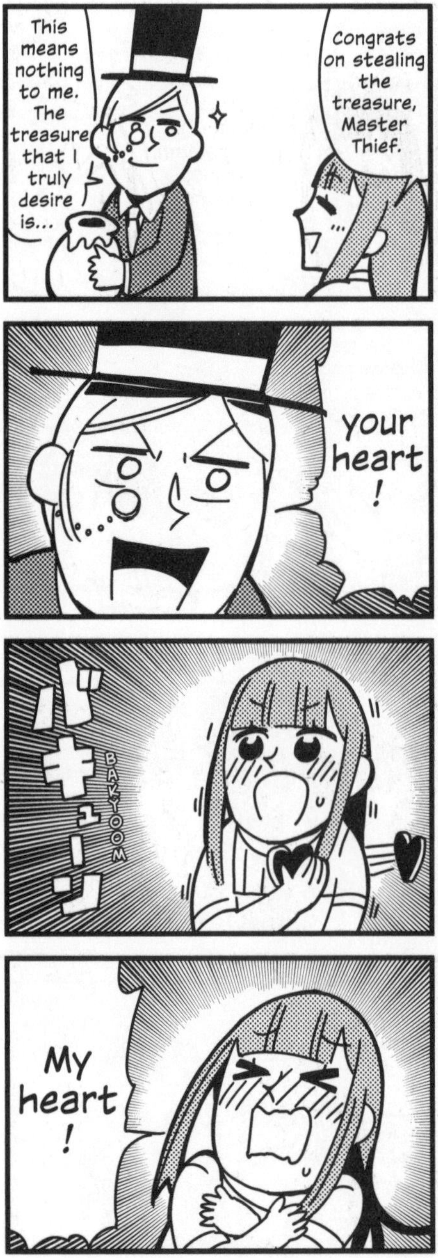
Congrats on stealing the treasure, Master Thief.
This means nothing to me. The treasure that I truly desire is...
your heart!
バキューン
BAKYOOM
My heart!

95

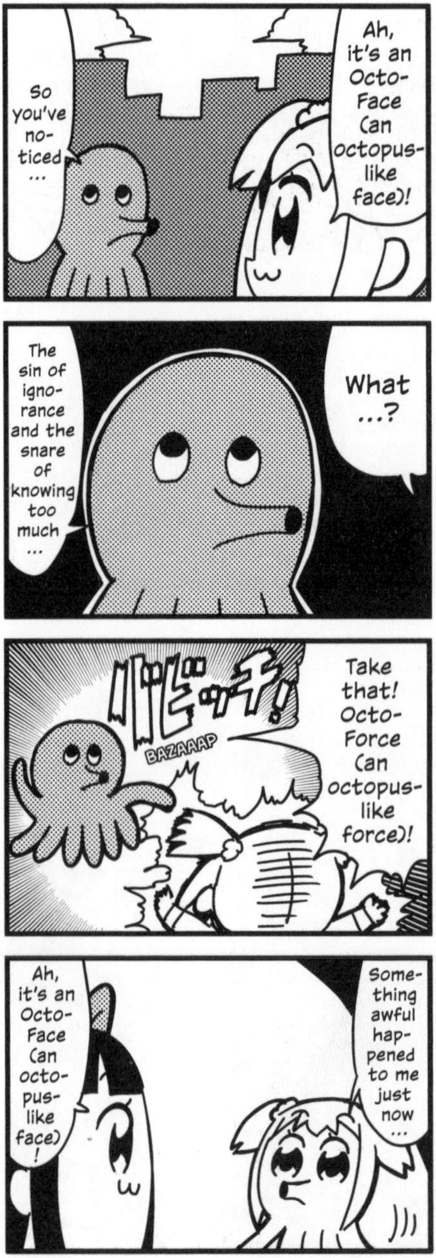
Ah, it's an Octo-Face (an octopus-like face)!
So you've noticed...
What...?
The sin of ignorance and the snare of knowing too much...
Take that! Octo-Force (an octopus-like force)!
BAZAAAP
Something awful happened to me just now...
Ah, it's an Octo-Face (an octopus-like face)!

96

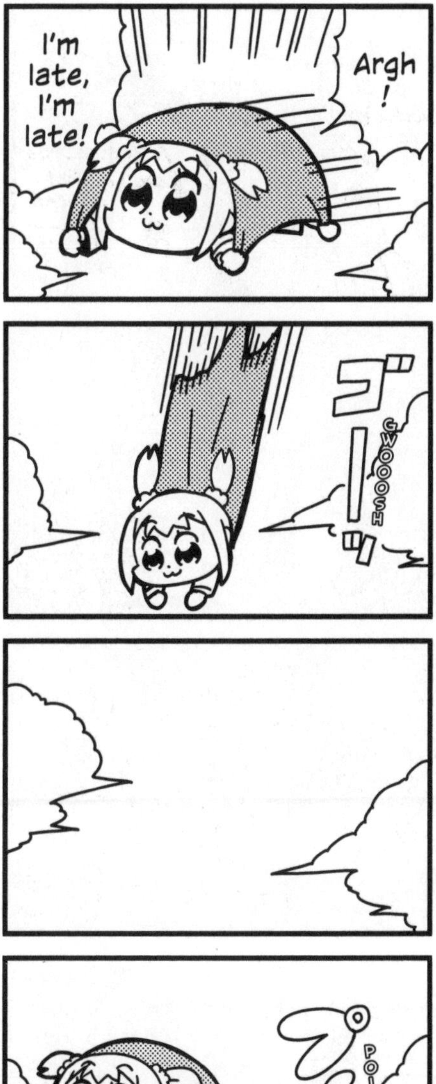
Argh!
I'm late, I'm late!
ゴーッ
GWOOOOSH
POING

97

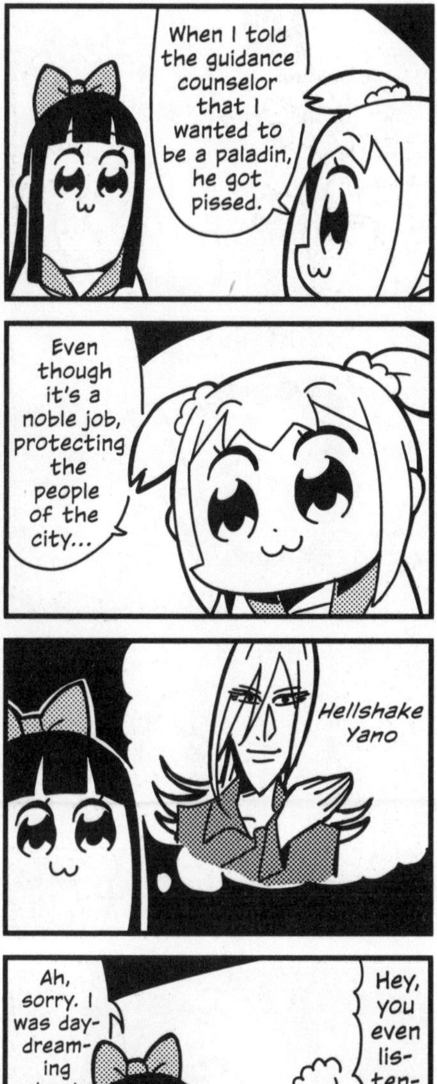
When I told the guidance counselor that I wanted to be a paladin, he got pissed.
Even though it's a noble job, protecting the people of the city...
Hellshake Yano
Hey, you even listening?!
Ah, sorry. I was daydreaming about Hellshake Yano.

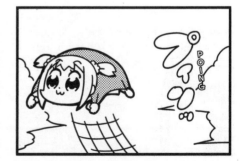

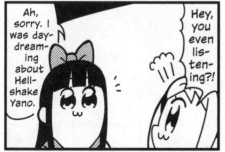

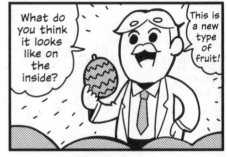

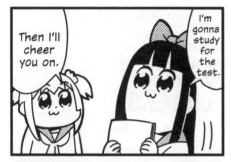

98

This is a new type of fruit!
What do you think it looks like on the inside?
Uhm, uhm …
Like an orange!
An orange, huh? Then let's cut it open and find out!
C'mon, take a look!
It's your face.

99

I'm gonna study for the test.
Then I'll cheer you on.
DUM GA DUM
HAH!
KLAK
Bet-tora Fish Cakes!
Way too obscure a reference.

To be continued…

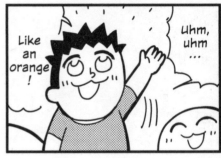

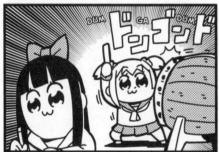

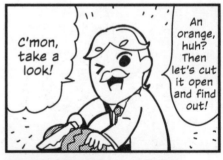

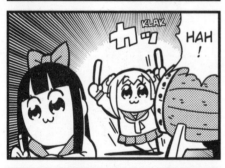

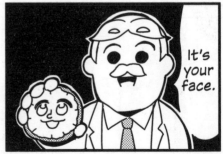

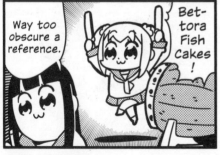

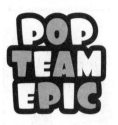

POP TEAM EPIC

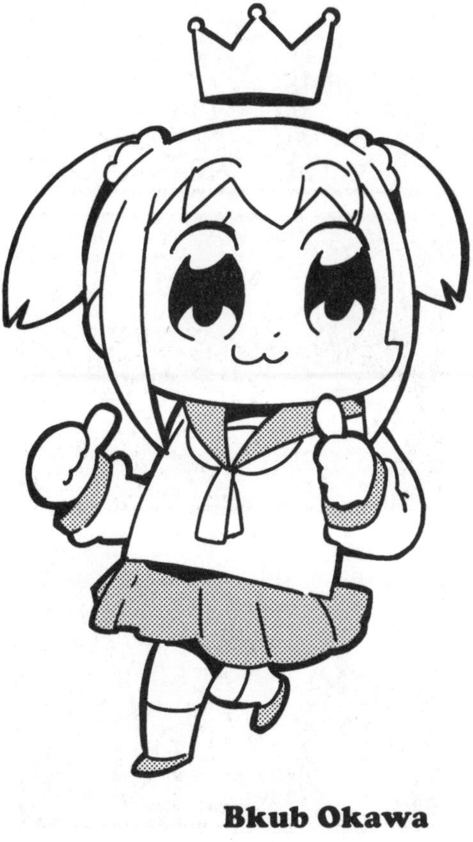

Bkub Okawa

(100)

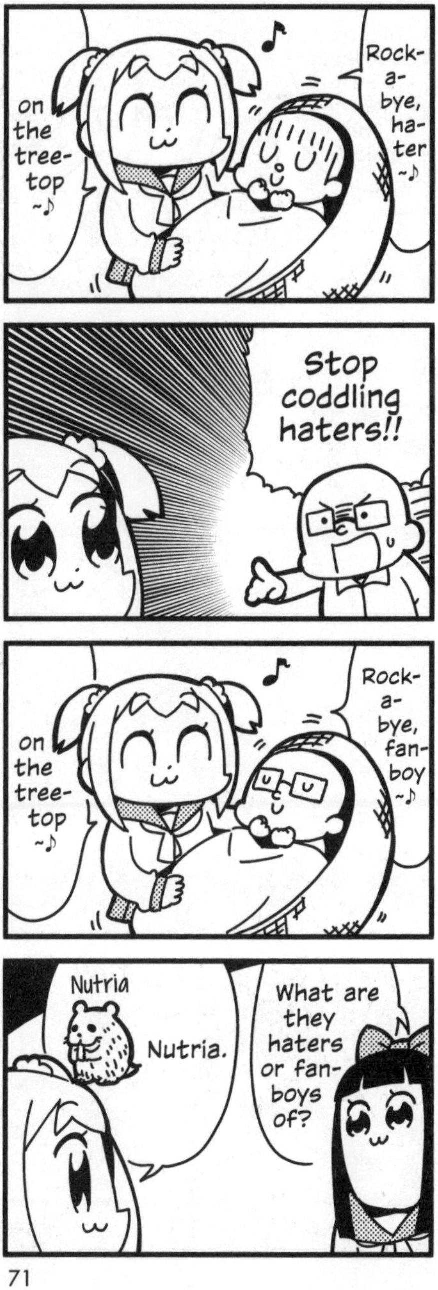
Rock-a-bye, hater ~♪
on the treetop ~♪
Stop coddling haters!!
Rock-a-bye, fanboy ~♪
on the treetop ~♪
What are they haters or fanboys of?
Nutria
Nutria.

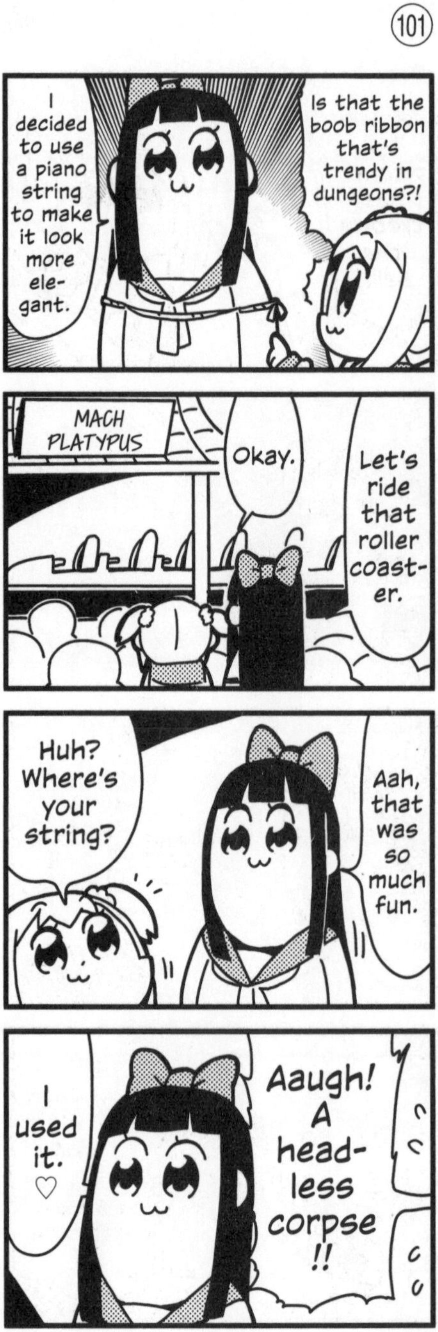
101
Is that the boob ribbon that's trendy in dungeons?!
I decided to use a piano string to make it look more elegant.
Let's ride that roller coaster.
Okay.
MACH PLATYPUS
Aah, that was so much fun.
Huh? Where's your string?
Aaugh! A headless corpse!!
I used it. ♡

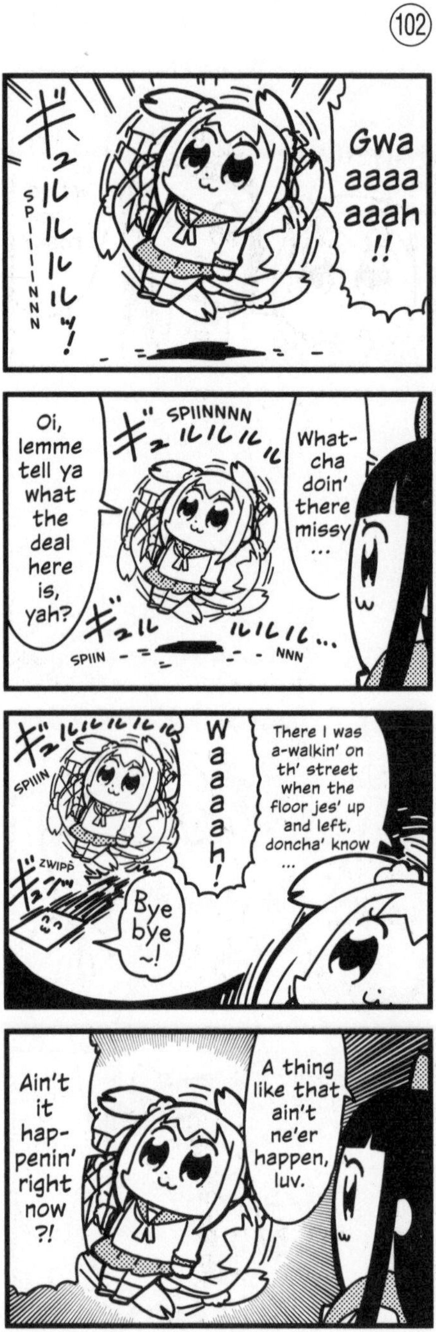
102
Gwa aaaa aaah!!
ギュルルルルッ!
SPIIIIINNN
Whatcha doin' there missy...
ギュルルルル SPIINNNNN
Oi, lemme tell ya what the deal here is, yah?
ギュル ルルル... SPIIN NNN
There I was a-walkin' on th' street when the floor jes' up and left, doncha' know...
Waaaaah!
ギュルルルルルル SPIIIN
ギュン ZWIPP
Bye bye ~!
A thing like that ain't ne'er happen, luv.
Ain't it happenin' right now?!

103

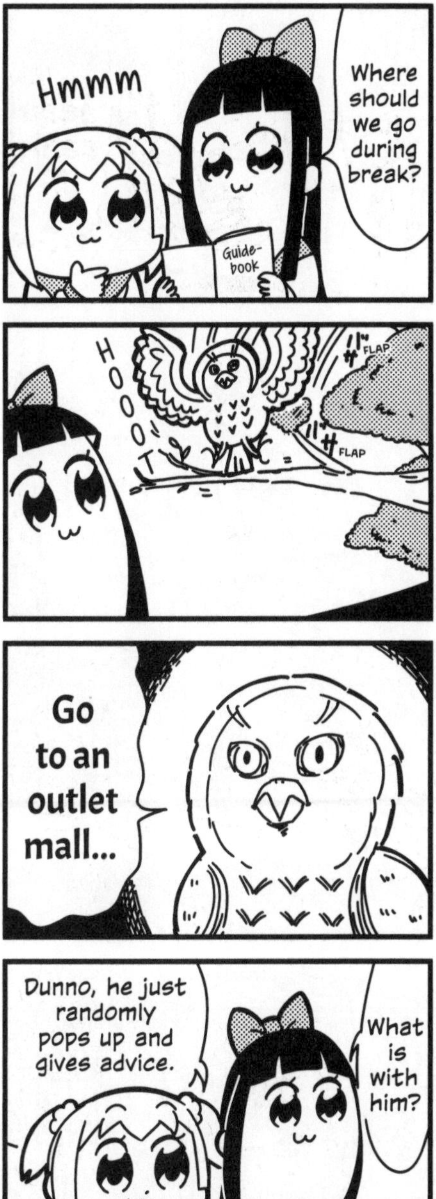
Where should we go during break?
Hmmm
Guide-book
HOOOT
FLAP
FLAP
Go to an outlet mall...
What is with him?
Dunno, he just randomly pops up and gives advice.
Guide-book

104

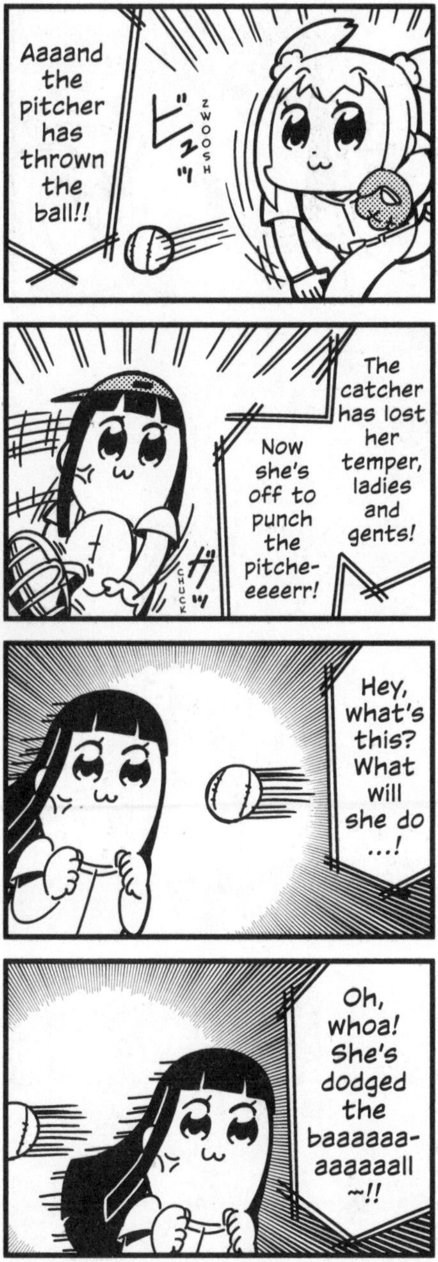
ZWOOSH
Aaaand the pitcher has thrown the ball!!
The catcher has lost her temper, ladies and gents!
Now she's off to punch the pitche-eeeerr!
CHUCK
Hey, what's this? What will she do ...!
Oh, whoa! She's dodged the baaaaaa-aaaaaall ~!!

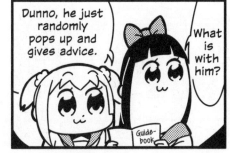

105

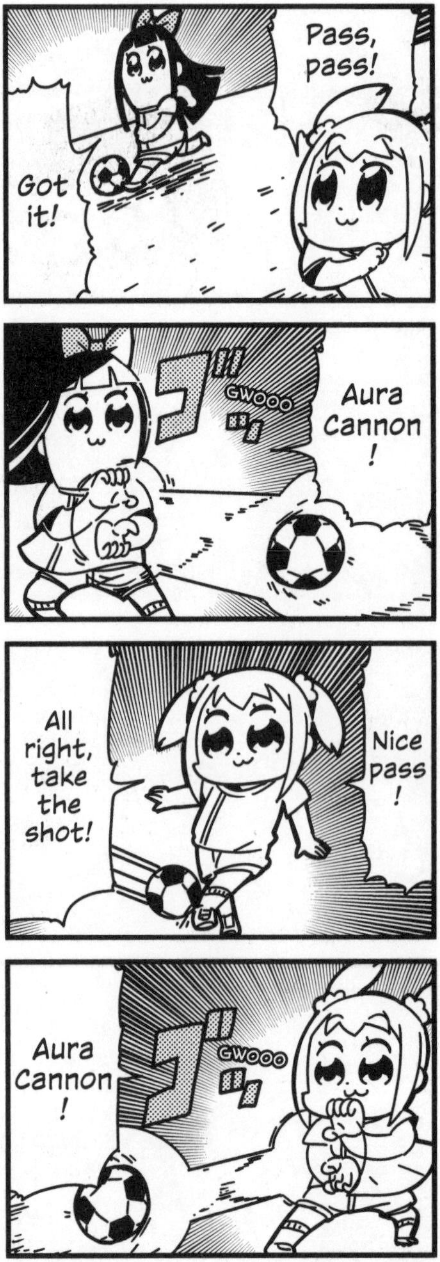
Pass, pass!
Got it!
Aura Cannon!
GWOOO
Nice pass!
All right, take the shot!
GWOOO
Aura Cannon!

106

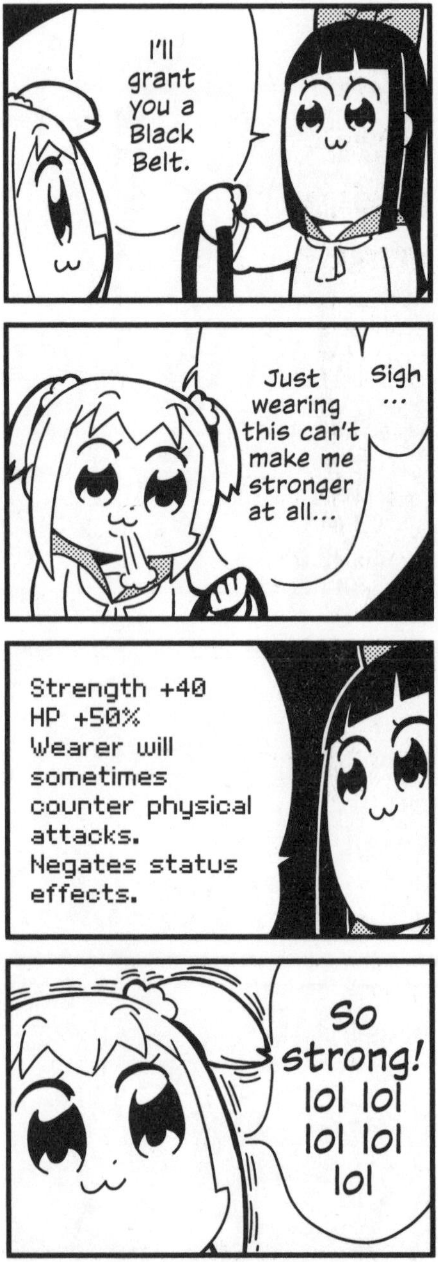
I'll grant you a Black Belt.
Sigh...
Just wearing this can't make me stronger at all...
Strength +40
HP +50%
Wearer will sometimes counter physical attacks.
Negates status effects.
So strong! lol lol lol lol lol

107

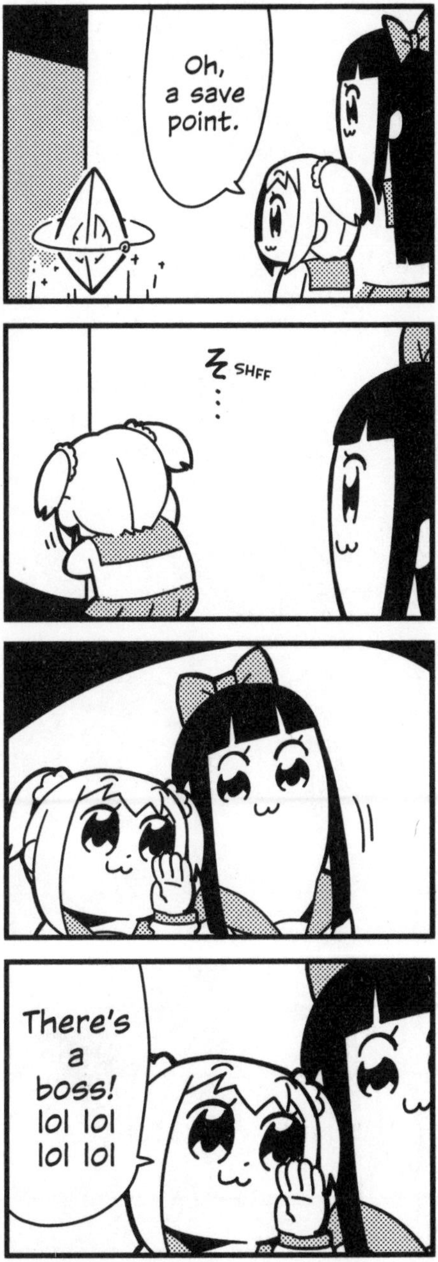
Oh, a save point.
SHFF
There's a boss! lol lol lol lol

108

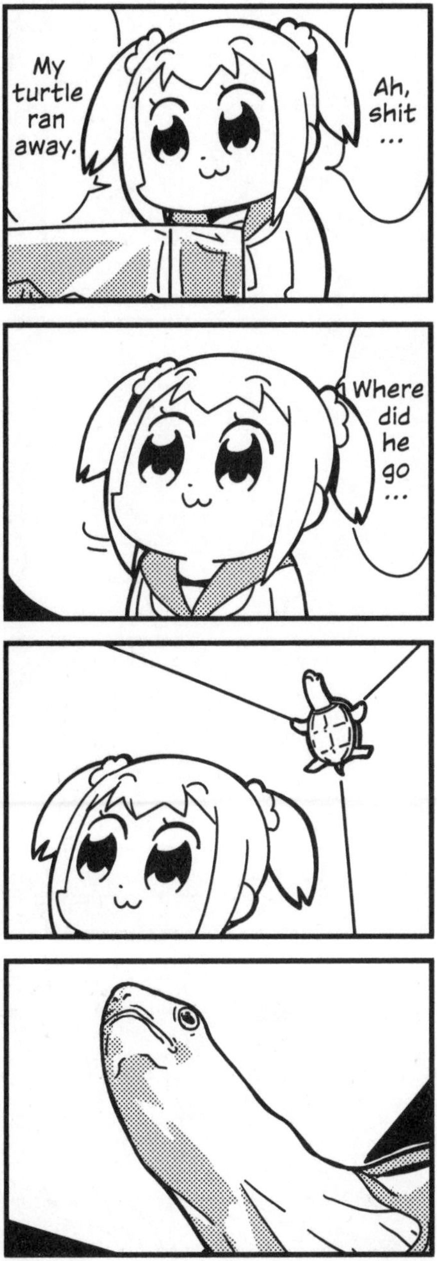
Ah, shit ...
My turtle ran away.
Where did he go ...

(109)

Hey, there's no smoking in here.
ザンッ
ZWAK
カチッ
KACHIK
ザンッ
ZWAKK

(110)

Ah! It's a monster !!
Woo-hoo! It's delicious in dungeon~!
ぐつぐつ
BRBLE BRBLE
Hey, ain't that a little too shameless ?
Hinna, hinna.

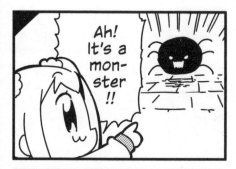

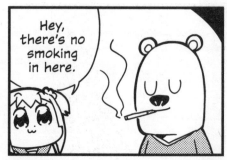

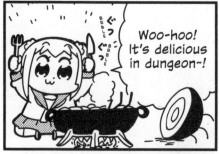

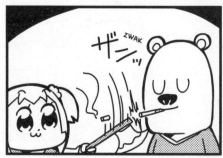

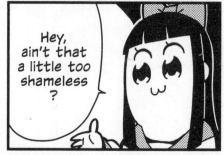

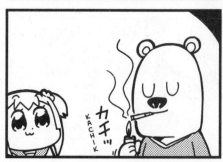

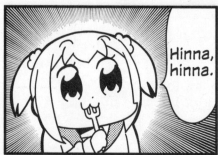

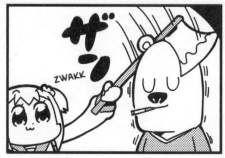

To be continued...

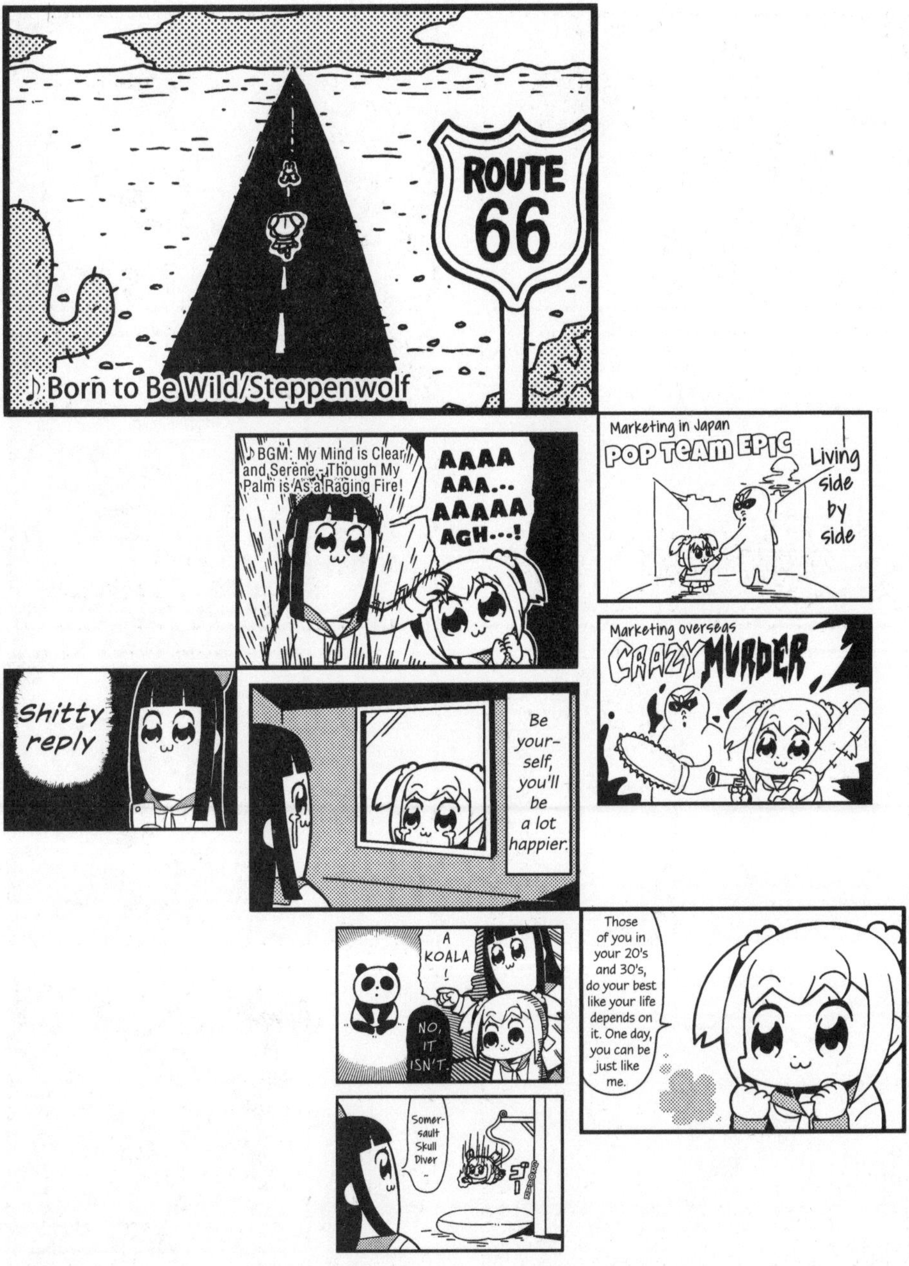
ROUTE 66
♪Born to Be Wild/Steppenwolf
Marketing in Japan
POP TEAM EPIC
Living side by side
♪BGM: My Mind is Clear and Serene - Though My Palm is As a Raging Fire!
AAAA AAA... AAAAA AGH...!
Marketing overseas
CRAZY MURDER
Be your-self, you'll be a lot happier.
Shitty reply
Those of you in your 20's and 30's, do your best like your life depends on it. One day, you can be just like me.
A KOALA !
NO, IT ISN'T.
Somer-sault Skull Diver ~

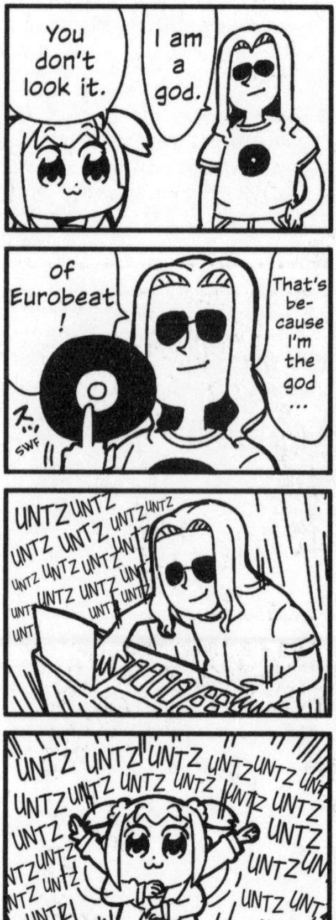
I am a god.
You don't look it.
That's be-cause I'm the god...
of Eurobeat!
SWF
UNTZ UNTZ UNTZ UNTZ
UNTZ UNTZ UNTZ UNTZ

(111)

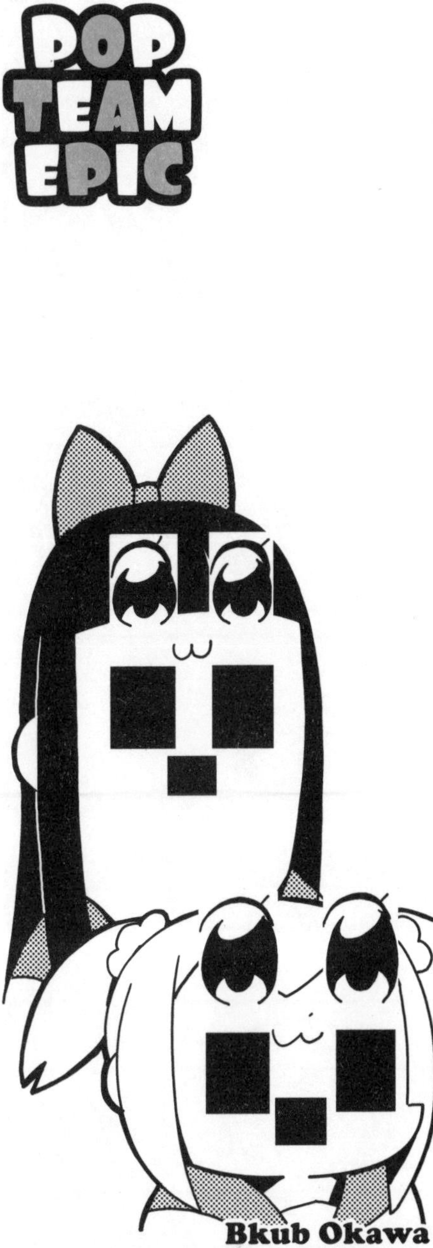
POP TEAM EPIC
Bkub Okawa

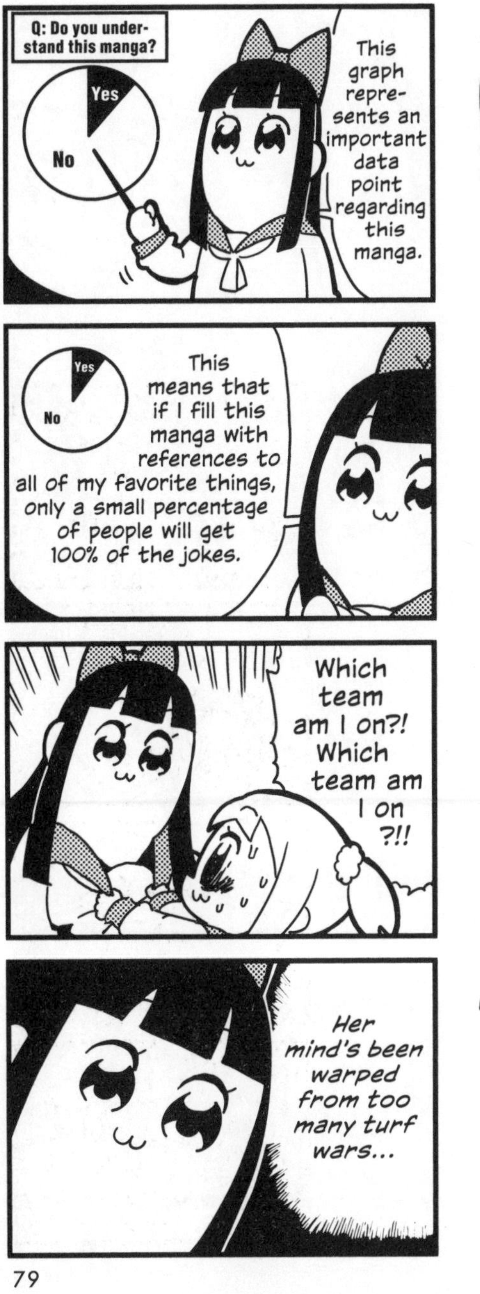
This graph repre-sents an important data point regarding this manga.
Q: Do you under-stand this manga?
Yes
No
This means that if I fill this manga with references to all of my favorite things, only a small percentage of people will get 100% of the jokes.
Yes
No
Which team am I on?! Which team am I on ?!!
Her mind's been warped from too many turf wars...

112

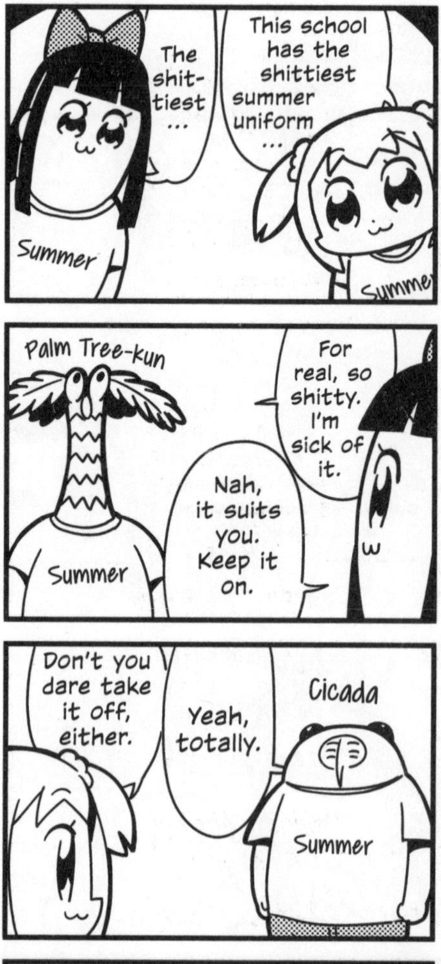
This school has the shittiest summer uniform...
The shit-tiest...
Summer
Summer
For real, so shitty. I'm sick of it.
Palm Tree-kun
Nah, it suits you. Keep it on.
Summer
Cicada
Yeah, totally.
Don't you dare take it off, either.
Summer
It's just awful, isn't it?
Hydrangea-chan
You... Huh, you're actually a borderline case...
Summer

113

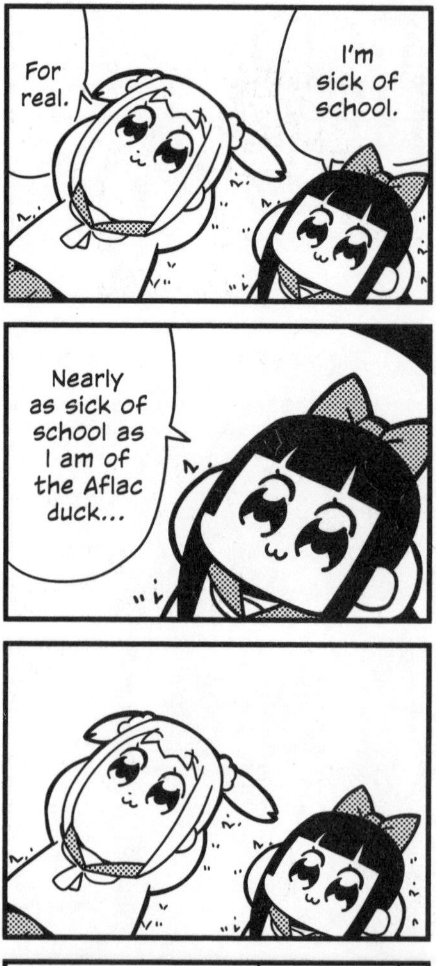
I'm sick of school.
For real.
Nearly as sick of school as I am of the Aflac duck...
That's like, plague levels of sick.

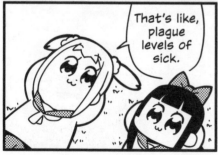

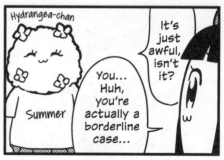

114

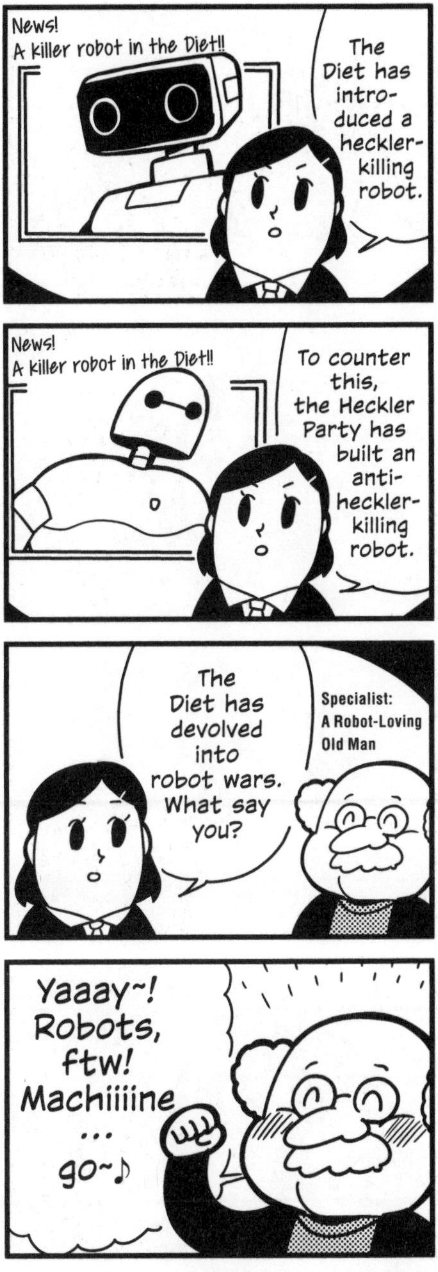
News!
A killer robot in the Diet!!
The Diet has introduced a heckler-killing robot.
News!
A killer robot in the Diet!!
To counter this, the Heckler Party has built an anti-heckler-killing robot.
The Diet has devolved into robot wars. What say you?
Specialist: A Robot-Loving Old Man
Yaaay~! Robots, ftw! Machiiiine ... go~♪

115

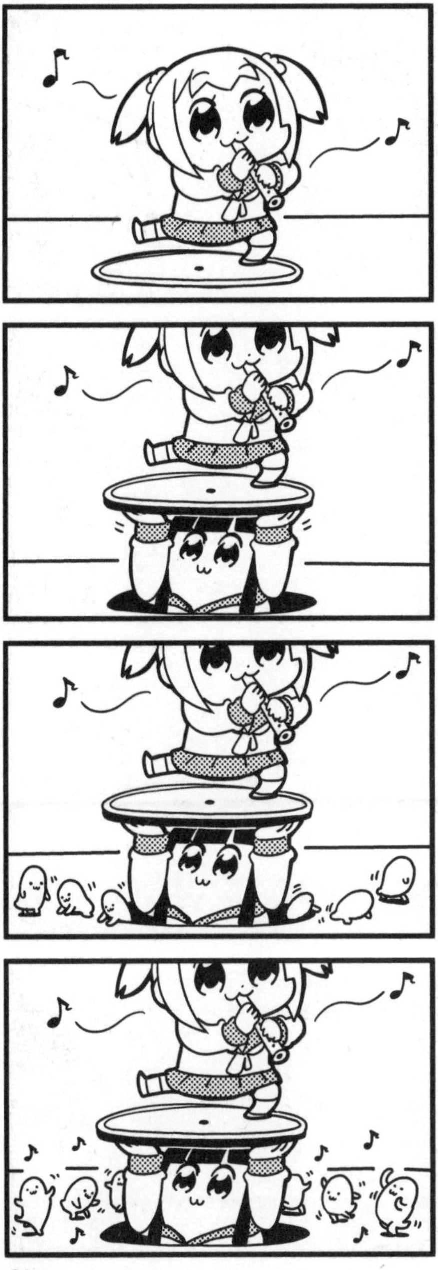

116

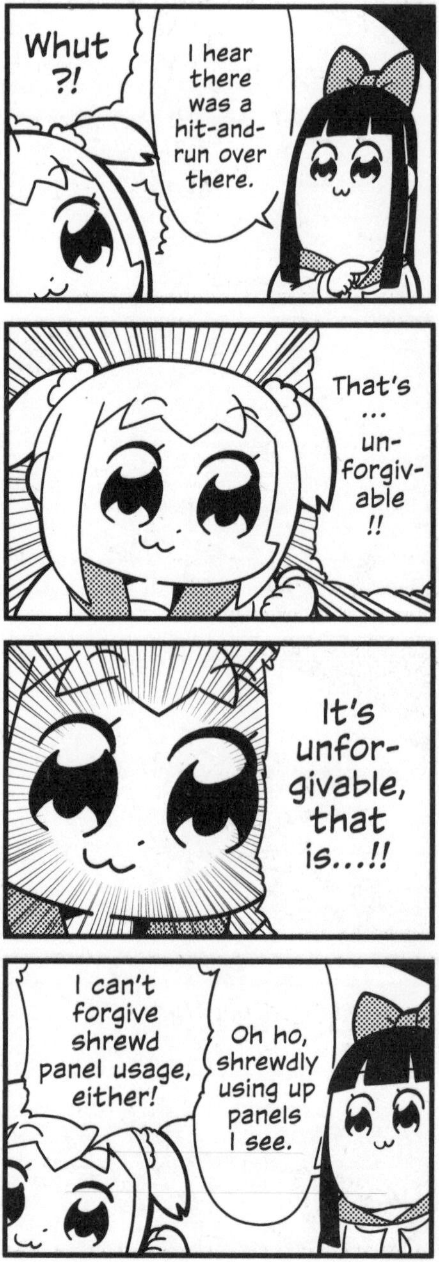
I hear there was a hit-and-run over there.
Whut ?!
That's ... unforgivable !!
It's unforgivable, that is...!!
Oh ho, shrewdly using up panels I see.
I can't forgive shrewd panel usage, either!

117

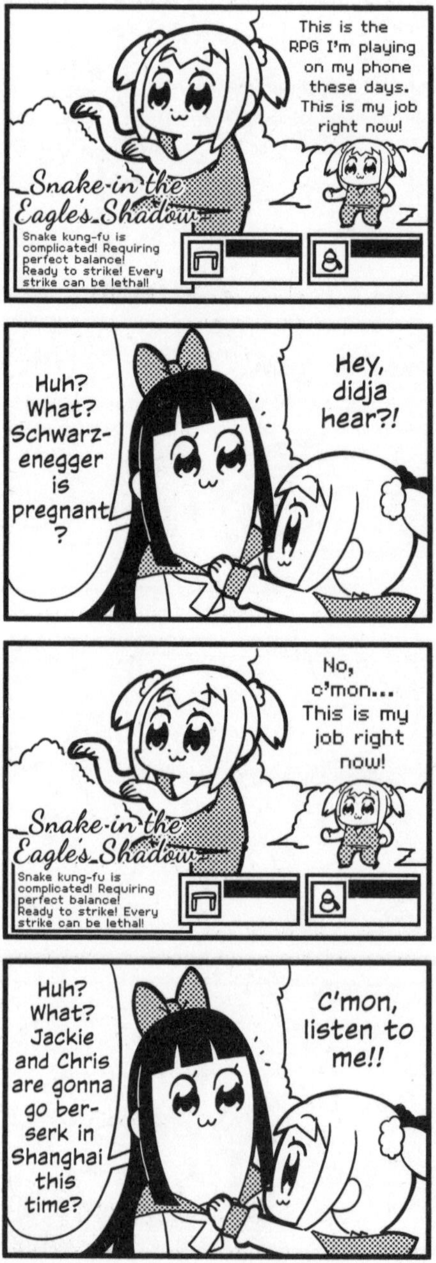
This is the RPG I'm playing on my phone these days. This is my job right now!
Snake-in the Eagle's Shadow
Snake kung-fu is complicated! Requiring perfect balance! Ready to strike! Every strike can be lethal!
Hey, didja hear?!
Huh? What? Schwarz-enegger is pregnant?
No, c'mon... This is my job right now!
Snake-in the Eagle's Shadow
Snake kung-fu is complicated! Requiring perfect balance! Ready to strike! Every strike can be lethal!
C'mon, listen to me!!
Huh? What? Jackie and Chris are gonna go ber-serk in Shanghai this time?

118

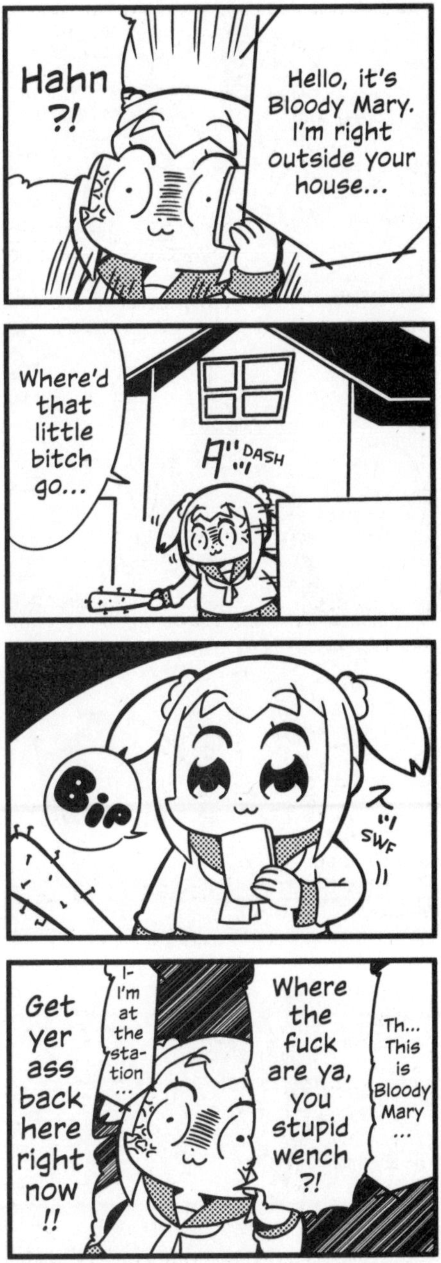
Hello, it's Bloody Mary. I'm right outside your house...
Hahn ?!
Where'd that little bitch go...
ダッ DASH
スッ SWF
Bip
Th... This is Bloody Mary...
Where the fuck are ya, you stupid wench ?!
I- I'm at the sta- tion...
Get yer ass back here right now !!

119

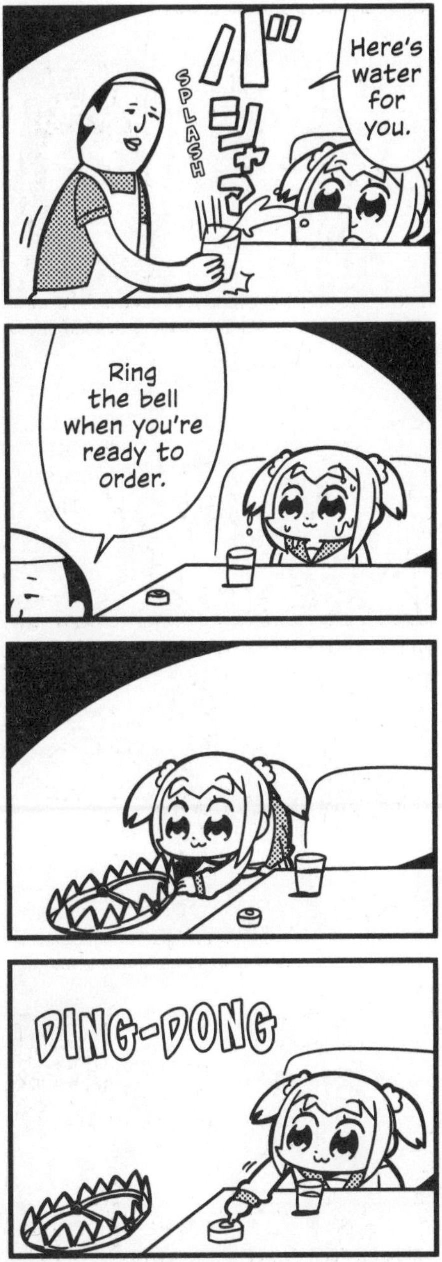
Here's water for you.
SPLASH
Ring the bell when you're ready to order.
DING-DONG

120

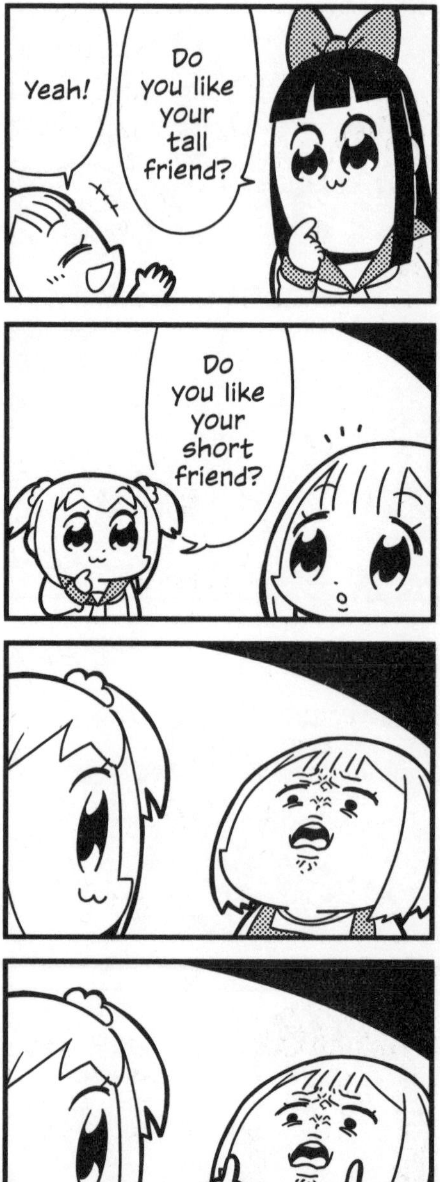
Do you like your tall friend?
Yeah!
Do you like your short friend?

121

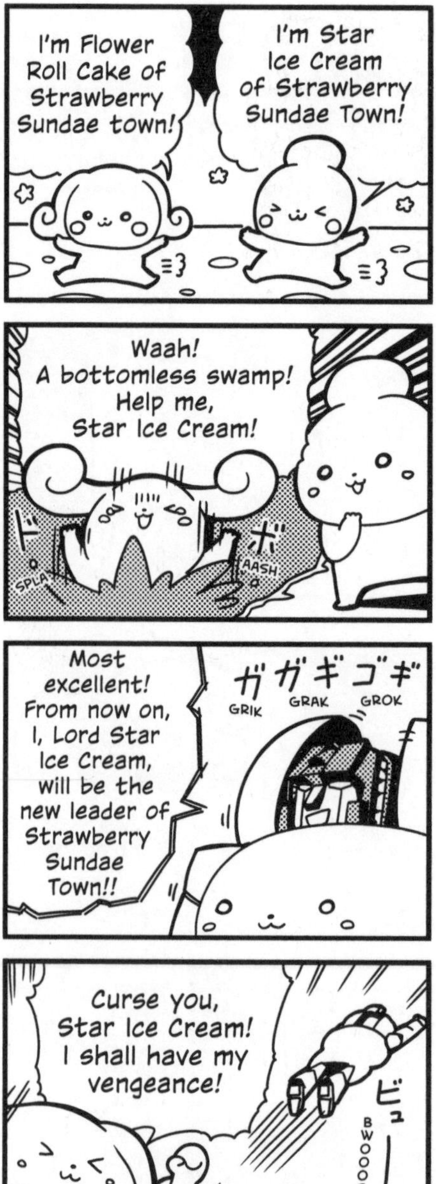
I'm Star Ice Cream of Strawberry Sundae Town!
I'm Flower Roll Cake of Strawberry Sundae town!
Waah! A bottomless swamp! Help me, Star Ice Cream!
ドボ
SPLA
ASH
ガガギゴギ
GRIK GRAK GROK
Most excellent! From now on, I, Lord Star Ice Cream, will be the new leader of Strawberry Sundae Town!!
Curse you, Star Ice Cream! I shall have my vengeance!
ビューン
BWOOOOSH

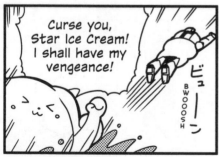

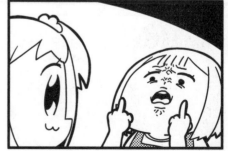

To be continued...

122

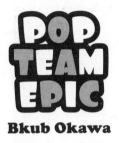

POP TEAM EPIC

Bkub Okawa

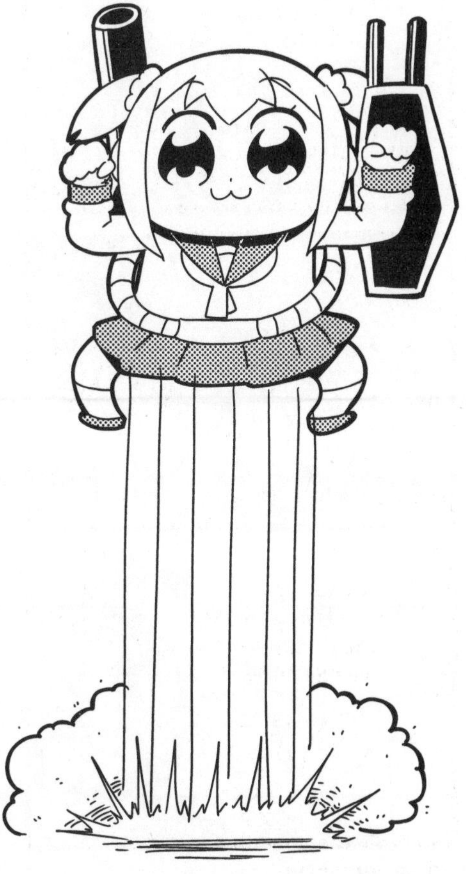

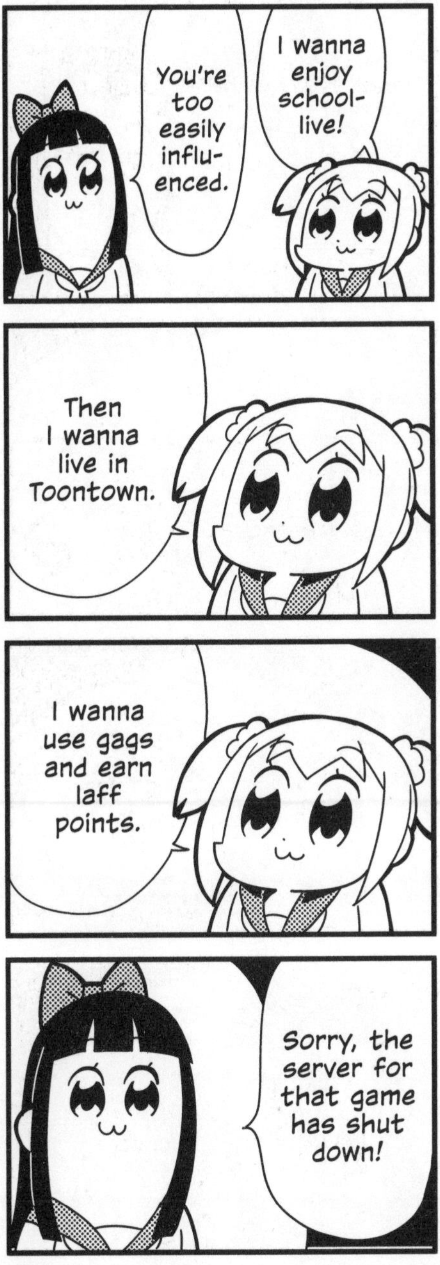

I wanna enjoy school-live!
You're too easily influenced.
Then I wanna live in Toontown.
I wanna use gags and earn laff points.
Sorry, the server for that game has shut down!

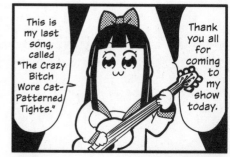

123

Thank you all for coming to my show today.
This is my last song, called "The Crazy Bitch Wore Cat-Patterned Tights."
LICK LICK
Lemon

124

Yo, Miss God of Death !!
Yeah ?
VWUMMM
I found a man from the B.C. era, let's play a game togeth-er.
Nice !
What should I use ...?
I'm using Zero Suit Samus.
Uhm, don't we need a game link cable?
Ah ha! Oh, you silly B.C. man!
Wick-ed funny !

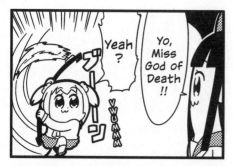

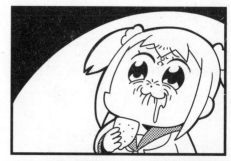

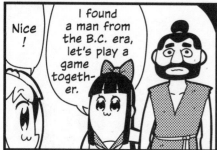

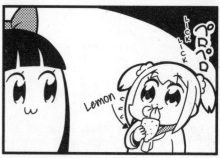

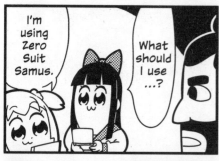

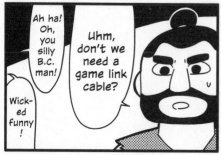

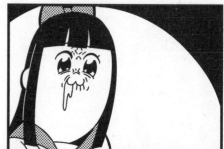

125

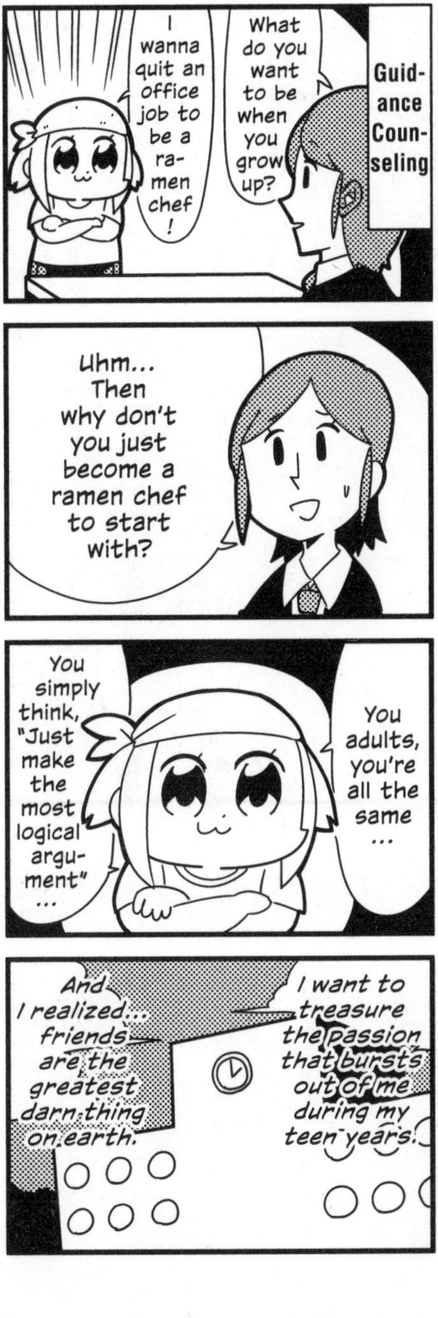
Guidance Counseling
What do you want to be when you grow up?
I wanna quit an office job to be a ramen chef!
Uhm... Then why don't you just become a ramen chef to start with?
You adults, you're all the same...
You simply think, "Just make the most logical argument"...
I want to treasure the passion that bursts out of me during my teen years.
And I realized... friends are the greatest darn thing on earth.

126

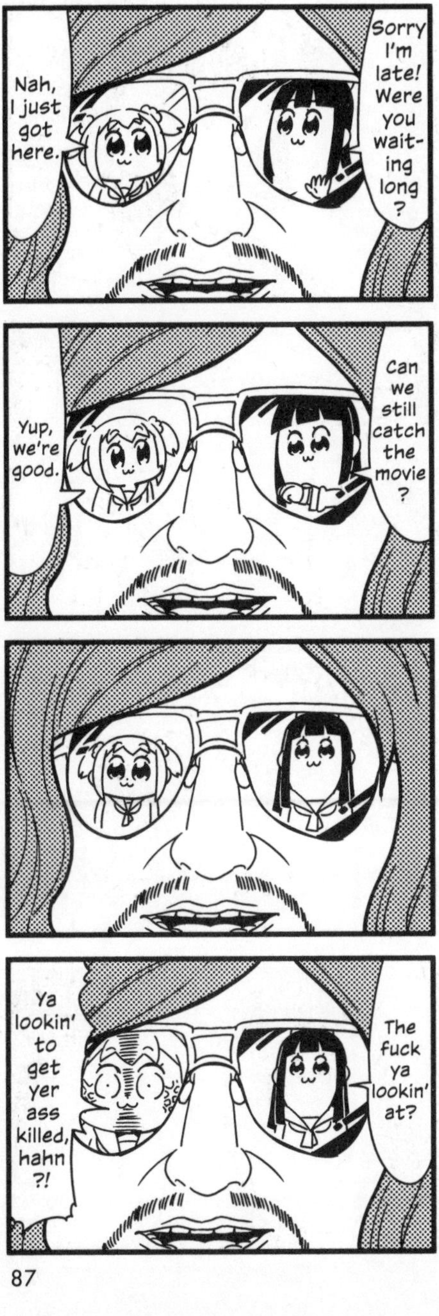
Sorry I'm late! Were you waiting long?
Nah, I just got here.
Can we still catch the movie?
Yup, we're good.
The fuck ya lookin' at?
Ya lookin' to get yer ass killed, hahn?!

128

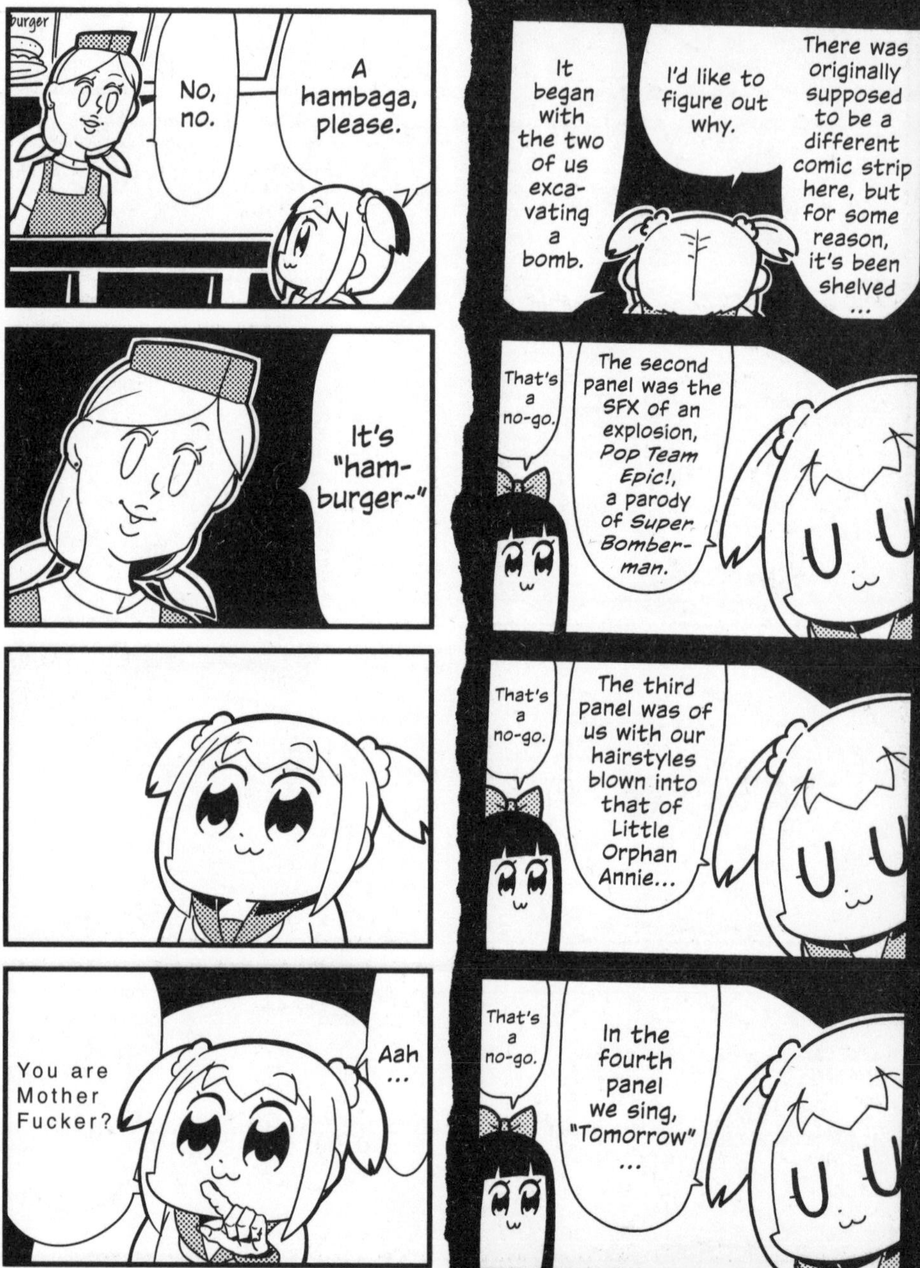

There was originally supposed to be a different comic strip here, but for some reason, it's been shelved ...
I'd like to figure out why.
It began with the two of us excavating a bomb.
The second panel was the SFX of an explosion, *Pop Team Epic!*, a parody of *Super Bomberman.*
That's a no-go.
The third panel was of us with our hairstyles blown into that of Little Orphan Annie...
That's a no-go.
In the fourth panel we sing, "Tomorrow" ...
That's a no-go.
A hambaga, please.
No, no.
burger
It's "ham-burger~"
Aah ...
You are Mother Fucker?

129

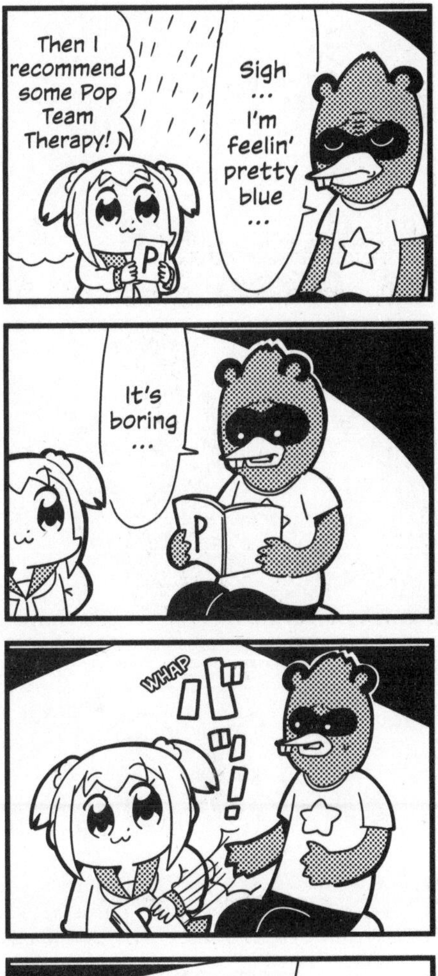
Sigh ... I'm feelin' pretty blue ...
Then I recommend some Pop Team Therapy!
It's boring ...
バッ!!
WHAP
Oh, so yer a hater.

130

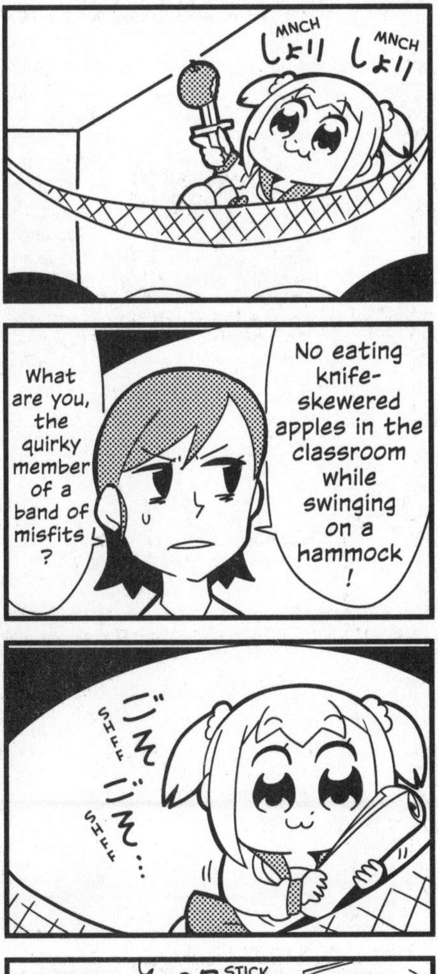
しょり
MNCH
しょり
MNCH
No eating knife-skewered apples in the classroom while swinging on a hammock!
What are you, the quirky member of a band of misfits?
ごそ
SHFF
ごそ...
SHFF
ペタ
STICK
ペタ
STICK
No hanging sexy posters on the classroom wall!!

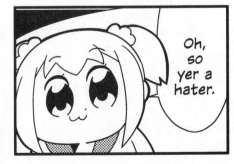

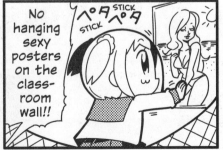

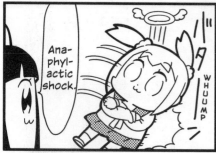

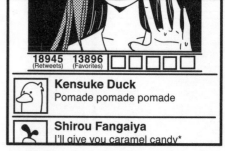

131

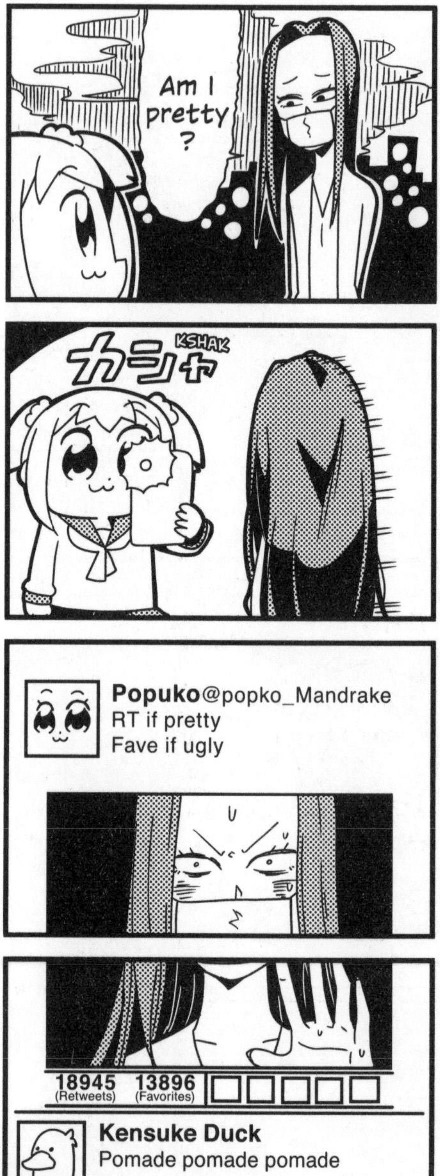
Am I pretty ?
KSHAK
カシャ
Popuko@popko_Mandrake
RT if pretty
Fave if ugly
18945 (Retweets)
13896 (Favorites)
Kensuke Duck
Pomade pomade pomade
Shirou Fangaiya
I'll give you caramel candy*

*Reference to tricks to ward off the Slit-Mouth Woman of urban legend.

132

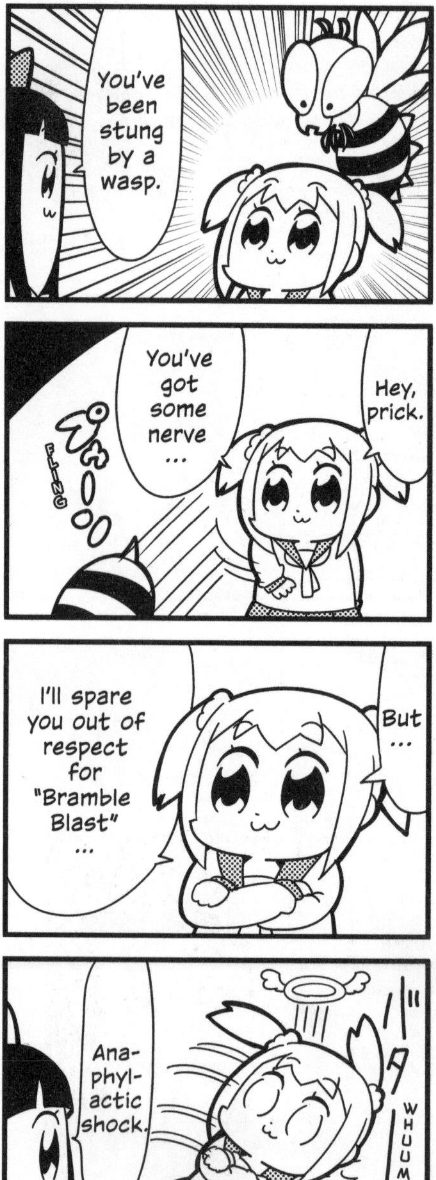
You've been stung by a wasp.
Hey, prick.
You've got some nerve ...
FLING
But ...
I'll spare you out of respect for "Bramble Blast" ...
Anaphylactic shock.
WHUUMP

To be continued...

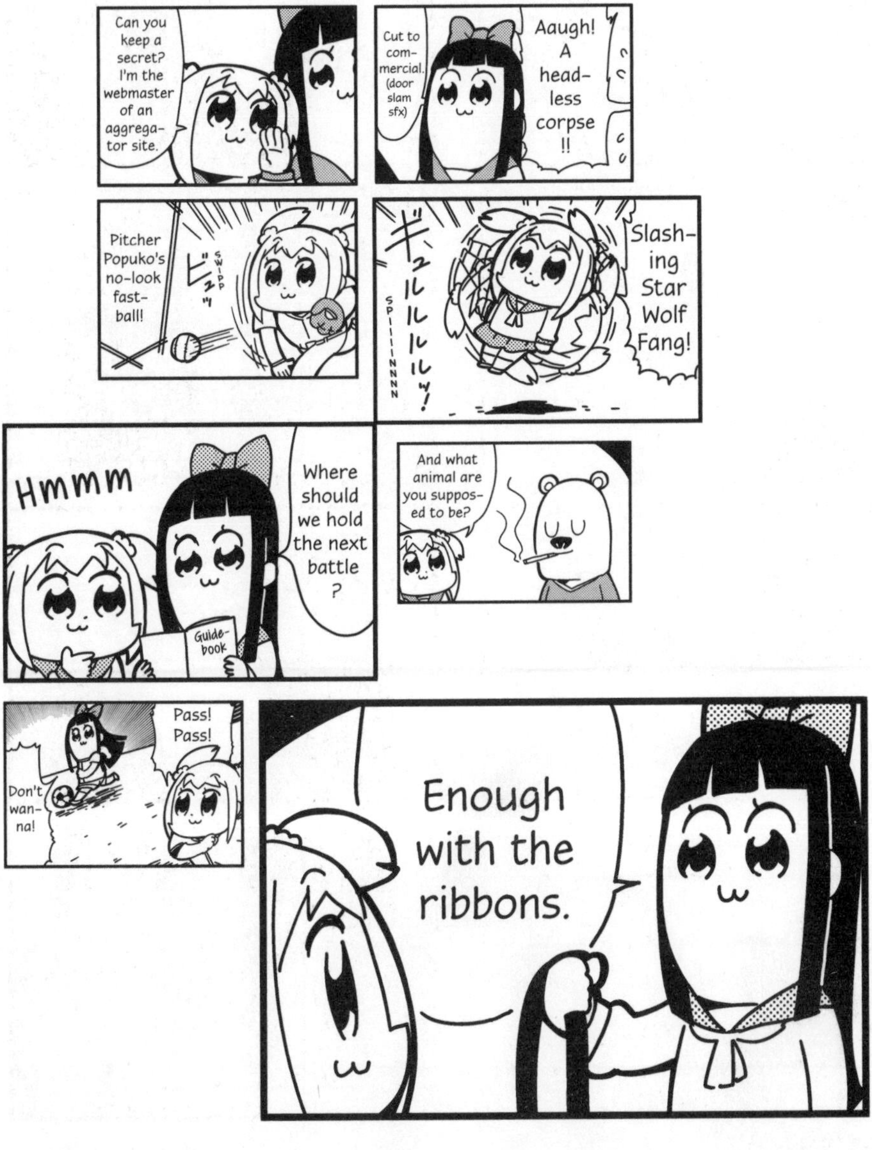
Aaugh! A headless corpse !!
Cut to commercial. (door slam sfx)
Can you keep a secret? I'm the webmaster of an aggregator site.
Slashing Star Wolf Fang!
ギュルルルルッ!
SPIIIINNNN
Pitcher Popuko's no-look fastball!
ビュッ
SWIPP
And what animal are you supposed to be?
Where should we hold the next battle ?
Hmmm
Guidebook
Enough with the ribbons.
Pass! Pass!
Don't wanna!

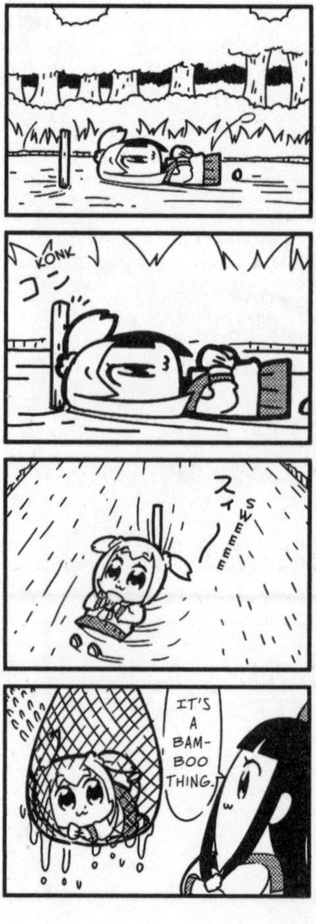
KONK
コン
スィー
SWEEEEE
IT'S A BAM-BOO THING.

(133)

POP TEAM EPIC

Bkub Okawa

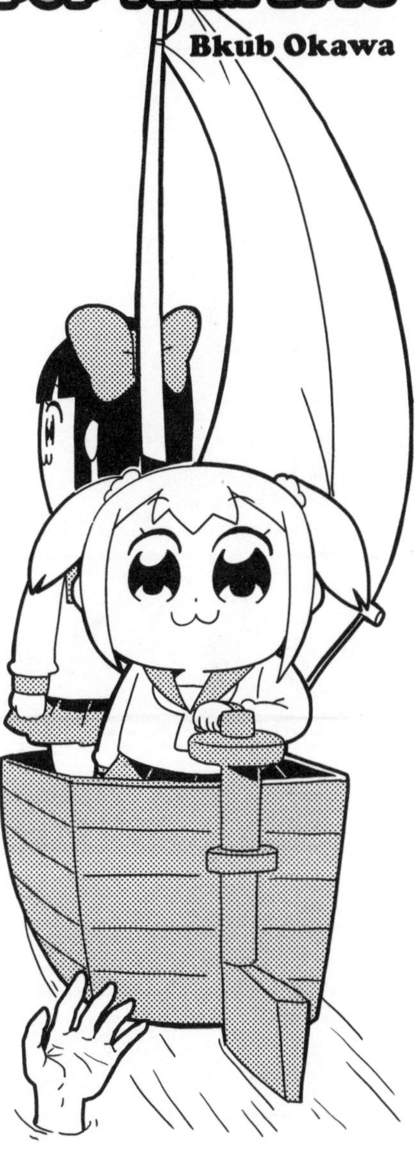

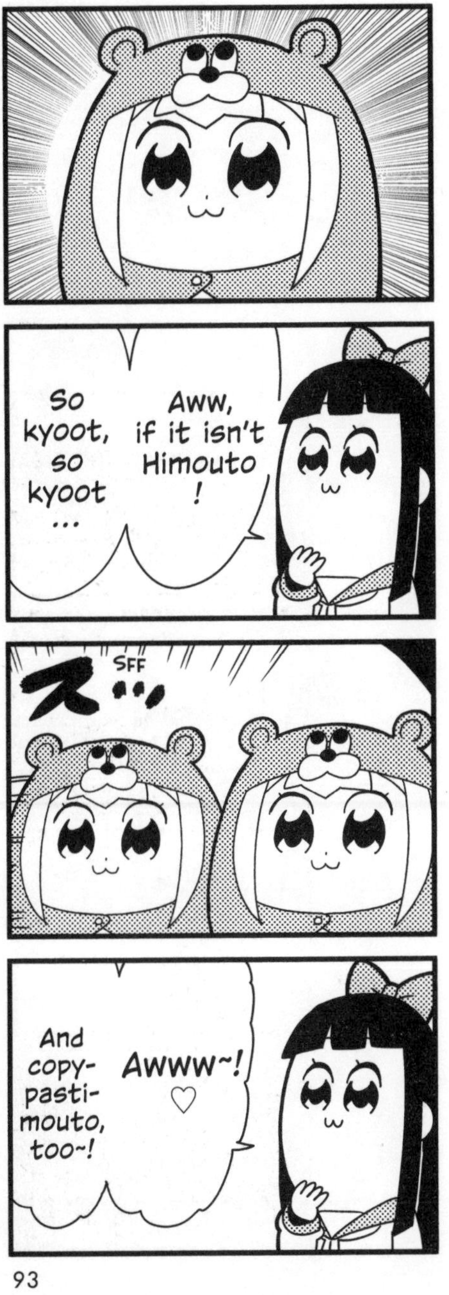
Aww, if it isn't Himouto!
So kyoot, so kyoot...
SFF
Awww~! ♡
And copy-pastimouto, too~!

134

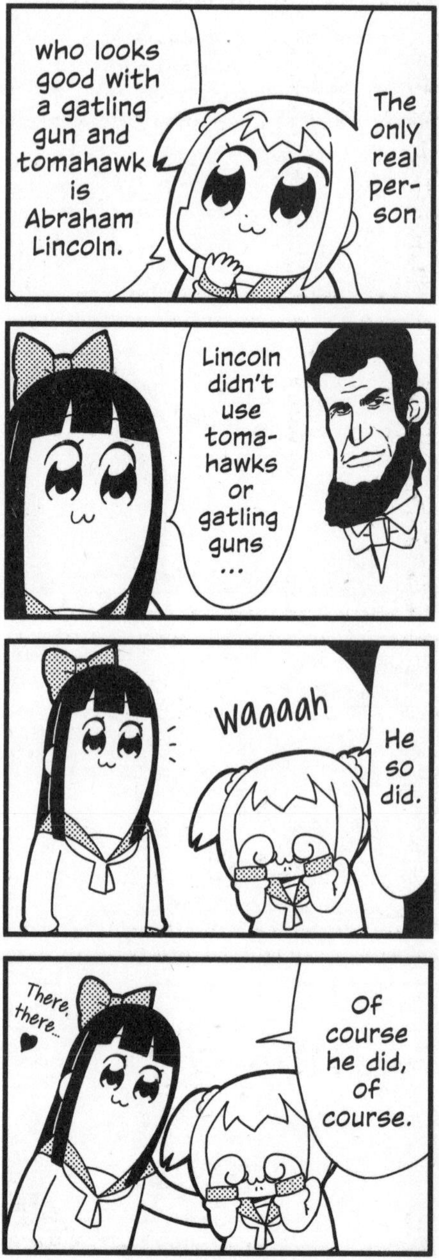
The only real person
who looks good with a gatling gun and tomahawk is Abraham Lincoln.
Lincoln didn't use tomahawks or gatling guns ...
He so did.
Waaaah
Of course he did, of course.
There, there... ♥

135

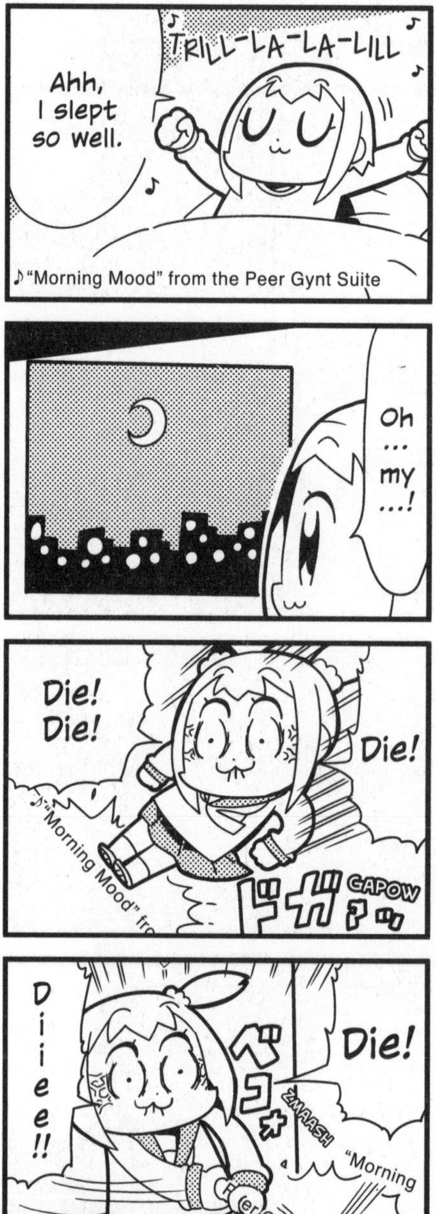
TRILL-LA-LA-LILL
Ahh, I slept so well.
♪"Morning Mood" from the Peer Gynt Suite
Oh ... my ...!
Die!
Die! Die!
ドガァッ
GAPOW
Die!
ベコォ
ZWAASH
Diiee!!

136

PIP
PIP
Grand-pa!
Please, open your eyes, Grand-pa!
EKG
BEEEEEP
Aaah!!
Grand-paaa!!!
ZAKA
BMM
ZAKA
BMM
YEAHHH!!
UNTZ UNTZ UNTZ UNTZ
GO GRAAAAMPS!!!!
UNTZ UNTZ UNTZ UNTZ UNTZ

137

TAKESHOBO
Publish the *tankobon* already, ya bastards!
Takeshobo
TAKESHOBO
Oh ho... Silent, are ya?
Takeshobo
SQK
SQK
Mafia-affiliated Takeshobo
Hello?
Police?

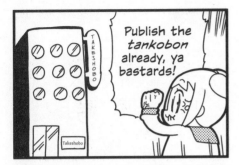

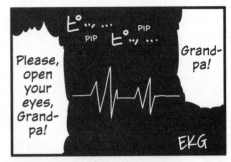

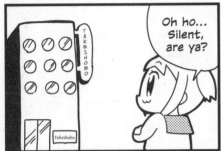

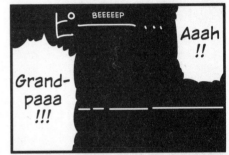

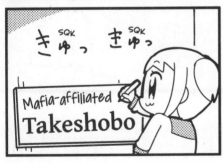

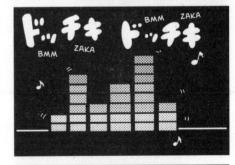

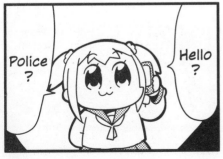

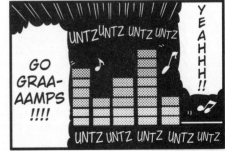

*Japanese publisher of *Pop Team Epic*

138

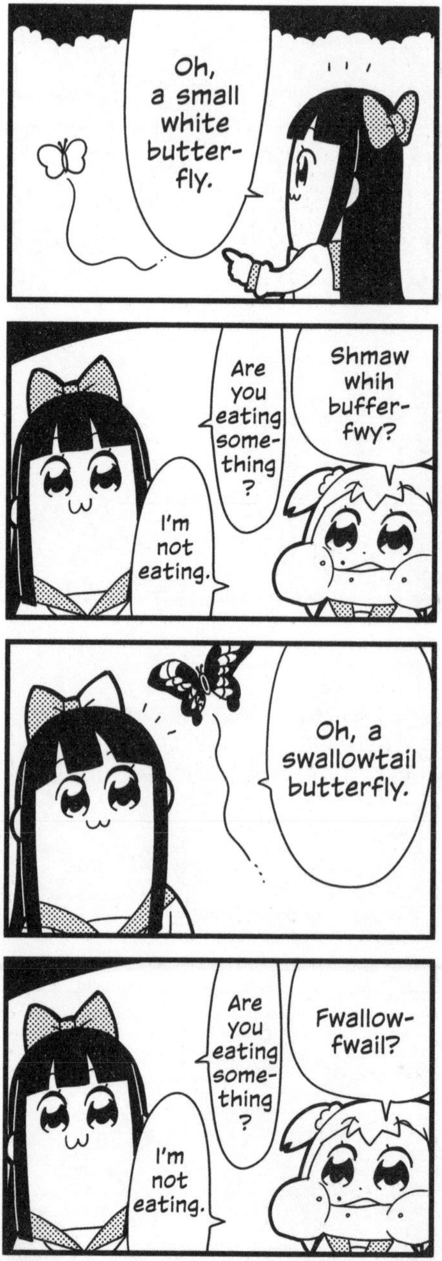
Oh, a small white butter-fly.
Shmaw whih buffer-fwy?
Are you eating some-thing?
I'm not eating.
Oh, a swallowtail butterfly.
Fwallow-fwail?
Are you eating some-thing?
I'm not eating.

139

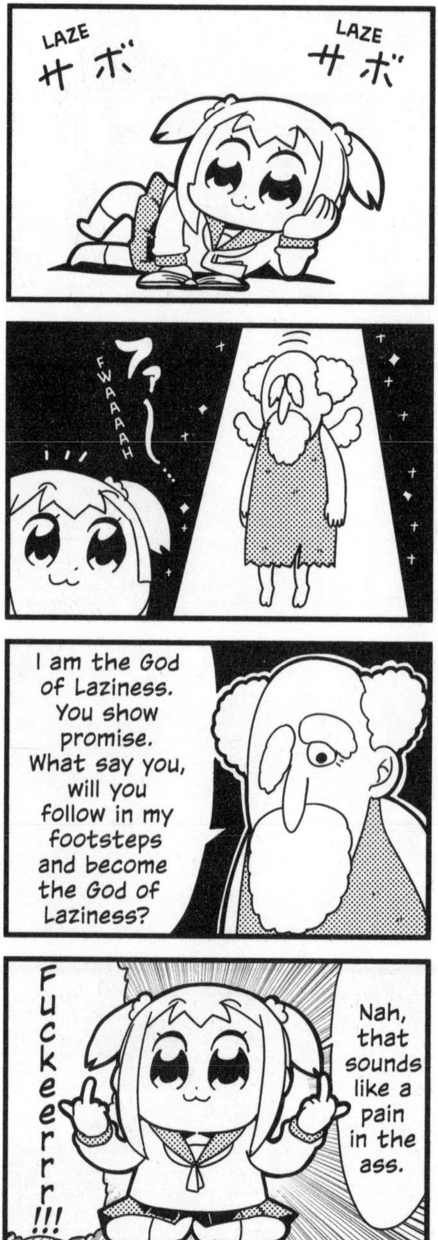
LAZE
サボ
LAZE
サボ
FWAAAAAH
ファー…
I am the God of Laziness. You show promise. What say you, will you follow in my footsteps and become the God of Laziness?
Nah, that sounds like a pain in the ass.
Fuckeerrr!!!

140

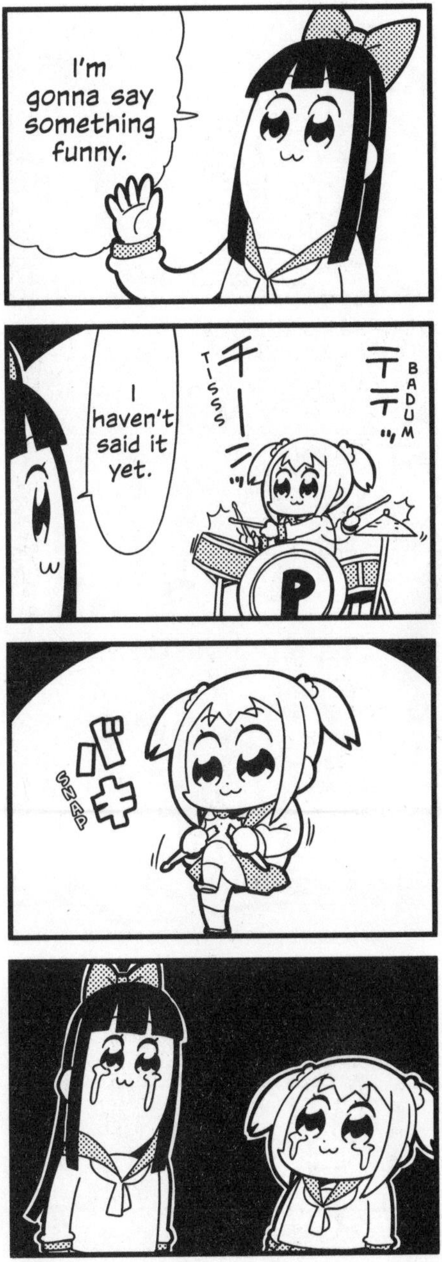
I'm gonna say something funny.
I haven't said it yet.
チーン
TISSS
テテ
BADUM
バキ
SNAP

141

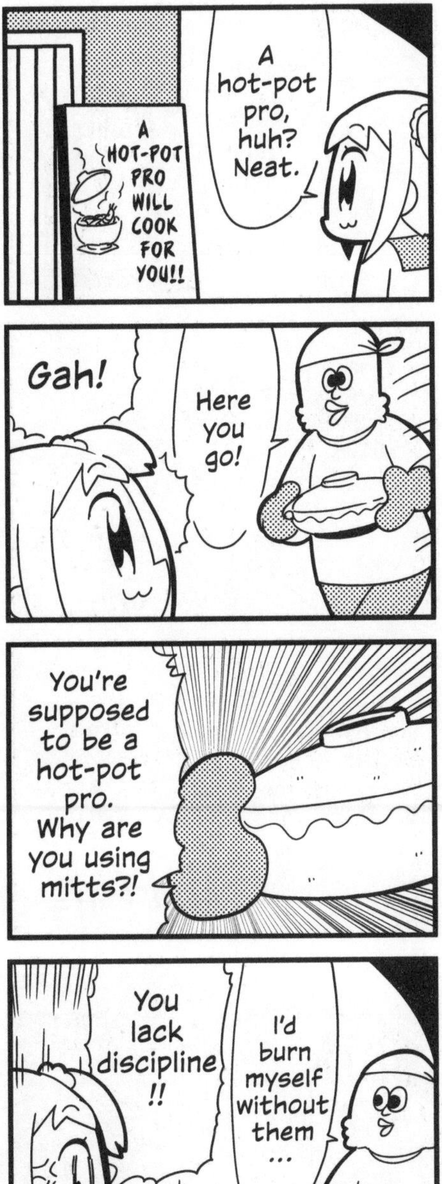
A hot-pot pro, huh? Neat.
A HOT-POT PRO WILL COOK FOR YOU!!
Here you go!
Gah!
You're supposed to be a hot-pot pro. Why are you using mitts?!
I'd burn myself without them...
You lack discipline!!

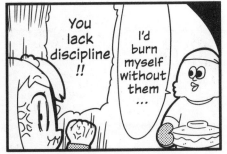

142

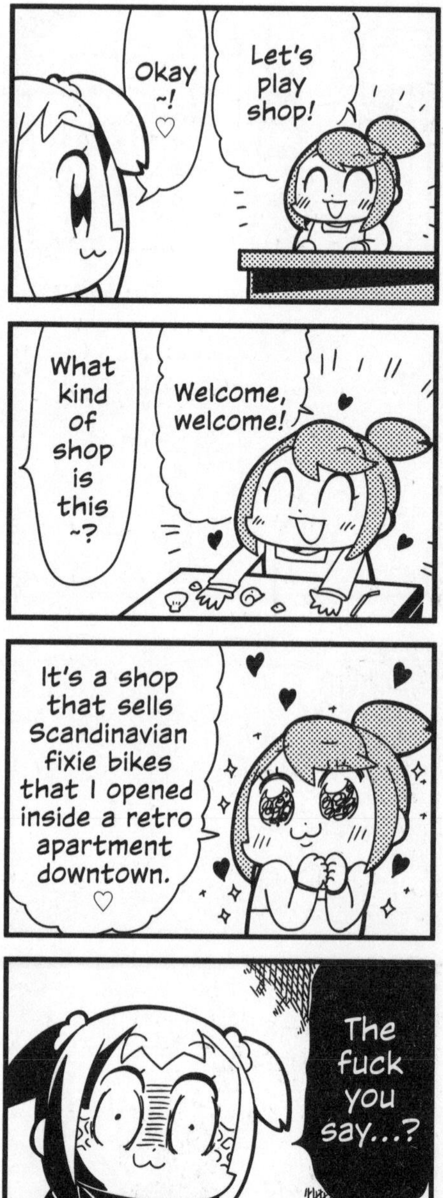
Let's play shop!
Okay ~! ♡
Welcome, welcome!
What kind of shop is this ~?
It's a shop that sells Scandinavian fixie bikes that I opened inside a retro apartment downtown. ♡
The fuck you say...?
Popuko snapped!!

143

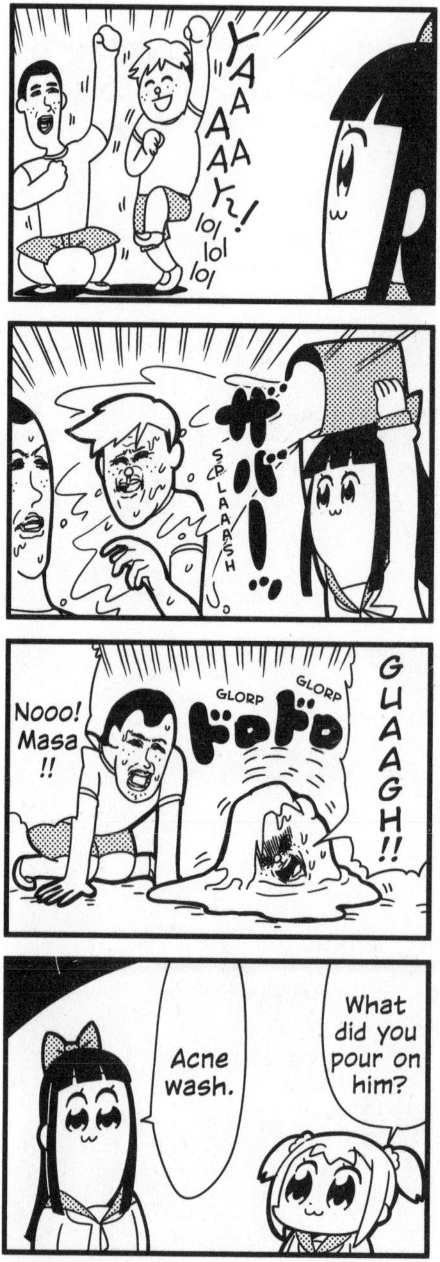
YAAAAAY?!
lol lol lol
ザバー…
SPLAAASH
GUAAAGH!!
GLORP GLORP
ドロドロ
Nooo! Masa!!
What did you pour on him?
Acne wash.

To be continued...

POP TEAM EPIC

Bkub Okawa

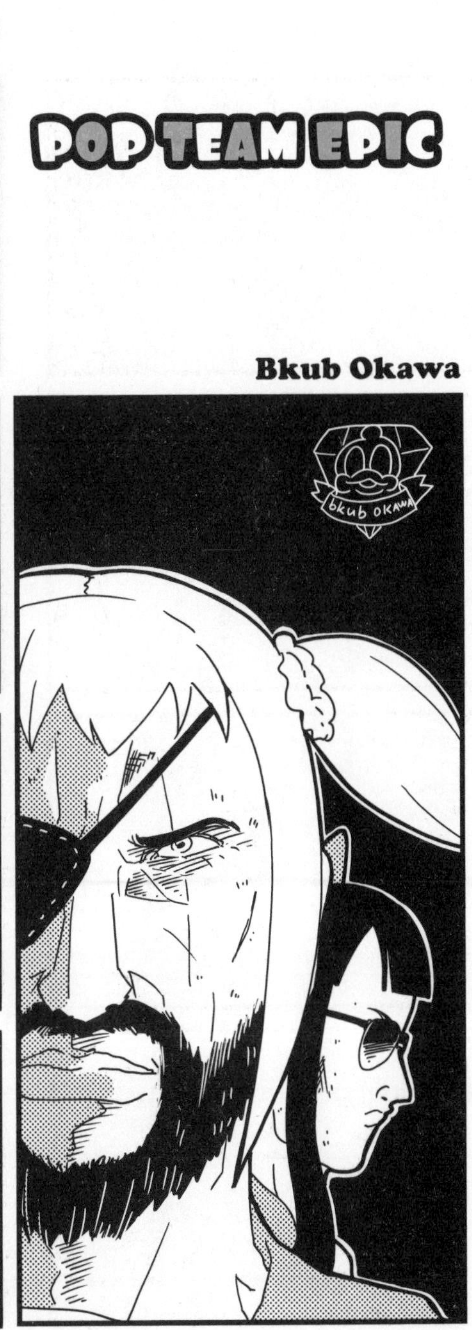
bkub OKAWA

144

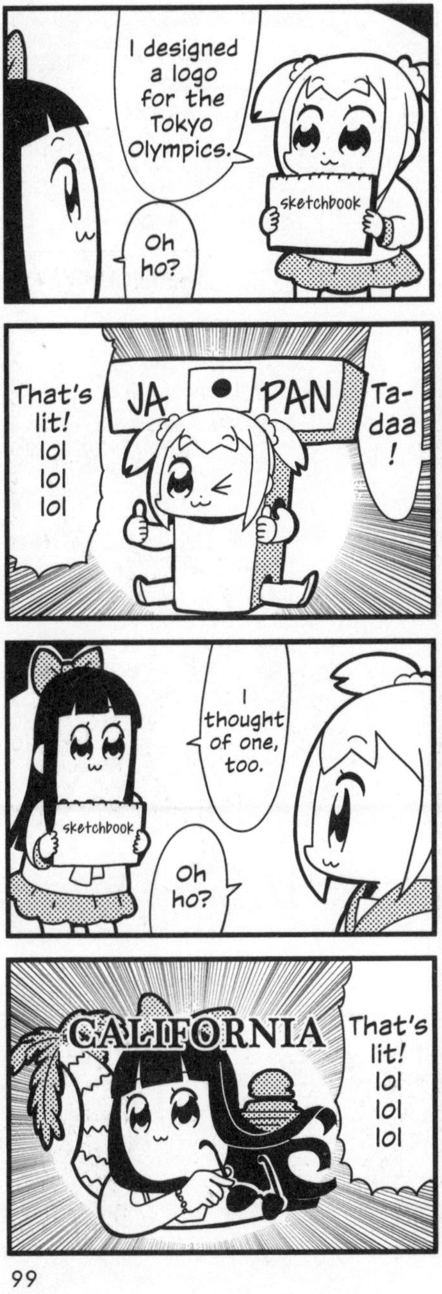
I designed a logo for the Tokyo Olympics.
sketchbook
Oh ho?
Ta-daa!
JA PAN
That's lit! lol lol lol
I thought of one, too.
sketchbook
Oh ho?
That's lit! lol lol lol
CALIFORNIA

145

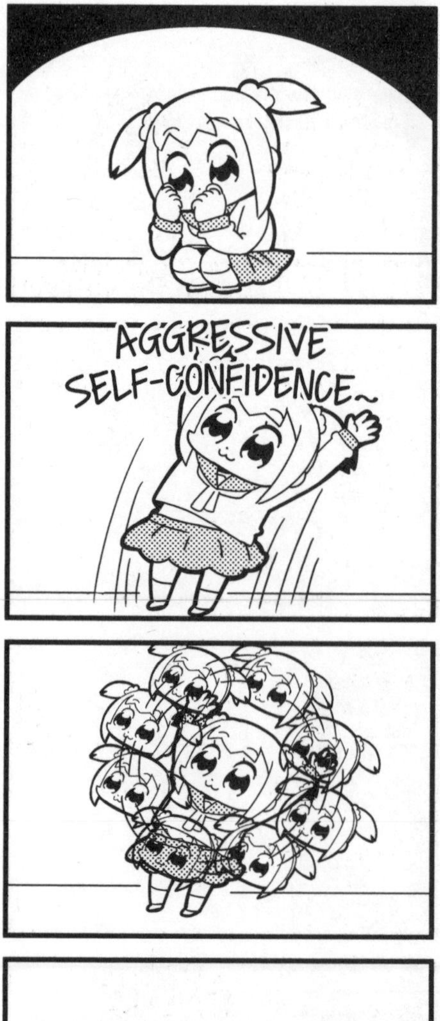
AGGRESSIVE SELF-CONFIDENCE~

146

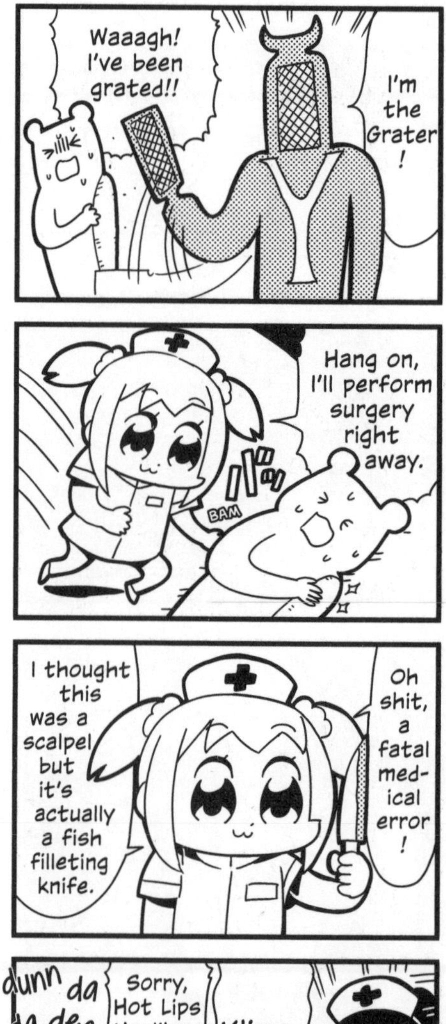
I'm the Grater!
Waaagh! I've been grated!!
Hang on, I'll perform surgery right away.
BAM
Oh shit, a fatal med-ical error!
I thought this was a scalpel but it's actually a fish filleting knife.
Kling-eee-errr~!!!
Sorry, Hot Lips Houlihan!!
dunn da da dee da dum dunnn

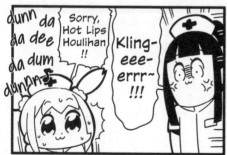

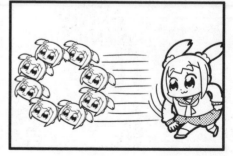

147

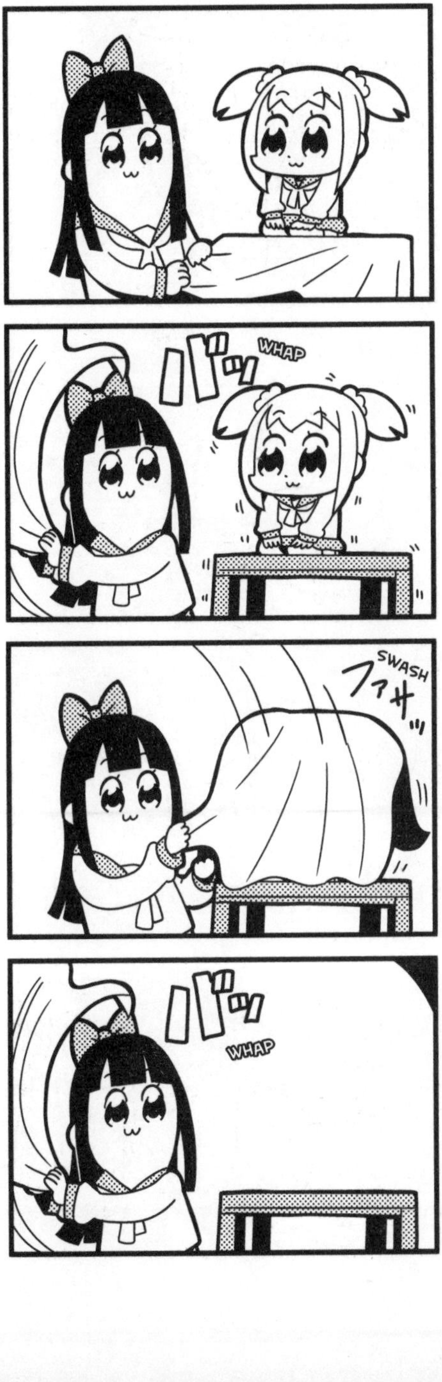

バッ
WHAP
ファサッ
SWASH
バッ
WHAP

148

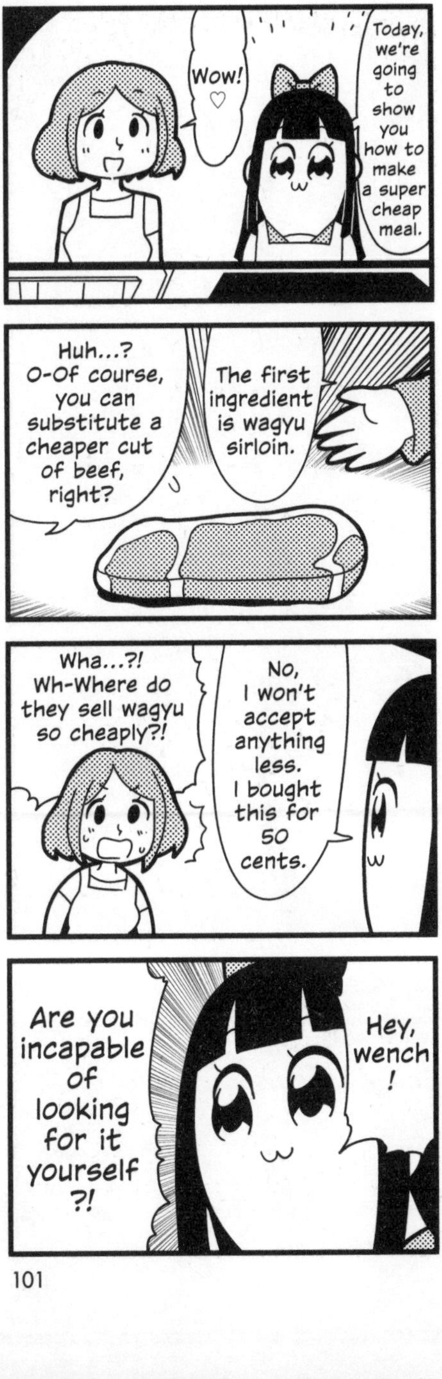

Today, we're going to show you how to make a super cheap meal.
Wow! ♡
The first ingredient is wagyu sirloin.
Huh...? O-Of course, you can substitute a cheaper cut of beef, right?
No, I won't accept anything less. I bought this for 50 cents.
Wha...?! Wh-Where do they sell wagyu so cheaply?!
Hey, wench!
Are you incapable of looking for it yourself?!

149

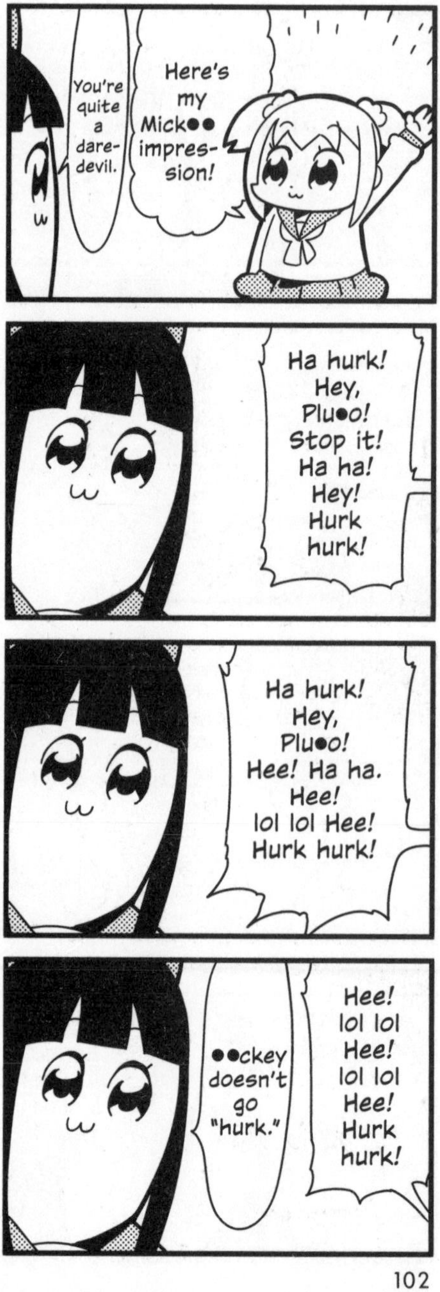

Here's my Mick●● impression!
You're quite a dare-devil.
Ha hurk! Hey, Plu●o! Stop it! Ha ha! Hey! Hurk hurk!
Ha hurk! Hey, Plu●o! Hee! Ha ha. Hee! lol lol Hee! Hurk hurk!
Hee! lol lol Hee! lol lol Hee! Hurk hurk!
●●ckey doesn't go "hurk."

150

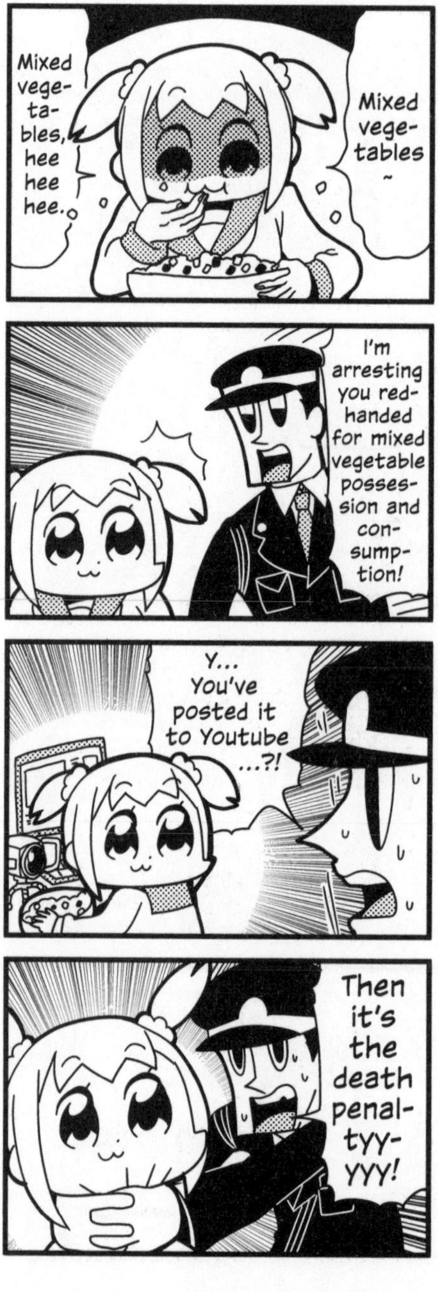

Mixed vegetables ~
Mixed vegetables, hee hee hee.
I'm arresting you red-handed for mixed vegetable possession and consumption!
Y... You've posted it to Youtube ...?!
Then it's the death penaltyyy-yyy!

151

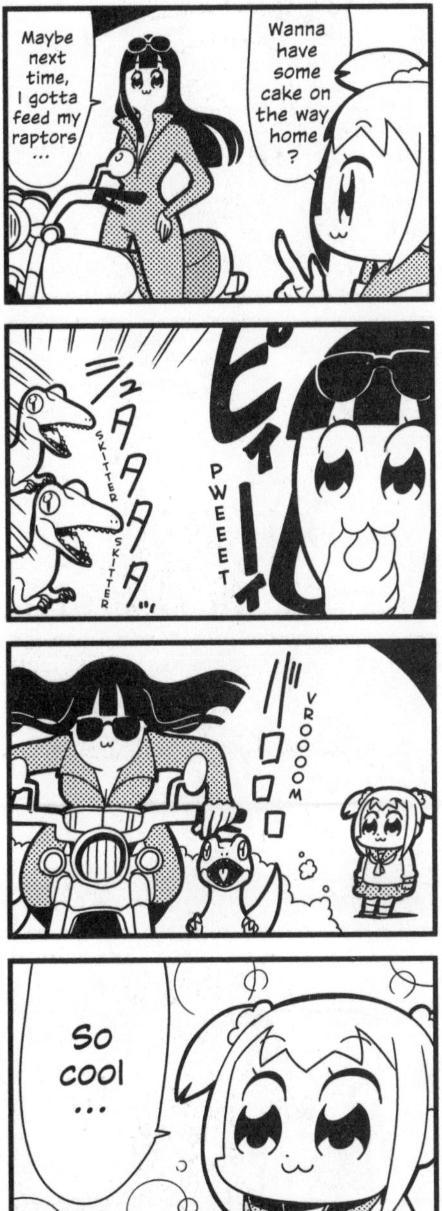
Wanna have some cake on the way home?
Maybe next time, I gotta feed my raptors ...
PWEEET
SKITTER
SKITTER
VROOOOOM
So cool ...

152

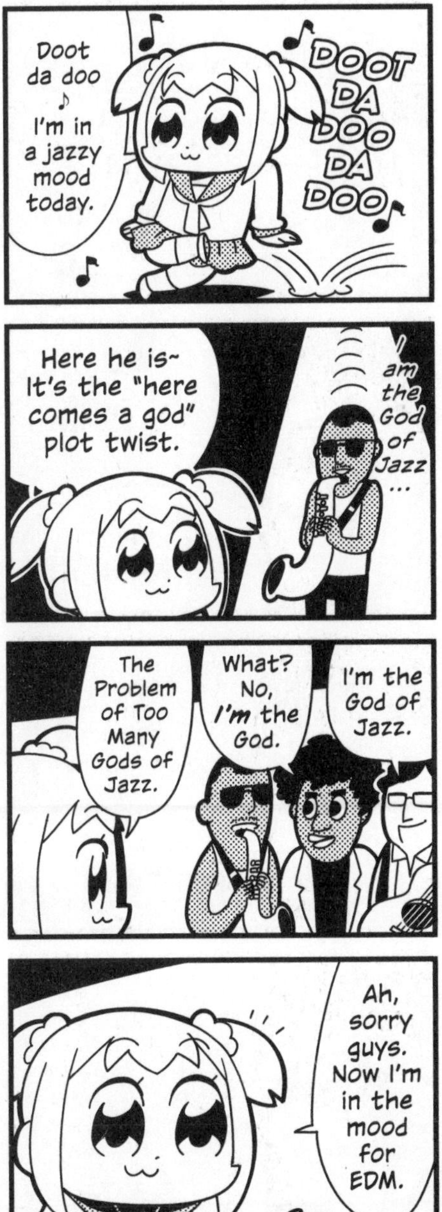
DOOT DA DOO DA DOO
Doot da doo ♪ I'm in a jazzy mood today.
I am the God of Jazz ...
Here he is~ It's the "here comes a god" plot twist.
I'm the God of Jazz.
What? No, *I'm* the God.
The Problem of Too Many Gods of Jazz.
Ah, sorry guys. Now I'm in the mood for EDM.

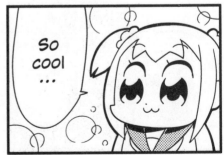

153

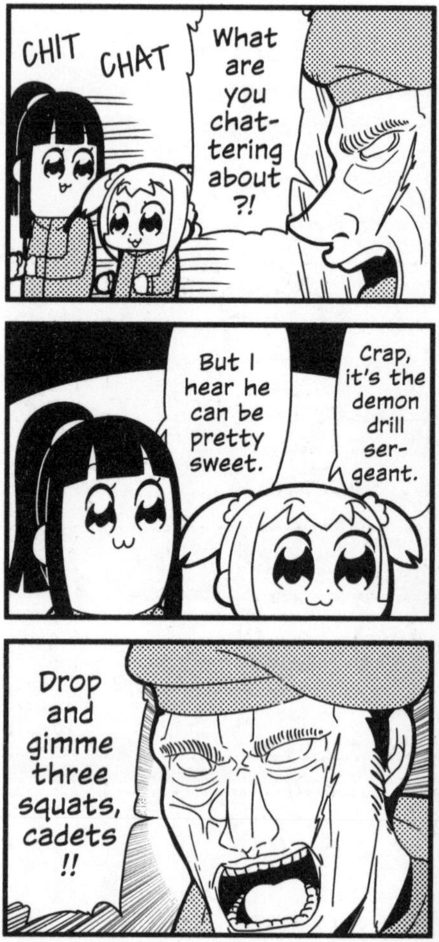
What are you chattering about?!
CHIT CHAT
Crap, it's the demon drill sergeant.
But I hear he can be pretty sweet.
Drop and gimme three squats, cadets!!
Sweet~
Sweet.

☆ **Looks like I'll be able to make a long-awaited announcement next time!**

154

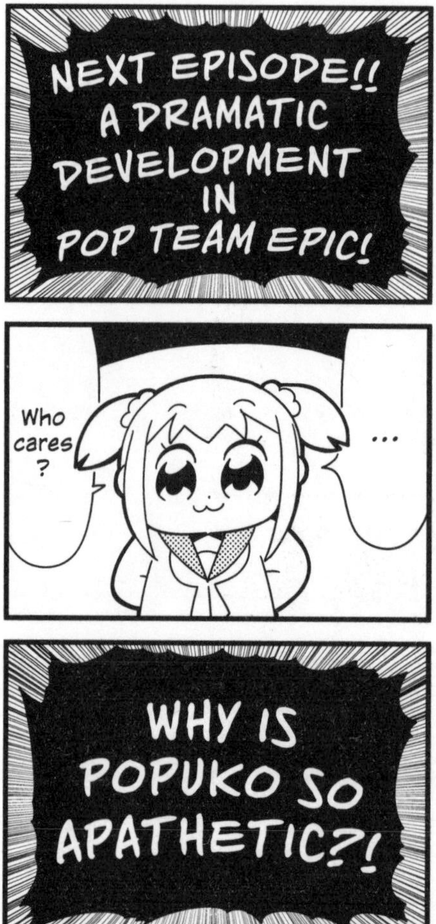
NEXT EPISODE!! A DRAMATIC DEVELOPMENT IN POP TEAM EPIC!
...
Who cares?
WHY IS POPUKO SO APATHETIC?!
Probs just announcing the *tankobon*, right?
It took waaay too long.

To be continued...

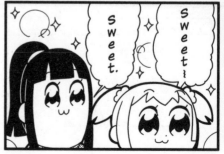

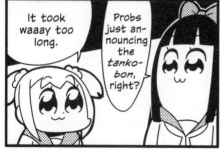

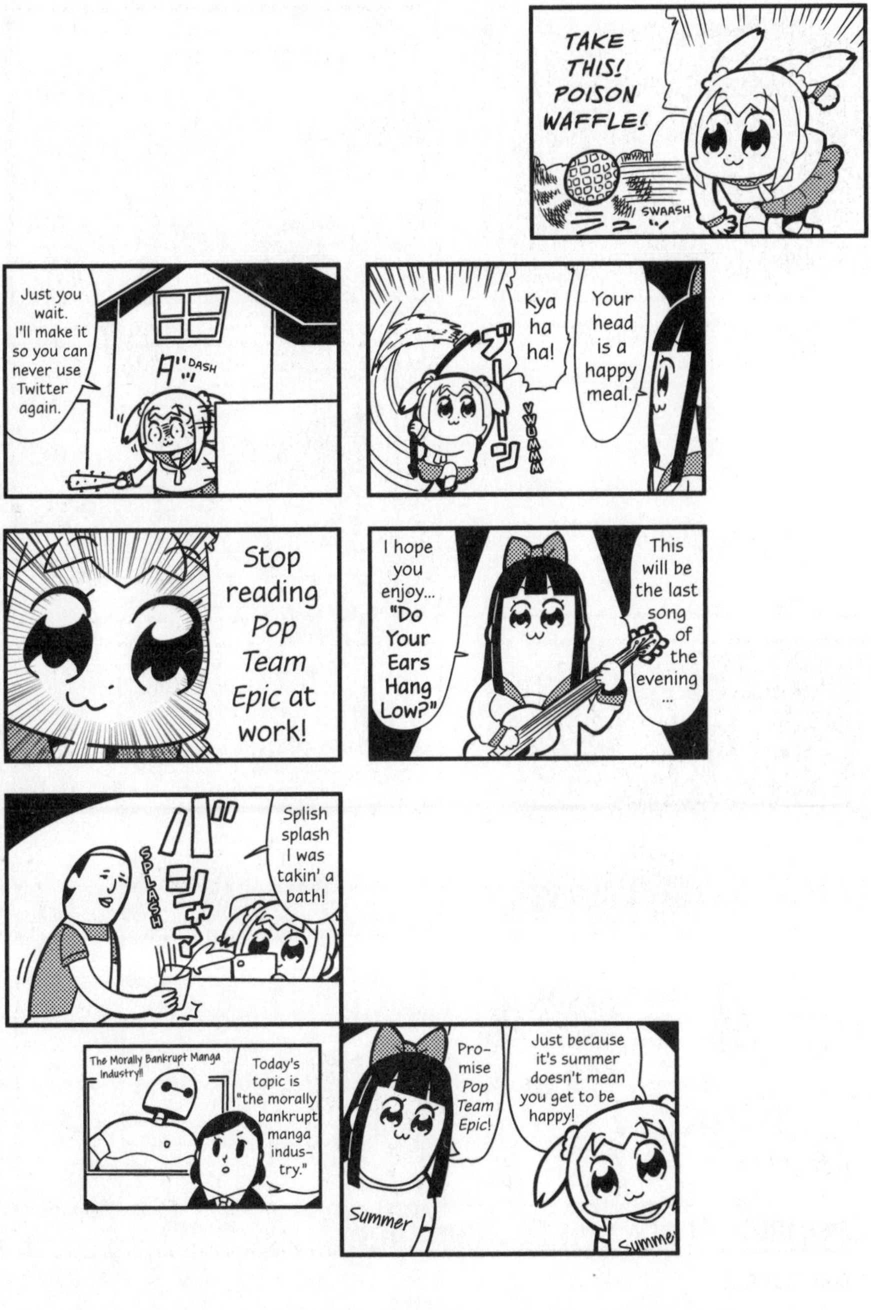
TAKE THIS! POISON WAFFLE!
SWAASH
Your head is a happy meal.
Kya ha ha!
VWUMM
Just you wait. I'll make it so you can never use Twitter again.
DASH
This will be the last song of the evening...
I hope you enjoy... "Do Your Ears Hang Low?"
Stop reading Pop Team Epic at work!
Splish splash I was takin' a bath!
SPLASH
Just because it's summer doesn't mean you get to be happy!
Pro-mise Pop Team Epic!
Summe
Summer
The Morally Bankrupt Manga Industry!!
Today's topic is "the morally bankrupt manga industry."

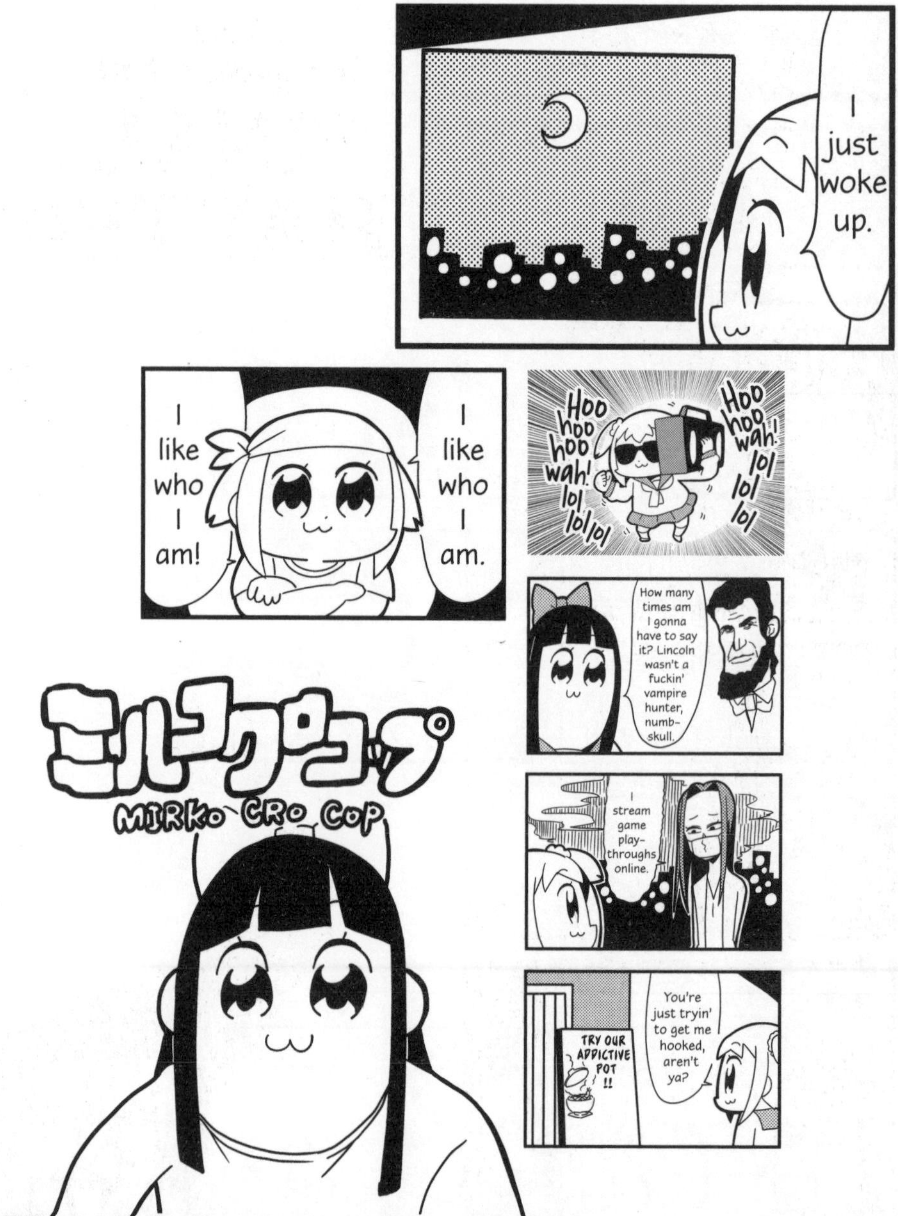
I just woke up.
Hoo hoo wah! lol lol lol
Hoo hoo hoo wah! lol lol lol
How many times am I gonna have to say it? Lincoln wasn't a fuckin' vampire hunter, numbskull.
I stream game play-throughs online.
You're just tryin' to get me hooked, aren't ya?
TRY OUR ADDICTIVE POT !!
I like who I am.
I like who I am!
ミルコクロコップ
MIRKO CRO COP
What the hell are you talking about?

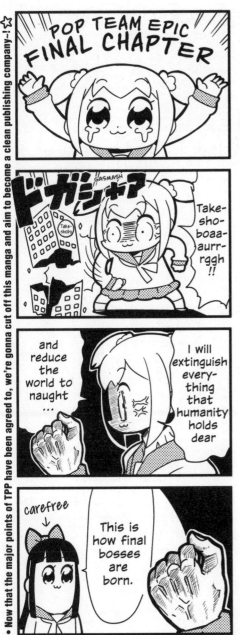

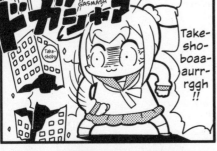

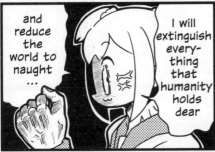

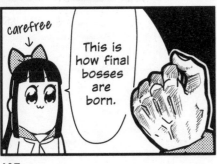

The long-awaited FINAL CHAPTER

POP TEAM EPIC

Bkub Okawa

155

POP TEAM EPIC FINAL CHAPTER
Take-shoboaa-aurrrggh !!
ドガシャア
GASMASH
Take-shobo
I will extinguish everything that humanity holds dear
and reduce the world to naught ...
This is how final bosses are born.
carefree

• Now that the major points of TPP have been agreed to, we're gonna cut off this manga and aim to become a clean publishing company~!☆

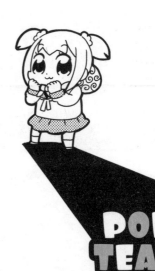

156

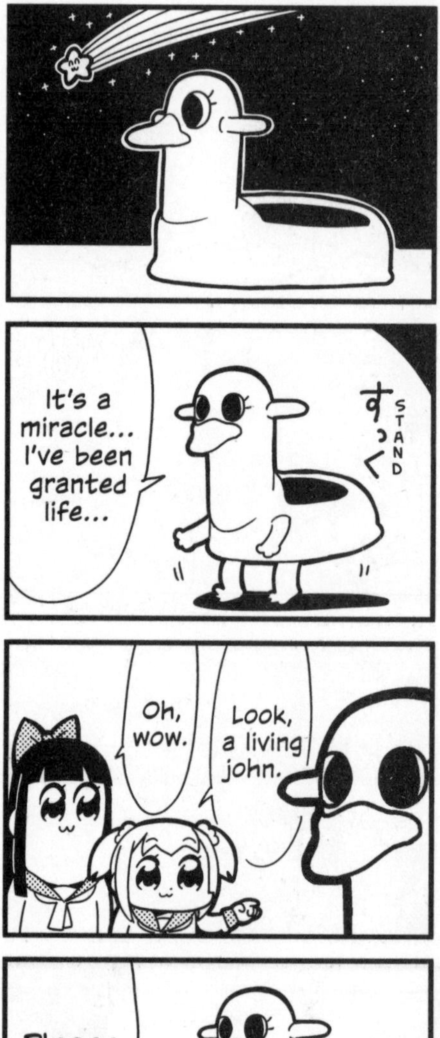
It's a miracle... I've been granted life...
すっく
STAND
Look, a living john.
Oh, wow.
Please kill me.

●The *tankobon* is real!

157

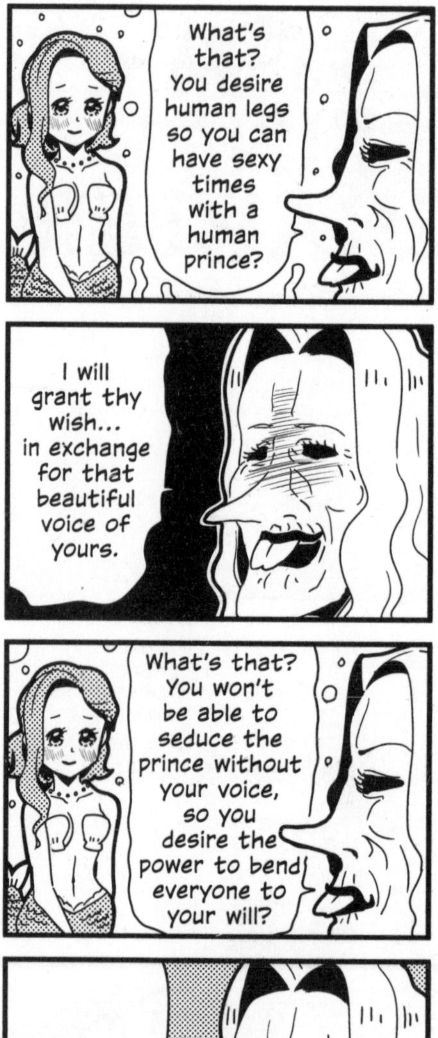
What's that? You desire human legs so you can have sexy times with a human prince?
I will grant thy wish... in exchange for that beautiful voice of yours.
What's that? You won't be able to seduce the prince without your voice, so you desire the power to bend everyone to your will?
Rape is a crime.

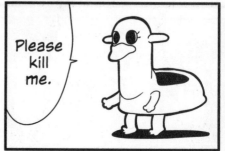

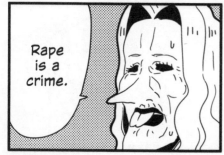

158

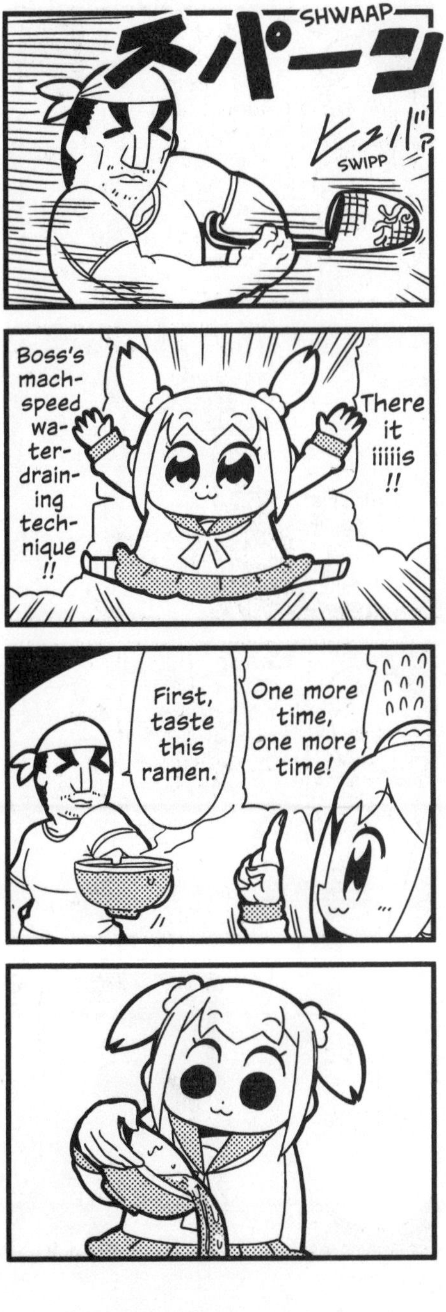

SHWAAP
スパーン
SWIPP
Boss's mach-speed water-draining technique!!
There it iiiiis!!
One more time, one more time!
First, taste this ramen.

159

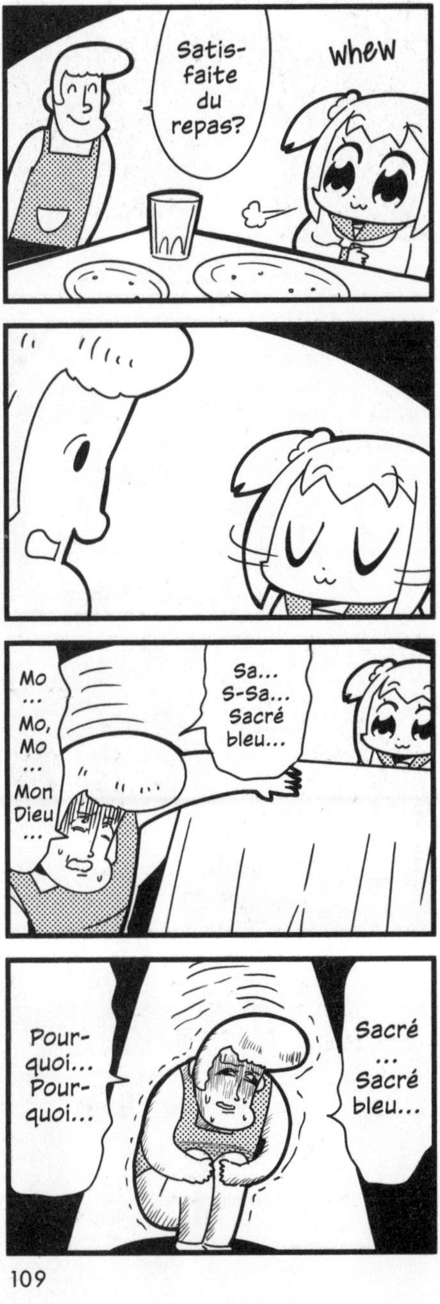

whew
Satisfaite du repas?
Sa... S-Sa... Sacré bleu...
Mo... Mo, Mo... Mon Dieu...
Sacré... Sacré bleu...
Pourquoi... Pourquoi...

160

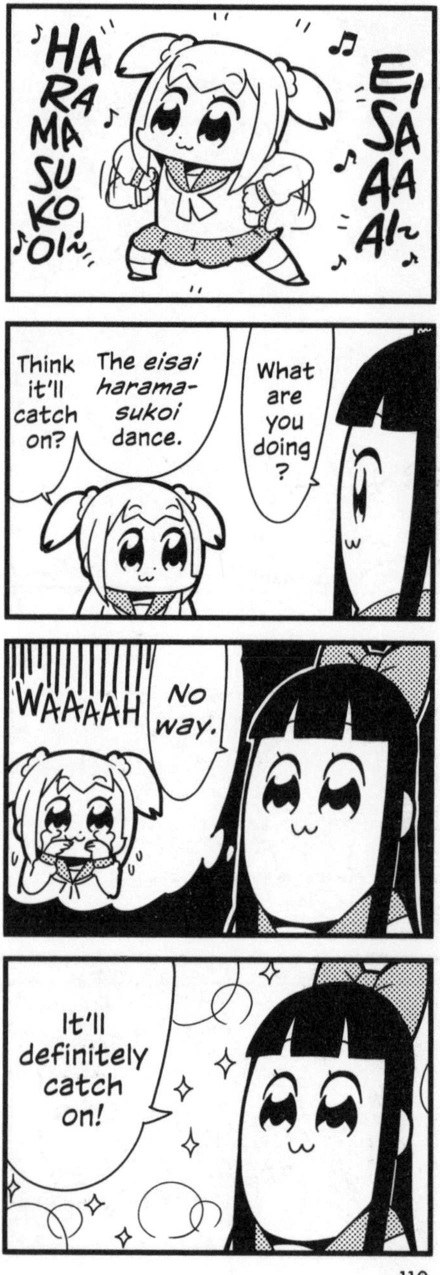
EISAAAAI~
HARAMASUKOOI~
What are you doing?
The *eisai harama-sukoi* dance.
Think it'll catch on?
No way.
WAAAAH
It'll definitely catch on!

161

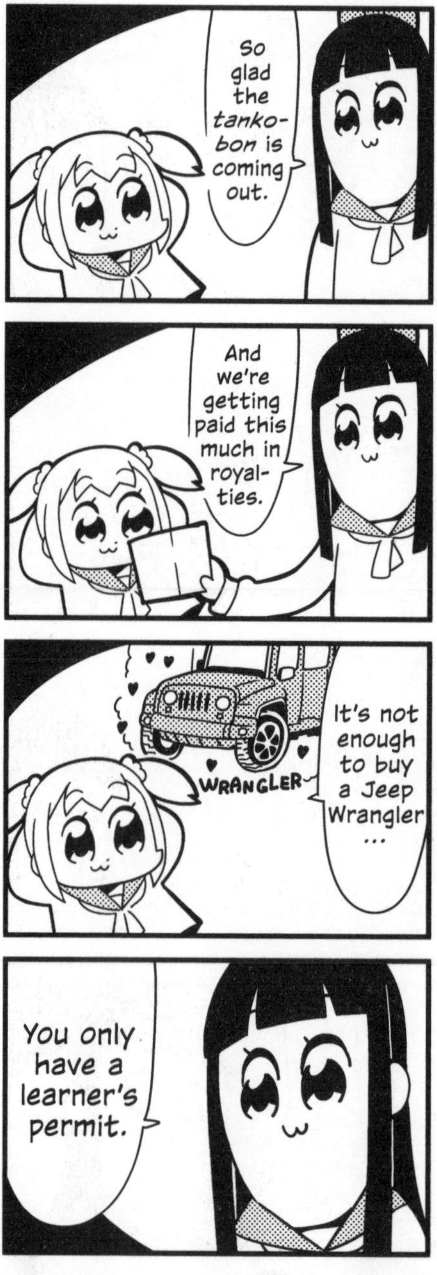
So glad the *tanko-bon* is coming out.
And we're getting paid this much in royal-ties.
It's not enough to buy a Jeep Wrangler...
WRANGLER~
You only have a learner's permit.

162

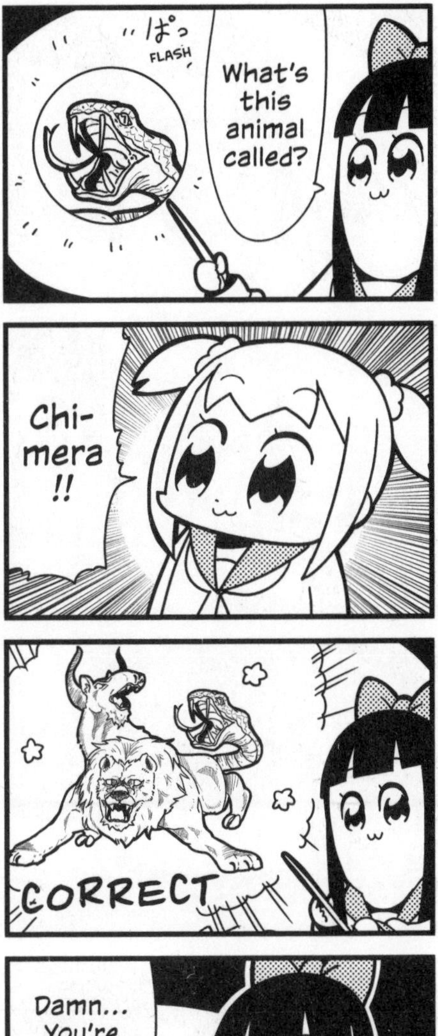
ぱっ
FLASH
What's this animal called?
Chi-mera !!
CORRECT
Damn... You're such a sharp little rascal ...

163

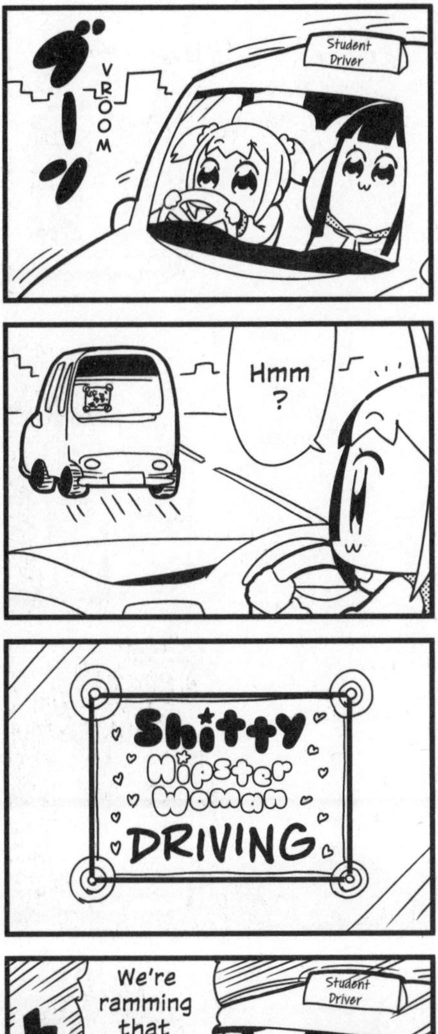
VROOM
Student Driver
Hmm ?
Shitty Hipster Woman DRIVING
Student Driver
We're ramming that bitch! Hold on tight!
VROOMM

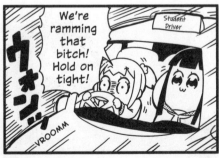

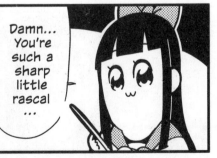

164

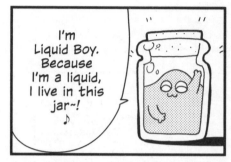

I'm Liquid Boy. Because I'm a liquid, I live in this jar~! ♪
Time for dinner, Liquid Boy.
YAAAAY

165

How did you like *Pop Team Epic*?
Feed-back on our end was in the "meh" range.
How are you doing, Popuko?
GRIK
GRIKK
Curse you, Take-shobo...
I will return to the pages of *Manga Life WIN**, whether it means crawling through dirt or drinking muddy water...
Well then, folks! Bye-bye! ☆
FIN
Please don't look forward to Bkub Okawa-sensei's next work!!

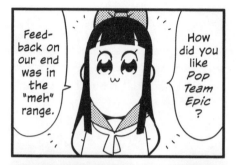

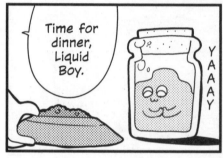

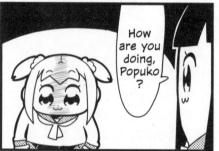

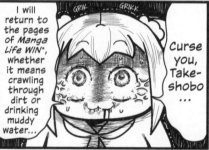

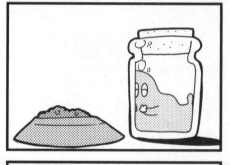

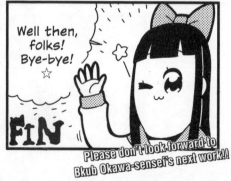

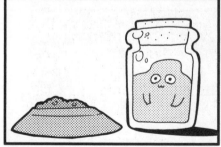

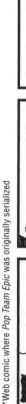

*Web comic where *Pop Team Epic* was originally serialized

■ The following two pages appeared in a separate manga magazine for a two-month run.

STARTING THIS MONTH, THE POP TEAM TABLE OF CONTENTS, FEATURING ALL YOUR FAVORITE THINGS!
BET IT'S RAMEN OR SOME SHIT ANYWAY.
Hang on.
There's a project proposal here.
"For two volumes," it says...
Just two volumes...?
A sudden farewell! Next volume will be the last installment...!

Hello all, the day has finally come.
It's our final ToC strip...
Looking back, so much hap-pened since the first ToC strip ...
Yeah ...
I'm sure all the writers whose work is serialized in this magazine have written thank-you notes to us on their comment pages!
Thank you, everybody ...!

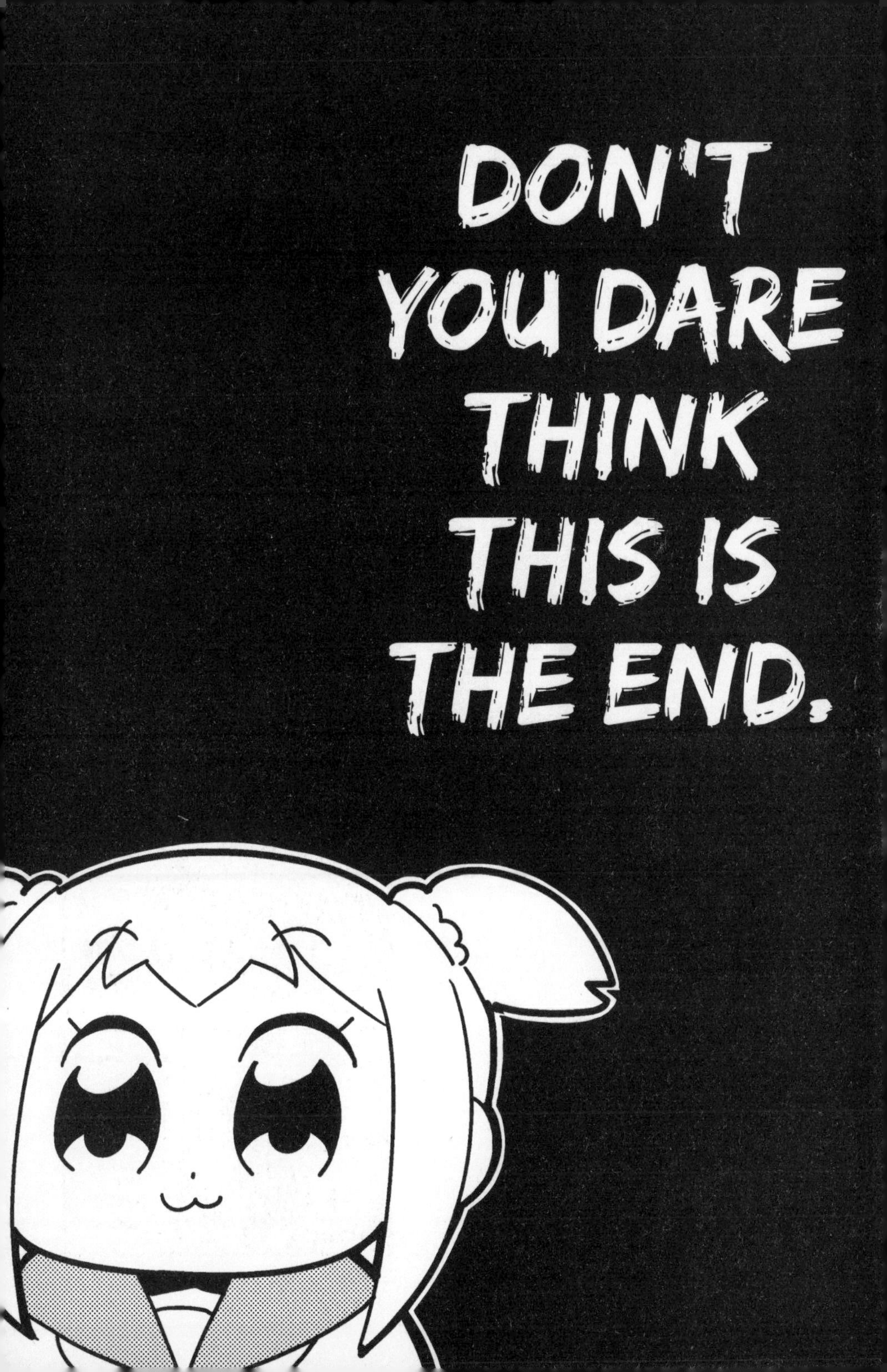
DON'T YOU DARE THINK THIS IS THE END.

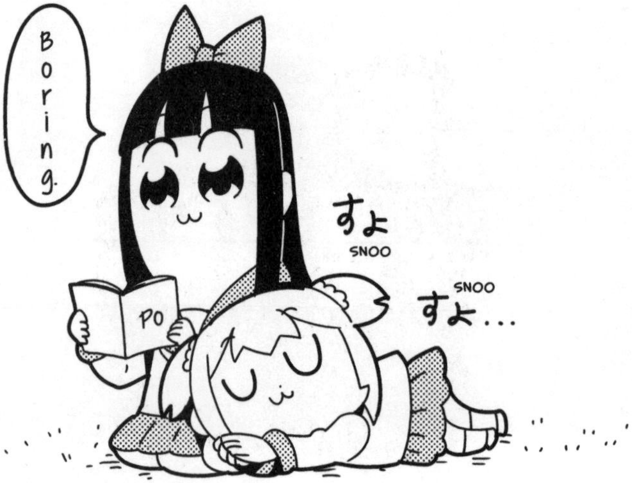
Boring.
すよ SNOO
SNOO すよ...
PO

POP TEAM EPIC

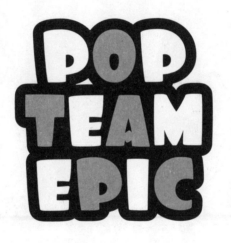

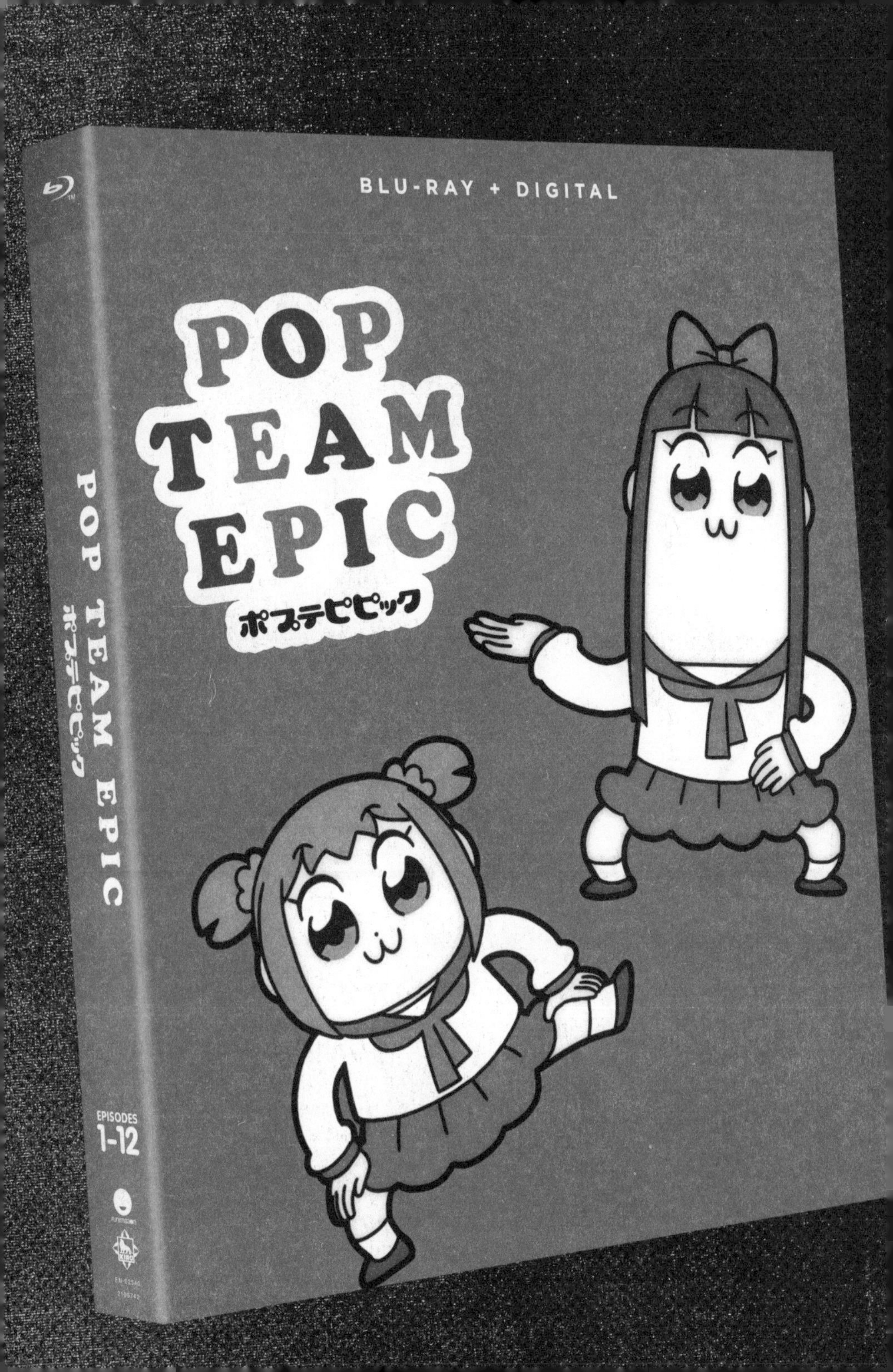
BLU-RAY + DIGITAL
POP TEAM EPIC
ポプテピピック
POP TEAM EPIC
ポプテピピック
EPISODES 1-12

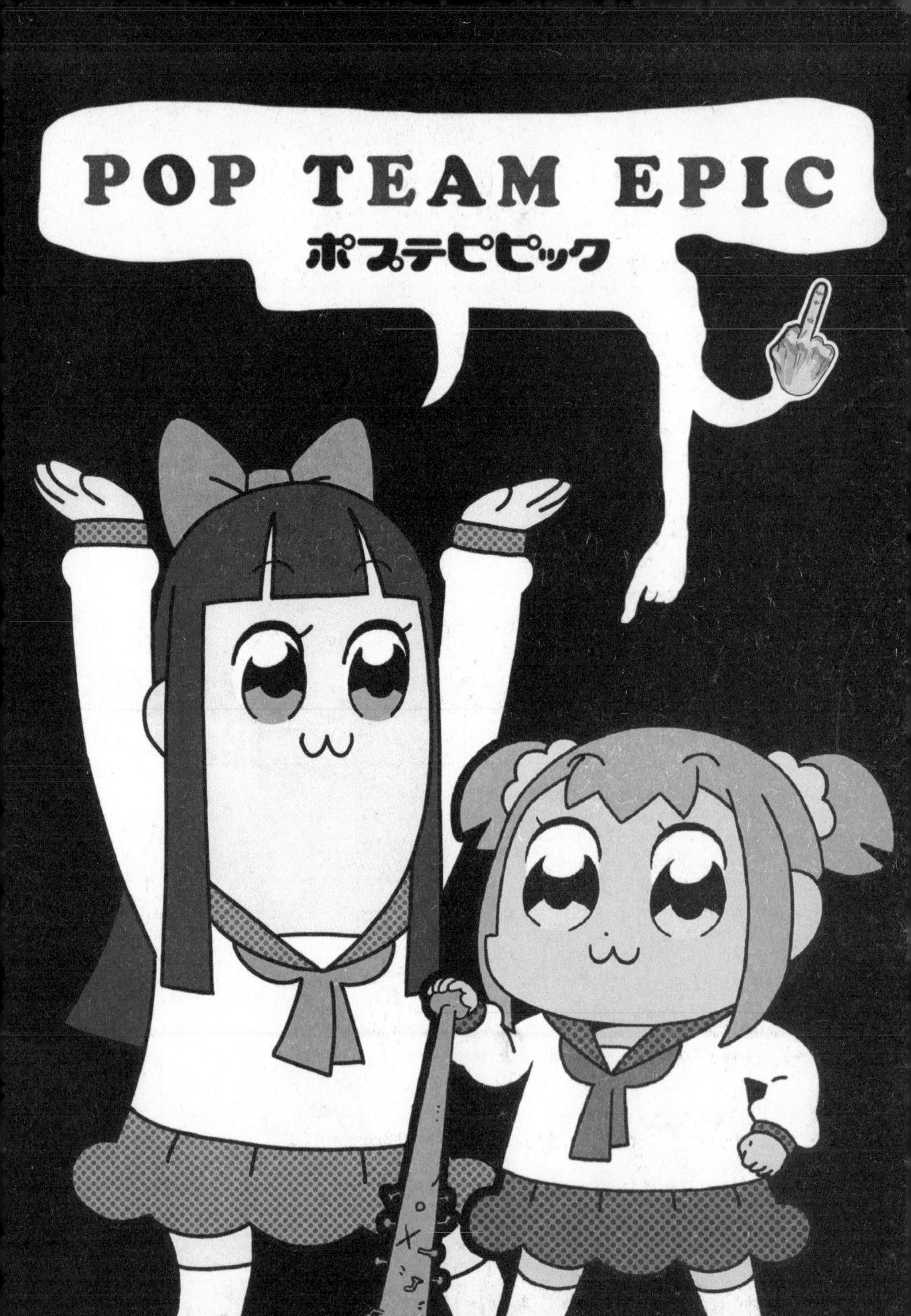
POP TEAM EPIC
ポプテピピック